BUILDING LAW FOR STUDENTS

The practising builder, perhaps more than in any other trade, is continually faced with problems whose successful solution involves a sound working knowledge of many different aspects of the law, in tendering, contracting, liability for accidents and faulty workmanship, building, planning and public health regulations, to name but a few. The legal aspects of building therefore form an important part of any building student's education.

The author's method is to proceed from a general view of the law and the organization of the courts and government both national and local, to company law, contracts, and sale of goods, and then to devote the bulk of the book to matters of special concern to the practising builder.

This book, which has been written in response to a long-felt need for guidance on the vital subject of building and the law, has been specially designed to cover the requirements of the law papers of the Institute of Building's professional qualifying examinations, the Higher National Certificate and Diploma in Building, and Degrees in Building.

The author is a visiting lecturer in Law in the Department of Civil Engineering, University of Salford, and is also a qualified lawyer.

This fifth edition has been revised to take account of the developments in building law which have occurred since the last edition. New case law has been considered, especially on the important topic of liability for defective building work (Chapter 8). New statutes such as the Latent Damage Act, 1986 and the amendments to existing statutes such as the Employment Protection (Consolidation) Act, 1978 have been included and their particular applications to building law are explained.

BUILDING LAW FOR STUDENTS

5th Edition

Keith Manson LL.B., D.P.A.

OF GRAYS INN, BARRISTER

Visiting Lecturer in Law, Department of Civil Engineering,
University of Salford

CASSELL

Cassell Publishers Limited
Villiers House, 41–47 Strand, London WC2N 5JE

First published 1968
Second edition 1971
Third edition 1974
Third edition, second impression, 1977
Fourth edition 1981
Fourth edition, second impression, 1984
Fourth edition, third impression, 1986
Fifth edition 1989
Fifth edition, second impression, 1990
Fifth edition, third impression, 1991
Fifth edition, fourth impression 1993

British Library Cataloguing in Publication Data
Manson, Keith
  Building law for students.—5th ed.
  1. England. Law
  I. Title
  344.2

ISBN 0–304–31815–9

Phototypeset by Input Typesetting Limited
Printed and bound in Great Britain by
Biddles Limited, Guildford and King's Lynn

Contents

Preface

This book has been written for building students who are studying for the examination in Law Subjects of the Institute of Building and for Higher National Certificate and Higher National Diploma examinations in building law. It is hoped, however, that the book will be of some assistance to others in the building industry for whom a knowledge of building law is necessary.

The aim of the book is to present in simple form the essentials of building law. The presentation in simple form, the desire to deal with all the essential law, and the wish to keep the book within reasonable length, have meant that certain matters may have been dealt with more briefly than some would deem desirable. Where this occurs reference to the particular statute or case for greater detail is recommended.

The point should be made that the book is not intended to provide the reader with sufficient knowledge to dispense with professional assistance should that need arise.

Finally, I wish to express my gratitude to RIBA Publications Limited for their kind permission to reproduce extracts from the JCT standard form of contract and the associated forms NSC/1/2/2a/3 which are their copyright, and to the National Federation of Building Trades Employers for their kind permission to reproduce extracts from the sub-contract forms NSC/4/4a which are their copyright.

University of Salford,
Lancashire

KEITH MANSON

Preface to Fifth Edition

Since the production of the first edition of this book building law has in no way diminished in importance to builders and others. Indeed, it has increased in importance not just from the greater detail and complexity of building law but also from the recent evidence of builders and others being held liable for constructing defective buildings. The courts have awarded considerable sums of damages to owners of buildings who have found, often many years after completion, that these buildings were built in a negligent way. A sound knowledge of building law therefore remains an essential part of every builder's ability to do his work competently. I hope that this new edition will, as in the past, provide a helpful guide to those students who seek to obtain such knowledge.

University of Salford, Lancashire   Keith Manson
February 1989

Table of Cases

Table of Statutes

Glossary

Articles of Association: these are regulations which govern the management of a company. A specimen set of articles are contained in the Companies Act, 1985.

Assignment: a term meaning the transfer of property. The person making the transfer is known as the assignor, the person receiving the transfer of the property is the assignee.

Bona fide: good faith. A person acting bona fide is acting honestly.

Breach of Warranty of Authority: an action brought against a person who has held himself out as an agent for another when in fact he had no authority to act.

Caveat Emptor: a buyer must be on his guard.

Chattel: property which does not form part of the freehold.

Contributory negligence: the negligence of the plaintiff which in part contributed to the injury for which an action for damages is being brought. Since the Law Reform (Contributory Negligence) Act, 1945, contributory negligence no longer defeats the plaintiff's claim.

Copyhold: a tenure of land, now abolished, where land was held at the will of the Lord of the Manor.

Corporate Bodies: a collection of persons who, in the eyes of the law, have a separate legal existence to the members who constitute that collection from time to time.

Covenant: a promise which is made in a deed. The person making the promise is the covenantor and the person receiving the benefit of the promise is the covenantee.

Curtilage: the area adjoining a house.

Debenture: usually used to describe an instrument issued by a company as security for a loan to the company. The person holding the debenture is usually given a charge against the property of the company for repayment.

Demise: usually refers to a grant of a lease.

Domicile: the place the law presumes a person intends permanently to reside.

Estate: has the following meanings: an area of land; the extent of a deceased person's property; the extent of a person's interest in land.

Estoppel: a rule in the law of evidence that a person cannot deny something he had previously stated.

Extraordinary Resolution: a resolution used at company meetings. It is passed by a majority of three-fourths of members entitled to vote at a general meeting at which notice has been given of the intention to propose the resolution as an extraordinary resolution.

Fee Simple: the highest estate in land. In practice is equivalent to ownership of land.

Fieri Facias: usually known as fi.fa. A court order to the sheriff or other officer to take goods in payment of a judgment debt.

Firm: a person or persons carrying on business; a partnership.

Fixture: a chattel which has become so connected with land as to form part of the land.

Garnishee: a person who has been required by a court order, known as a garnishee order, to pay a debt he owes not to the creditor but to another who has obtained judgment against the creditor.

Independent Contractor: a person who has agreed to carry out a task for the person by whom he was engaged but not in such a manner as to be under that person's control. Independent contractors are in general liable for their torts.

Lands Tribunal: a tribunal set up by statute to deal with the extinguishment or modification of restrictive covenants under the Law of Property Act, 1925; and to settle compensation for the compulsory purchase of land.

Lessee: a person who accepts the grant of a lease.

Lessor: a person granting a lease to another.

Lien: a right a person possesses against the property of another to settle a debt owed to him by the owner of the property.

Liquidated Damages: an agreed amount to be paid as compensation for breach of contract.

Memorandum of Association: a document required by the Companies Act, 1985, which the persons wishing to form a company must sign. The document must also contain certain information describing the company.

Natural Justice: rules of law which must be followed in the settlement of disputes.

Offer: usually the first move in the formation of a contract. The person making the offer is the offeror, the person receiving the offer, the offeree.

Option: a right given to a person in return for consideration whereby a purchase can be made within a specified time.

Ordinary Resolution: a resolution passed by a simple majority of the members present at an ordinary meeting of a company.

Personal Representatives: persons appointed to see to the distribution of the estate of a deceased person. When appointed by the will of the deceased person they are known as executors; when appointed by the court, where there is no will or persons have not been named in the will, they are known as administrators.

Private Act of Parliament: an act passed by Parliament which has reference to one particular area only. Frequently the means of giving a local authority special powers in its area.

Privity of Contract: the relationship between the two parties to a contract which excludes those who are not parties to the contract from bringing an action on the contract.

Privity of Estate: the relationship which exists between lessor and lessee. This relationship is essential to enforce the terms of a lease.

Quantum Meruit: as much as he has earned. A claim for payment for work done or services rendered where the contract has been ended before it could be completed.

Res Ipsa Loquitur: the thing speaks for itself. A claim made that, until the contrary is proved, it must be presumed that from the facts the other party was negligent.

Riparian Rights: the rights possessed by the owner of land through or past which a river runs in connection with the use of the river.

Special Resolution: a resolution used at company meetings. It is passed by three-fourths of the members entitled to vote at a general meeting where not less than twenty-one days' notice of the intention to propose the resolution has been given.

Sub-lease: a lease granted by a person who is himself a lessee of the same property. The term of the sub-lease is shorter than the main lease.

Subpoena Ad Testificandum: a writ or summons requiring a person to appear and give evidence in judicial proceedings.

Subpoena Duces Tecum: a writ or summons requiring a person to appear and produce certain documents at judicial proceedings.

Tenure: the manner of holding an estate in land.

Truck: a system where employers paid wages to their employees in goods or made the employees purchase goods in the employers' shops. A number of statutes were passed to abolish this practice.

Uberrimae Fidei: of the utmost good faith. A contract *uberrimae fidei* is one which requires a party to the contract to reveal facts which would influence the other party in deciding whether or not to enter the contract. This applies in contracts of insurance.

Ultra Vires: beyond the powers. Applies where a corporation enters into an agreement which it does not have power to enter. The court will declare such agreement to be void.

Vested: denotes that a person has become entitled to an estate in land or to a right.

Vicarious liability: the liability of a principal to answer for the acts of his agent when acting within his authority. Of importance in the relationship of employer and employee.

Volenti Non Fit Injuria: no injury is done to a willing person. A person who consents to run a risk cannot sue in tort if he suffers injury from that risk.

Abbreviations

The references given for the cases mentioned in the book refer to the law reports which are abridged records of cases. The numbers after the date of the case refer to the volume of the report, the letters to the name of the report, and the numbers which follow the letters to the page of the volume at which the case is mentioned. These law reports are kept at the larger reference libraries and may be consulted for greater detail. The system of law reports is now in official hands. The earlier reports were often compiled by individuals who then published the work. These reports usually carry the name of the reporter.

A.C.	House of Lords Appeals from 1891.
App. Cas.	House of Lords Appeals 1875–1890.
A. & E.	Adolphus and Ellis.
All E.R.	All England Law Reports.
B. & S.	Best and Smith.
Beav.	Beavan.
Bing.	Bingham.
C.B.,N.S.	Common Bench, New Series.
Ch.	Reports of Chancery Division from 1891.
Ch.D.	Reports of Chancery Division 1875–1890.
C.L.	Current Law.
C.P.D.	Common Pleas Division.
Exch.	Exchequer Reports.
Ex.D.	Exchequer Division.
H. & C.	Hurlstone and Coltman.
H.L.C.	House of Lords Cases 1847–1866.

K.B.	King's Bench Division.
L.G.R.	Local Government Reports.
L.J.Ex.	Law Journal Exchequer.
L.R.Ex.	Law Report Exchequer.
L.R.H.L.	Law Report, House of Lords 1865–1875.
L.T.	Law Times.
Ph.	Phillips.
Q.B.	Queen's Bench Division.
Vern.	Vernon.
W.L.R.	Weekly Law Report.

1

Law and the Legal Profession

The Nature of Law

It has been recognized for centuries that it is an essential element of community life to have a set of minimum standards to regulate the conduct of the persons forming that community. These standards or laws are needed to enable the community to function properly and to develop without undue friction. The Bible gives clear evidence of the recognition by the Christian community of the need for laws. The Romans, before the birth of Christ, had laws enabling people to live peaceably and to trade knowing that in the event of a dispute the matter could be settled by reference to law.

Law is not a static body of rules disregarding the changes taking place in the social structure of a free and flourishing community. It is flexible so that where social changes have occurred and the law is no longer relevant, or is inadequate, changes can be made so that the law represents the needs of the day. Law does not aim to govern all conduct in a community; some matters are left to the rules of social conduct, the penalty here being the disapproval of the other members of the community. The development of the law, particularly in recent times, has created the situation whereby much of our conduct, in many cases unknown to us, brings us into conflict with the law. An example of this is a person singing loudly in the streets late at night; he is not only a social nuisance but an offender against the law for disturbing the peace of the community. Many aspects of law have been developed to deal with the needs of different sections of the community: the taxation system requires the authority of law to function properly, and the needs of commerce have to be met by law, enabling disputes to be settled.

It sometimes happens that the enforcement of a law may lead to a decision which appears to society to be unduly harsh, this possibly by reason of change in the social conditions and needs of the community since the law was made. The remedy here is to amend the law so that it is more in accord with the social conditions of the day and the desire of the community. A flexible system will enable such a change to be made without undue delay.

For any law to function properly it must carry with it a power of punishment to be administered to the offender. The purpose of the punishment is to deter others from breaking the same law and to reform the offender so that he will not be tempted to break the law again.

We can see therefore that the nature of law is the protection of the community; while it has to be sufficiently rigid to be certain it must not be so rigid as to be incapable of amendment where the need of the community requires its alteration.

The Sources of Law

The law of England and Wales, unlike that of many other countries, owes its existence or creation to varying origins. Other countries have a system whereby the whole of their law is contained in a code which is the sole body of law. France is one such country, one code having been introduced by Napoleon.

The development of the law of England and Wales has been such that, as the occasion demanded, a new source of law has arisen, usually to overcome an inadequacy or harshness of law created by a prior existing source. We can find evidence of this development in the use of Roman law, and in the willingness of the courts to look at the decisions of the courts of other countries in dealing with a similar dispute.

We have in this country a body of law brought together from different sources which has, in its process of growth, rejected that which was unsatisfactory and retained that which is good. The fact that it is drawn from different sources has not hampered the courts in dispensing justice, and the law has not shown itself to be unwieldy.

Common Law

Before the Norman Conquest there existed in England a system of local courts in which judicial matters that had arisen in that locality were determined. There was no strong central judicial body imposing its will over the whole of the country. Each local court operated in isolation from the others.

After the Norman Conquest a system of rule by kings with strong wills came about. The change was not made overnight, nor was it sweeping in its effect; the process was gradual, the system of courts continuing to function. The kings used a system of rule having a council known as the King's Court. This King's Court at first acted as an advisory body and also as a place where affairs of state could be transacted; later it developed judicial power, with authority to act in these matters being placed in the hands of certain officials. These officials or commissioners went round the country administering business in the King's name. This system was the beginning of the assizes system which continued until 1972.

The effect of this introduction of central direction on judicial affairs, which was a gradual process, was the replacement of local courts administering local law in different areas by a system of judicial administration applying law which was common to all the land. So the system of common law was built up. In the process the assizes system arose and courts were formed to deal with the common law; some of these courts remained until the Judicature Acts, 1873–75, when a fusion of the administration of justice took place.

Common law is a term often used to show that the law is unwritten, that is, not statute law. This form of law is made up of many decisions made in particular cases, these decisions giving the principles of law.

The law made by legislation statutes has tended to supplant the common law, in fact in many matters it has been used to remedy defects found to exist in the common law. An example of common law still remaining is to be found in the law of torts, or civil wrongs.

Custom

Custom is usage which has been granted recognition by the law. By that we mean that when a certain thing is done and it satisfies certain conditions, the law has granted recognition to the usage and will deal with it as a custom, so making it part of the common law. Custom is either general or local.

General custom is not restricted to a particular locality or body of persons and its recognition has helped to build up the common law of England. What happened was that someone would dispute the custom, with the result that the matter would be brought before the court. If the custom was recognized, this meant that it was given the force of law. This process of recognition of customs no longer forms an important part of the creation of English law, the usages capable of being recognized as customs having nearly all been dealt with by the courts.

Local customs differ from general customs in that they apply to a particular locality or class of persons. An example of a local custom existing at the present time is the right of fishermen living in certain villages to hang out their nets to dry on land belonging to a private owner. In the many cases dealing with local customs the courts have laid down tests to be satisfied before the local custom will be granted legal recognition. These are that it must be certain in its nature, that is, it must be such as not to appear incapable of precise definition; it must be reasonable, for the law cannot be expected to uphold a right that is unreasonable; the right should have been enjoyed without dispute, for what has been established by force can hardly claim recognition from the law; the custom must have been recognized as being compulsory and the right to the custom to have been in existence from time immemorial. 'Time immemorial', in law, means from the earliest time of the reign of Richard I (1189). An exception to these rules is to be found in the practice of the courts in granting recognition to a custom which has existed, not from 1189, but for some substantial period usually evidenced by the oldest inhabitant. The court will not, however, grant recognition to a custom which could not have existed until after 1189.

Another addition to the common law has been the adoption by the courts of the customs that existed between the merchants trading in the seventeenth century. Certain aspects of banking and insurance can be traced directly to a custom existing between merchants many years ago.

Judicial Precedent

When a case is before a court the judge will reach a decision based on a legal principle; this decision is entered on the court records and is a judicial precedent on the legal principle involved which will bind all lower courts when considering the same legal principle. Judicial precedent arose in the common law courts and has since been used in interpreting statutes and in equity. It is claimed for judicial precedent that it makes the law certain, in that lawyers may consult reports of cases, and the decision reached, to determine how the courts will deal with a similar case.

The fact that the system is capable of growing with changes in society is one advantage. In the case of *Haynes v Harwood*, 1935 the court had to consider, for the first time, the legal principle involved where a person is injured in attempting to rescue another. A new statement was made regarding this legal principle, the court consulting reports of similar American cases to help it each its decision.

The system of English courts is that they are so formed as to be related to each other. The highest court is the House of Lords, its decisions being binding on all lower and inferior courts. Below the House of Lords is the Court of Appeal, which is divided into Criminal and Civil Divisions. These Divisions are superior to the lower courts and their decisions are binding on the lower courts. This process of higher courts making decisions which are binding on lower courts is repeated down to the lowest court. The House of Lords were formerly bound by their own decisions, which in many cases were decisions made many years earlier. The effect of this principle of binding precedent was to produce a rigidity in law which prevented the House of Lords from recognizing the social changes which had occurred since the earlier decisions were made; social changes which, it must be said, were such as to require the law to be altered. To remedy this matter the House of Lords, in 1966, decided that they would no longer be bound by earlier decisions, but that they would not readily depart from those decisions unless it seemed right to do so. Before 1966 the only exceptions to the doctrine of binding precedent were where a decision was made in ignorance of some provision in an Act of Parliament or of a decision binding on the House of Lords.

Legislation

This forms the main source of English law. Legislation is the passing of an Act of Parliament so as to make law to deal with some social need or to alter or repeal the existing law. An Act of Parliament is made by the sovereign power of Parliament, and it is worded with great precision so as to prevent, as far as possible, any evasion of the aims of Parliament expressed in the Act.

In many matters Parliament has thought it necessary to provide in the Act for ministers and others to make orders and regulations which have the force of law. This is known as delegated legislation and usually deals in great detail with technical matters. An example of this is the Factories Act, 1961, Section 7 of which gives power to the Minister of Labour to make regulations for determining the number of sanitary conveniences to be provided in factories. If the validity of some delegated legislation is questioned the court must decide whether the delegated legislation has been made in the manner intended by the Act.

It is usual practice to have an interpretation section in the Act so that the precise meaning of certain words is made clear. In addition to this, reference may be made to the Interpretation Act, 1978, which gives guidance to the courts in the interpretation of Acts of Parliament.

A list of the Acts of Parliament passed each year is published by Her Majesty's Stationery Office.

Equity

In the thirteenth, fourteenth and fifteenth centuries the common law became rigid. This rigidity of law was encountered particularly in the bringing of an action and the procedure of the trial. Actions were brought which would fail by reason of some imperfection in the writ commencing the action, the courts being so rigidly bound as to be unable to overcome this imperfection, notwithstanding the justice of the claim. To overcome these difficulties application would be made to the Council of State, in which the royal justice resided, for relief from the injustices of the common law. This process of petitioning passed to the Lord Chancellor, as the Keeper of the King's Conscience. Lord Chancellors, in turn, continued to hear petitions and grant relief from injustices of the common law, and extended the principles where this form of justice, known as equity, would apply. This resulted in a system of equitable doctrines which were almost as rigid as the rules of common law that equity had originally sought to modify.

Equity developed its own exclusive jurisdiction where the common law was unable to give relief. This may be seen in the enforcement of trusts. The Court of Chancery, where equity was enforced, had the power to aid the common law where the common law had recognized the right but was unable to provide an adequate remedy. In the case of breach of contract the common law remedy was damages, which were not always appropriate. Here equity was able to grant the remedy of specific performance. This is a decree of the court ordering a party to the contract to carry out his obligations under the contract.

As we can now see, there existed two systems of courts, each one dealing with law which was somewhat similar in nature. This was wasteful and unnecessary and the passing of the Judicature Acts, 1873–75, which created a single system of courts, with power to administer both equity and common law, fused the administration but not the principles of equity and common law. The Judicature Act of 1873 made provision that when the court was dealing with a matter where the principles of equity and common law came into conflict then the rules of equity should prevail. Thus the supremacy of equity is maintained. We shall see later that the development of the law of land owes much to equity.

European Law

The most recent addition to the body of English law is that introduced by the European Communities Act, 1972. By this Act we became a member of the European Economic Community and subject to Community laws. Community legislation may be by way of regulations which usually apply as part of our law; by way of decisions which apply to particular circumstances; or by way of directives which require some action by Parliament to become part of our law. An example of the application of European law is the restriction on building contracts being open to companies in our country only.

The Legal Profession

The legal profession in England is divided into two branches, solicitors and barristers. In many countries there is no such division, the whole of the legal work being conducted by the same person. The term 'lawyer' means either a solicitor or barrister. No person may at the same time be a barrister and a solicitor. It is possible, however, for a person to change from one branch of the profession to the other. Each branch has its own system of examination and admittance. Not all those who qualify as solicitors or barristers practise as such. Many of them work as legal advisors to local authorities, government departments and companies, or teach in colleges of further education and universities.

Solicitors are constantly dealing with the public, not always in connection with legal matters. Often they advise their clients on financial matters and try to prevent clients starting legal actions which are not likely to succeed. Solicitors spend much of their time acting for clients in conveying houses, investigating the titles of houses to make certain the sellers have the right to sell them, in this way protecting the clients; making clients' wills and acting as executors when the wills become operative; and appearing in the magistrates' court if clients are charged with minor criminal matters.

A person becomes a solicitor by serving articles with a solicitor and passing the necessary examinations. When this is done the articled clerk applies to the Law Society for admission to the Roll of Solicitors. Solicitors who practise must take out a certificate each year with the Law Society. The Law Society is the body who not only deals with the education of solicitors but acts, if the need arises, as a disciplinary body; it has a fund to meet the demands of clients who have suffered by reason of a solicitor's dishonesty. The Law Society also has a scheme of compulsory insurance for professional negligence by solicitors.

Barristers have the right to conduct cases in all the courts in England. Solicitors may conduct cases in the county courts, magistrates' courts and in certain limited circumstances crown courts. In general, a barrister must take instructions from a solicitor, since he is not allowed to deal with the public except through a solicitor. The solicitor collects the evidence and arranges for the barrister to appear in court and represent the client. Barristers are not always engaged in court cases; much of their work is conducted in their chambers on such work as drafting documents or pleadings, and giving legal opinions. A barrister is not allowed to advertise, nor can he form a partnership or company.

A Queen's Counsel is a senior barrister appointed by royal patent. He receives higher fees but the work he can undertake is limited. When he appears in court he is usually accompanied by a junior counsel, who is an ordinary barrister.

A person becomes a barrister by joining as a student one of the four Inns of Court. These Inns have their origins in the fourteenth century. A student must keep terms by dining in the inn a specified number of times over a period of three years. Two examinations must be passed before the student becomes a barrister by being called to the Bar.

Before a newly-called barrister is allowed to practise he must be a pupil for twelve months in the chambers of an experienced barrister. In this way he becomes properly trained in his profession.

Judges and Magistrates

The independence and quality of the judiciary in England and Wales is a source of justifiable pride. Their decisions are not affected by factors such as public pressure or political opinion. There is a great tradition of resistance to any efforts to sway the judges from the right and proper conduct of cases.

The judges who sit in the High Court are appointed by the Crown on advice tendered by the Lord Chancellor. Appointments are made from the leading barristers, who often suffer financial losses in income on being so appointed. The barrister appointed must have been practising as such for not less then ten years. On being appointed to the High Court the judge is knighted and surrounded, both in the court and outside, by an aura of traditional ceremony and respect. Judges are appointed for life and can only be removed by the Crown for misconduct or on addresses of the houses of parliament.

The Lord Chief Justice is appointed by the Crown. He sits as a judge in the High Court, is head of the Queen's Bench Division, and arranges the business of the High Court.

Judges are appointed to one of the three Divisions of the High Court; they may be transferred from one Division to another but usually stay in one Division. One judge only is used to try a case. In the Criminal Division of the Court of Appeal, at least three judges must sit to hear the appeal.

The head of the Family Division of the High Court is known as the President; he, too, is appointed by the Crown.

The judges sitting in the Court of Appeal are the Master of the Rolls and the 23 Lords Justices of Appeal. Each of the Lords Justices of Appeal has been a High Court Judge or a barrister of fifteen years' standing. The Master of the Rolls exercises certain duties concerning the admission of solicitors to the Roll of Solicitors.

The Lords of Appeal in Ordinary, thirteen in number, are appointed by the Crown from persons who have been High Court Judges or Lords Justices of Appeal for at least two years, or from barristers of fifteen years' standing.

The Lord Chancellor is appointed by the Government. This is a combined political and judicial office, the Lord Chancellor being responsible for appointing justices of the peace and advising on the appointment of certain other judicial officers.

Circuit judges, who sit in Crown and County Courts, are appointed on the recommendation of the Lord Chancellor from barristers and solicitors of at least ten years' standing. There are almost 400 circuit judges sitting in different parts of the country. Some sit regularly in one place, others travel from one court to another on a circuit.

Recorders sit at Crown Courts situated in certain towns. These are practising barristers and solicitors appointed by the Lord Chancellor who are paid a small sum for their duties which are part-time.

Justices of the peace are appointed by the Lord Chancellor from people in all walks of life. Most of them are untrained and unpaid yet deal with the majority of criminal cases in England. They have limited powers of punishment and can deal only with the less serious criminal offences. A justice of the peace on reaching the age of seventy-five can no longer sit on the bench. A minimum of two justices of the peace is required to sit and try a case, but it is usual to have more than two.

Stipendiary magistrates are appointed by the Lord Chancellor from solicitors and barristers of seven years' standing. A stipendiary magistrate is paid, the appointment is full-time and he sits in court on his own and has the same power to punish as two justices of the peace. The practice of appointing stipendiary magistrates is declining, so that they are now only to be found in the bigger cities and boroughs.

2

Court Procedure

The Organization of the Courts

The courts in England and Wales are so arranged as to allow minor crimes or simple disputes in civil matters to be dealt with as quickly and cheaply as possible. More serious matters are dealt with in the higher courts where the procedure is slower and more expensive. In whatever court a matter is decided the same principles of English law apply. The courts are formed in two sections, one dealing with civil matters, the other with criminal matters. For each section there is a division in the court of appeal and further appeals are decided by the House of Lords.

The whole system of courts is arranged in the form of a pyramid with the lower courts at its base, the higher courts on the level above, the court of appeal above that, and finally at the apex of the pyramid the supreme court of appeal, the House of Lords.

We will now look more closely at the individual courts, starting with the courts dealing with criminal matters.

Magistrates' Court

Magistrates' courts deal with the majority of criminal cases, most of which are a question of very minor offences. These courts are presided over by a stipendiary magistrate or by lay justices of the peace; in a few matters a single lay justice of the peace may sit, but his power of punishment is very limited. In general magistrates' courts have power to impose imprisonment of up to six months. For a statutory offence the amount of punishment, either a fine, or imprisonment, or both, is set out in the statute under which the offence is charged.

Sometimes statutes make offences triable in the magistrates' court or in a higher court; an example of this is the offence of theft. Here, if the defendant agrees, the prosecution may bring the case as an ordinary case in the magistrates' court. If the defendant is found guilty, and the court feels that a more severe sentence is needed than it has power to impose, he may be sent for sentence to the Crown Court.

The court will sit as a juvenile court when it is dealing with a charge made against a child over ten and under fourteen years or a young person over fourteen and under seventeen years. There are restrictions on the publication of the name and address of a person charged in a juvenile court, and on those who may be present in court during the hearing.

As we shall see, the court may deal with civil matters regarding domestic affairs and similar restrictions to those mentioned above apply.

Certain rights of appeal exist from the decisions of magistrates' courts. An appeal against the conviction or the sentence imposed may be made by the accused to the Crown Court; no such right exists for the prosecution where the case is dismissed. If either the prosecution or the defendant believes that the court has made an error in law, a special form of appeal known as a 'case stated' may be made to the Queen's Bench Division. This appeal requires the magistrates' court to state a case for the opinion of the Queen's Bench Division on the point of law in issue. The decision of the Queen's Bench Division, which hears the appeal by a Divisional Court of two judges, is final.

An important function of magistrates' courts is to act as examining justices. This they do when a person is charged with a serious crime, for example, murder or burglary; what is known as a preliminary examination then takes place and the court hears the evidence against the person accused, and then decides whether the evidence is sufficient to justify sending the accused for trial at the Crown Court. The court can commit the accused for trial only if it is satisfied that the evidence is sufficient to justify this. A preliminary examination is not a trial, it is solely an examination of the evidence.

Crown Courts

The system of courts for the trial of serious crimes became the subject of increasing criticism. The belief was that a system formed hundreds of years ago was ill-suited to modern needs. It was felt that the system was unnecessarily expensive and on occasions so slow as to involve the accused in long delays before they were brought to trial. A report on the system was called for and a body under the chairmanship of Lord Beeching undertook this task. The report was made in 1969 and suggested radical reforms of the system. In effect a new modern and more efficient system was suggested. These suggestions were given statutory force by Parliament passing the Courts Act, 1971, which required that a new system of courts, known as Crown Courts, should be introduced from 1972.

A large number of Crown Courts have been set up throughout the whole country. This means that trial courts are readily available, so reducing the distances witnesses and others have to travel. The structure of the Crown Courts is that they are divided into four tiers. The purpose of this arrangement is to ensure that offences are tried before an appropriate judge according to their gravity. For example, the first tier Crown Court, which must have a High Court Judge, deals with murder. The second tier, which is usually presided over by a High Court Judge but occasionally a circuit judge, tries manslaughter and other serious crimes. The third-tier Crown Court, under a High Court Judge or a circuit judge, tries less serious crimes, and finally the fourth tier, under a High Court Judge or circuit judge, deals with the remainder of the serious crimes. In some circumstances a part-time judge known as a Recorder may try cases. The first-tier Crown Court has certain civil jurisdiction.

Court of Appeal, Criminal Division

The Criminal Division of the Court of Appeal was created in 1966. Appeal may be made to this Division by persons convicted on indictment against conviction or sentence imposed at the Crown Court. There are certain restrictions regarding the appeals which may be made. Appeals are heard by the Master of the Rolls and the Lords Justices of Appeal, supplemented as required by the judges of the Queen's Bench Division. The Court may allow or dismiss the appeal but in no case may it increase the sentence beyond that imposed at the trial.

House of Lords

The House of Lords was made the final Court of Appeal in criminal matters in 1907. It hears appeals from the Court of Appeal, Criminal Division, and from the Divisional Court of the High Court. An appeal to the House of Lords may only be made with its consent or with the consent of the Court of Appeal, Criminal Division. Such right of appeal will be granted only on a point of law of exceptional public importance.

Both prosecution and defence may appeal in this case. The court consists of at least three, selected from the Lord Chancellor, the Lords of Appeal in Ordinary and any peer who has held high judicial office.

Civil Courts

The courts dealing with civil matters follow much the same pattern as the courts dealing with criminal matters. The final court of appeal is the House of Lords; it hears appeals from the Court of Appeal. At the lowest level the magistrates' court deals with many small civil matters in domestic affairs. An appeal from such a hearing is to a Divisional Court of either the Queen's Bench Division or the Family Division, according to the matter being deal with.

County Courts

County courts were established in 1846 as a system of local courts dealing with civil matters. At the present time the country is divided into districts which are arranged into some fifty-four circuits. Each circuit has one or more circuit judges assigned to it. The court's jurisdiction is limited in claims for tort or breach of contract to those not exceeding £5000. Some of the more serious civil matters such as libel or slander cannot be brought in the county court. The county courts provide an accessible means of settling disputes in matters such as debts, rents and possession of houses. The circuit judge usually sits on his own, but there is power to summon a jury. Appeals from the county courts are made to the Court of Appeal, Civil Division.

High Court

The High Court provides the jurisdiction to deal with serious civil matters; it consists of the Family Division for matters concerning adoption, divorce and settling matters on guardianship; the Chancery Division for dealing with trusts, mortgages and land disputes; and the Queen's Bench Division for dealing with those other civil matters which cannot be brought in the county courts. All the divisions are presided over by High Court judges. Appeals are to the Court of Appeal, Civil Division. The court may sit with a jury, but the question as to whether there should be a jury or not is decided by the court.

Court of Appeal, Civil Division

The Court of Appeal, Civil Division, may only hear appeals on civil matters. These appeals come from the county courts and from the High Court. Either party to the action may appeal to the court which is empowered to order a new trial. The composition of the court is not less than three, drawn from the Lord Chancellor, the Lords Justices of Appeal, the Lord Chief Justice, and the President of the Family Division; High Court judges may also be required to sit in the court. Appeals from the decisions of the Court of Appeal, Civil Division, may, subject to certain conditions, be made by either party to the action to the House of Lords.

House of Lords

The House of Lords hears appeals from the Court of Appeal by its leave or by leave of the Court of Appeal. The same judicial officers deal with civil appeals as with criminal appeals.

Criminal and Civil Procedure

The procedures of criminal and civil cases differ greatly. Both are detailed in their respective requirements, but share a common factor in that they seek to provide a simple system of procedure.

Criminal procedure is different for cases triable on indictment and those tried summarily in a magistrates' court. Unless the accused is arrested without a warrant he is brought before the court by a summons or by a warrant. A summons is signed by a justice of the peace and requires the person named in the summons to appear in court at a place, date and time set out in the summons. A warrant is signed by a justice of the peace and directs certain persons to arrest the person against whom the warrant is issued. The summons and the warrant must state the offence with which the accused is charged, together with particulars of the offence. A police officer may arrest, without a warrant, a person found committing a serious crime; a similar power, somewhat restricted, is given to private persons. A person so arrested must be informed of the reason for his arrest and be taken before a justice or police officer, who has power to grant bail, as soon as is reasonably possible.

When the accused is brought before the magistrates' court he will be tried there unless the charge is one where the court has no jurisdiction; in which case the court will conduct a preliminary examination to determine whether or not there is sufficient evidence to justify sending the accused for trial on indictment to the Crown Court.

Procedure in Magistrates' Court

If the offence is one which can be tried summarily in the magistrates' court the procedure is simple. The trial begins by the clerk to the justices reading out the charge, to which the defendant makes his plea. If the plea is one of not guilty the prosecutor gives brief details of his case and calls and examines his witnesses. These witnesses may be cross-examined by the defence as to the evidence they have given to the court. The defence may at this stage submit that there is no case to answer. If this submission is over-ruled or no such submission is made, the defendant opens his case by calling and examining his witnesses, who may be cross-examined by the prosecutor. If the accused has not previously addressed the court he may do so at this stage. If additional witnesses – other than the defendant and witnesses as to his character – are called by the defence, the prosecutor may call witnesses in reply. The prosecutor may only address the court after the accused has done so twice.

The court having heard the evidence retires to consider its verdict. If the court finds the accused guilty it hears evidence as to any previous convictions, details of his character, and anything the defendant or his lawyer wishes to say in mitigation, following which the court imposes sentence.

A preliminary examination begins by the prosecution calling witnesses; each gives his evidence which is taken down in writing and signed by the witness and the justice. The witnesses are then bound over to attend and give evidence at the Crown Court; the purpose of this is to form a deposition which may, in certain circumstances, be used in evidence in another court without the witness being present. The justice next reads the charge to the accused and explains it to him in ordinary language. The accused is cautioned that he need not say anything, but that if he does it will be taken down and may be used in evidence. Following this the evidence of the accused and his witnesses if any, is taken down in the form of a deposition and the accused's solicitor and then the prosecution addresses the court. The justices then decide whether to commit the accused for trial at the Crown Court, or to dismiss the charge. It is more usual now to use the provisions in the Magistrates' Courts Act, 1980, and the Criminal Justice Act, 1982, which allow the accused to be committed for trial without the magistrates considering the evidence. In this circumstance the defendant and his lawyer must agree and all the evidence must be in the form of written statements.

In the case of an offence which may be tried summarily or on indictment the Criminal Law Act 1977 now requires that the magistrates' court, before deciding which method of trial should be used, must hear representations from both the prosecution and the defence.

Procedure on Indictment

A trial at the Crown Court is by jury on indictment. The indictment is a formal document charging the accused, in the name of the Queen, with committing a specified crime, particulars of which are briefly given. The trial begins by the clerk of the court reading the indictment to the accused and asking him to make his plea. If the accused pleads guilty the judge hears the facts of the case, details of any previous convictions and of the accused's character, and anything the defendant or his lawyer wishes to say in miti-gation, following which the judge imposes sentence. Where the plea is 'not guilty' a jury of twelve members is sworn in to try the case. The defence may challenge the selection of a jury member without giving a reason on not more than three occasions, but any number of jury members may be challenged if proper cause can be shown, for example, because the jury member knows the accused. The prosecution barrister opens the case and calls his witnesses who may be cross-examined by the defence barrister. At the conclusion of the prosecution's evidence the defence may submit that the evidence does not show there is any case to answer. This is decided by the judge alone; if he agrees with the defence submission he stops the case and orders the jury to bring in a verdict of 'not guilty'; otherwise he directs that the case shall continue. The defence now calls its witnesses who give evidence and may be cross-examined by the prosecuting barrister. At the end of the case for the defence the prosecuting barrister then addresses the jury, followed by the defence barrister. This order of speeches is required by the Criminal Procedure (Right of Reply) Act 1964 and is considered to be of some importance. The import-ance of this is the belief that the barrister speaking last to the jury has an advantage, his words are fresh in their minds when they retire to consider their verdict. The judge sums up the evidence to the jury, drawing their attention to important features and direct-ing them as to any law involved. The jury then retire to consider their verdict. If the verdict is 'not guilty' the accused is immediately released; if he is found guilty the judge hears evidence of any previous convictions; details of the accused's character, and any facts put forward in mitigation; and then imposes a sentence which he believes is appropriate, in accordance with the maximum pre-scribed by law.

Civil Procedure

The civil procedure used in civil actions in the Queen's Bench Division of the High Court is governed by a detailed system of procedure known as the Rules of the Supreme Court, arranged in Orders which are sub-divided into rules. The aim of the rules is to regulate civil procedure so that it is conducted in an orderly manner as simply as possible. An immense amount of work is done before a case is dealt with in court; the issue has been reduced to its bare facts so permitting the matter to be resolved as cheaply and quickly as possible.

The parties to a civil action are known as the plaintiff and the defendant, the plaintiff bringing the action against the defendant. There are special arrangements for persons who are under a disability (infancy or mental disorder) so that they may bring an action or defend through some other person.

A civil action in the High Court commences with a Writ of Summons. A writ is a formal document commanding the defendant, in the name of the plaintiff, within fourteen days to return an acknowledgement of service in which the defendant must say whether he intends to contest the claim. The writ must bear the name and address of the plaintiff and his solicitor, if any, the name and address of the defendant, and the Division of the High Court in which the action is to be brought. The writ is issued by being stamped at the Central Office of the High Court or, for matters outside London, at a District Registry Office. Once the writ is issued it may be served on the defendant. Details of when and how the writ was served are entered on the back of the writ within three days of the service. The writ must either have details of the claim endorsed on it, or be accompanied by a statement of claim. The statement of claim sets out the plaintiff's claim and particulars of the claim. The acknowledgement of service is returned to the Central Office or District Registry.

At this stage the pleadings are exchanged, the purpose of which is to reduce the dispute to its material facts. Pleadings consist of the statement of claim, the defence and the reply. The statement of claim must be delivered within fourteen days of service of the writ. The defence, which must be delivered within fourteen days of the statement of claim, may have a denial, known as a 'traverse'; or 'confession and avoidance', which admits the facts alleged but destroys their effect by showing some additional facts which show justification on the part of the defendant; or an objection on a point of law. The rules permit the defendant to enter on his defence any set-off or counterclaim; a set-off is where the defendant claims the plaintiff owes him a sum of money, while a counterclaim is a separate claim by the defendant against the plaintiff. The reply to the defence must be delivered within fourteen days of delivery of the defence. The purpose of the reply is to answer the points raised in the defence and to further reduce the issue to its facts. In general, this marks the close of the pleadings.

The next stage is that within one month of the closing of the pleadings the plaintiff must take out the summons for direction. The purpose of this is to finalize the procedural matter before the court action. A Master of the Queen's Bench Division, who is appointed by the Lord Chancellor from barristers of at least ten years' standing, gives directions for amendments of the pleadings, settles matters of evidence and the place and mode of trial. There is no right to claim trial by jury.

The importance of the preliminary work done in the pleadings and in other ways should not be ignored; it reduces the issue to its simplest form, keeps the cost to a minimum, and enables a decision to be more speedily reached.

The trial of a civil matter begins by the plaintiff's counsel setting out the facts of the case; he then calls his witnesses who are examined and may be cross-examined by the defendant's counsel. At the close of the plaintiff's evidence the defence may submit that there is no case to answer; the judge decides this. If the submission is rejected the defence counsel opens his case and calls his witnesses whom he examines; they may be then cross-examined by the plaintiff's counsel. The defendant's counsel then addresses the judge and jury, after which the plaintiff's counsel does likewise. If the judge is sitting with a jury he sums up the case to the jury who then retire to consider their verdict. Having reached their decision they return to the court and inform the judge who gives the judgment. If the judge is sitting without a jury he reaches his decision alone and informs the court of his judgment. The award of costs is at the judge's discretion but in general they are awarded to the successful party.

The procedure for a claim in the County Court is similar to that just described but much simpler. Indeed the system is constructed with the intention of keeping the use of lawyers to a minimum. An increasing development is that of settling small claims, presently those below £500, by an arbitration arrangement within the court system.

Elements of the Law of Evidence

The law of evidence is composed partly of statutes and partly of common law. It aims to exclude evidence that is not relevant to the issue and to achieve, so far as is possible, a fair trial of any issue.

An important feature is the burden of proof; this is the burden of establishing the guilt of a person or, in a civil case, proving an issue. In a criminal case the duty is to prove the guilt of the accused beyond all reasonable doubt, otherwise the accused must be found 'not guilty'. In civil cases the guilt is established by a preponderance of evidence, so the burden is not as great.

Evidence may be divided into various classes: direct, circumstantial, documentary, primary and secondary. Direct evidence is where a person states in evidence what he actually saw, for example, a car being driven at a fast speed. Circumstantial evidence is evidence which may be inferred from certain facts, such as skid marks made by a car on the wrong side of the road. Documentary evidence is that derived from a document. Primary evidence is the best available evidence of a specific fact; this means in the case of a document the production of the original document. Where the original document cannot be produced, and the court is satisfied as to the reason for failure to produce it, the court will permit the introduction of secondary evidence to prove the contents of the original document.

Hearsay evidence is when a witness tells the court not what he saw, but what he was told by another person. In general, hearsay evidence is not admissible on the grounds that the person who made the original statement was not on oath; that he is not in court so that the court may see his demeanor; and that a tale retold is often altered. There are, however, many exceptions to this rule; many statements made by persons who subsequently die are admitted – failure to allow them might exclude the only available evidence in the case.

The opinion of witnesses is in general inadmissible since it is the court's duty to decide on the evidence and not on the opinions of the witness. There is, however, an exception to this: the opinion of an expert will be admitted as evidence if it concerns a matter where he is competent to form an opinion by reason of his special study or experience.

Certain evidence will be excluded on the ground that the evidence is privileged. Matters of public policy are thus protected; it would not for example, be in the best interests of the country to disclose certain affairs of state. In the case of *Duncan* v *Cammell, Laird & Co. Ltd.*, 1942, the court upheld the refusal of the Admiralty to give information concerning a submarine disaster where a claim for damages was being made by a relative of one of the victims. A similar privilege exists regarding meetings and documents when a person consults his legal advisor. This is held to be professional privilege and the court will not allow evidence to be given unless the person who has the privilege, the client, wishes to waive the privilege.

An important feature in the law of evidence is the protection given to negotiations conducted to settle a dispute without going to court. Any admissions made in the course of such negotiations will be protected and cannot be given in evidence in court, provided the documents are marked with the words 'without prejudice'. The same protection applies to oral negotiations. The law may imply that the negotiations are 'without prejudice' from their nature even though the documents have not been so marked. Furthermore, if a series of correspondence is started by marking the first letter 'without prejudice', all subsequent letters, even if not so marked, are similarly protected. This protection cannot be claimed unless a dispute exists. So the marking of a document 'without prejudice' when no dispute existed would not be accepted by the court. It would be an attempt to claim protection for a possible dispute which might arise and, as such, is outside the scope of protection.

A witness's attendance in court may be secured by serving a *subpoena ad testificandum*; a *subpoena duces tecum* requires a witness to attend and produce documents for the court. Failure to obey these subpoenas may be held to be contempt of court.

3

National and Local Government

Government Departments

The law concerning the Government is partly written in statutes and partly unwritten. Many measures in use in Parliament do not have the force of law but are recognized and obeyed; these are known as conventions. Government departments are still under the control of the law even though they are connected with the main law making body in the country. In some respects they have certain privileges but in general their position is the same as that of the ordinary man.

The individual is protected from arbitrary action by the state by such statutes as: the Magna Carta, 1215, requiring that no man shall be imprisoned, executed or deprived of his property except by the law of the land: the Petition of Rights, 1628, preventing taxation except by consent of Parliament; the Habeas Corpus Act, 1679, requiring the release from prison of a person not lawfully detained. Only in times of exceptional danger, for example in 1940, has Parliament made laws to reduce or remove this protection given to the individual.

Government departments in general obtain their powers from statutes. These statutes are made in the normal manner by Parliament. Subject to discussion and opposition, each part is examined carefully to determine exactly what its full effect will be when in force.

Each government department has a Minister or some other political head who is in charge of the department and answers for its actions to Parliament. There is also a permanent civil servant who is responsible for seeing that the policy of the Minister is carried out and who may be called upon to advise the Minister. The political head may change with an election or he may be removed by the Prime Minister, but the permanent civil servant remains. The Government of the day decides the number and type of departments it will have. New departments may be created where there is felt to be a need to provide such a department. Other departments may be enlarged to take in a new function. At other times departments are given more importance by having their Ministers included in the Cabinet.

The Civil Service of this country is much admired by other countries. Our Civil Service is efficient despite what is said to the contrary, its honesty is beyond question and cases of corruption are almost unknown. Since 1855 civil servants have entered the service by qualifying examination, and from 1870 the system of open competition has been in use. There are three main classes of civil servant:

1. The Administrative class which is made up of university graduates and those who have qualified to enter from the Executive class. Their concern is with making decisions and they consequently occupy the important positions in the civil service.
2. The Executive class is composed of persons who are not usually university graduates but are of G.C.E. A level standard of education. They may, in fact, have entered the class by competitive examination from the Clerical class. Their responsibilities are the more important functions of the day to day work of the service.
3. The Clerical class is composed of persons who have had a secondary school or similar type of education bringing them up to G.C.E. O level standard of education. Their duties are the routine work of the departments.

Many departments recruit technical officers as the work of the department may well be such that it cannot function properly without proper technical staff. The best example of this is the Department of the Environment where a staff of architects and surveyors, among others, is employed.

It should not be thought that government departments and civil servants are solely concerned with the procedure for making law or the administration of law; many departments act in an advisory capacity, seeking to bring about an improvement in technical knowledge by means of lectures and discussions. Again, the Department of the Environment is a good example of such a ministry.

Local Government

A great deal of the capital works, such as schools, public buildings, housing developments and road construction, being carried on in the country at the present time is under the control of local authorities and their importance should not be underrated.

The earlier system of local government had its origins in Acts of Parliament passed in the nineteenth century. These local government units existed until recently. Changes were made from time to time but in the main these were minor changes which did not bring about the major reorganization of the structure of local government which many people felt to be essential. The question as to the form of the new local government was to be considered by a review body. A review commission was appointed by the Local Government Act, 1958, but before the work of the Commission was completed a Royal Commission was set up to review local government. The report of the Royal Commission was very comprehensive, but in general it said that there were too many local government authorities and many of the authorities were too small to function properly. The aim was to re-structure local government so that it was more efficient.

The Local Government Act, 1972, which has been amended by the Local Government Act, 1985, created the present system of local government. The aim is to have large efficient local government units. The system consists of two main local authorities, county councils and district councils. There are also parish councils and meetings which have very limited powers and which, for our purposes, can be excluded from further consideration.

There are 47 county councils and 369 district councils. The Local Government Act, 1985, abolished the Greater London Council and the 6 metropolitan county councils which had been created under earlier legislation. The functions these councils discharged have been allocated to district councils and to some specially created controlling bodies. An example is the police authority which controls the police function previously the responsibility of the metropolitan county council. Arrangements vary from one area to another.

County Councils

The new county councils do not follow the previous system of being based on geographical areas. Indeed the new areas include in many cases parts of several of the older administrative counties. Now the areas are made up so as to give areas of suitable size, population and resources.

County councils have the status of corporate bodies, that is, they are separate legal entities. Their financing comes from rates and grants and loans from the central government. The councils are made up of a chairman and councillors. The chairman is appointed from the councillors and is given an expenses allowance for his duties. Councillors are elected for the divisions making up the county. The councillors hold office for four years and all retire at the same time.

The functions of county councils are those that, it is believed, are best served by having large units over big areas. For example, the administration of the fire and police services is considered to be more efficient and economical in large units. County councils are the top tier of a two-tier system which has the finance, resources and experience to control essential public services over a wide area. Some functions are such that they can best be served by being shared with the bottom tier of the system, that is the district councils; for example, town and country planning functions are shared. The important matter of the preparation of the development plan is dealt with by the county council, with less important matters being left to the district councils.

District Councils

A district council is the bottom tier of the two tier system of local government. District councils are either metropolitan if within a former metropolitan county council area or non-metropolitan if in an ordinary county council area. The aim of the district council is to provide a local government unit which is in close contact with the public and therefore able to deal with the day-to-day matters which arise. Some matters are of considerable importance to the population of a locality and are of little interest to others.

District councils are corporate bodies. The financing of these councils is by rates and grants and loans from the central government. A rate is collected in these areas for the county council to pay for the services provided by that body. The council has councillors who are elected for four years with one of the councillors being the chairman. In a few of the older and more important towns the office of Lord Mayor has been retained. An expense allowance is paid to the chairman. In some areas there is a system of partial retirement with elections so that there is some continuity of membership of the council. Councillors are elected for parts of the district.

The functions of the district councils include such matters as housing, refuse collection, some town and country planning functions, environmental public health, and building regulations administration. In the case of metropolitan district councils additional functions apply. These are ones formerly the responsibility of the metropolitan county councils. An example is the responsibility of metropolitan district councils to administer all town and country planning provisions.

Local Government in Greater London

Until the Local Government Act, 1985, came into force there was a Greater London Council. This acted as the council for the Greater London area and was responsible for the major services in the area. The Greater London Council is now abolished. Its functions have been given to some special bodies and to the 32 London borough councils. These councils also exercise the usual functions of district councils.

Committees

The many and varied duties a local authority has to perform mean that it is not possible for the whole council to deal with its duties. The system has arisen, therefore, for councils to form committees to deal with a particular function or group of functions. A committee formed to deal with housing would, for example, be unlikely to be able to deal with any other function. The various committees report to the full council at a meeting, held as a rule once a month, when the reports and recommendations are discussed and action is authorized. Some committees may have certain functions, such as planning decisions, delegated to them for direct action.

Control of Local Authorities

A local authority is a corporation, which in the legal sense means that it has a separate existence from its members. It has a name and all legal transactions must be made in that name; even though its members die the corporation continues, this is known as perpetual succession. The evidence of the local authority's will is by the affixing of its seal on documents.

The power to act, to spend money, and to conduct its affairs is contained in an Act of Parliament. Unless the local authority can show statutory authority its act is illegal. This principle is the doctrine of *ultra vires*, which means 'beyond the powers', a breach of which will cause the courts to intervene to correct the matter. An example of this doctrine is to be seen in the case of *Prescott v Birmingham Corporation*, 1955, where Birmingham Corporation sought to give free travel on its buses to old-age pensioners. A ratepayer objected to this proposal and brought the matter before the court. The court ruled that the action was not in accordance with any statutory authority and so was *ultra vires*. (The law on this point has subsequently been changed and such action is now within a local authority's power.)

A very effective form of control in the case of the smaller units of local government is the District Audit. This is an annual audit of the accounts of the local authority conducted by a civil servant to ascertain if the local authority's spending has been in accordance with law; to disallow any item of expenditure not in accordance with law; and to surcharge that amount upon the person responsible for the expenditure. The district auditor's surcharge is made by his finding being authorised by a declaration of the High Court. This surcharge may be made on a member of the council or an official of the council. There is a right of appeal against a surcharge to the High Court.

Another important form of control is for the head of a Government department to withold the payment of a grant if he believes the local authority to be acting improperly in connection with that function for which the grant is made. This threat of withdrawal of the grant has been used successfully on several occasions by the Home Secretary where he disapproved of the choice made by a local authority for the appointment of its chief constable.

Local authorities are subject to the control of the courts by means of the High Court Orders of *Mandamus*, Prohibition and *Certiorari*. *Mandamus* is an order commanding the performance of some public duty. Prohibition is an order preventing an inferior court completing something already begun. The order of *certiorari* removes from the control of an inferior court matters it has decided for the review of the High Court. Actions of a local authority may also be tested by declaratory judgment; this is where the High Court gives its decision on a point of law or of rights. An injunction may also be granted to prevent the commission of a particular act.

In addition to the above powers of control many statutes giving power to local authorities also give a right of appeal to the courts to those persons aggrieved by the action of the local authority.

Control of Members of Local Authorities

As we have seen above members are subject, in certain cases, to the power of the District Auditor to surcharge. In addition to this, a means of proper control of business is the requirement in Section 117 of the Local Government Act, 1972: a member having a pecuniary interest, whether direct or indirect, in any matter under discussion, must declare his interest. This declaration may be related to the matter under discussion or be a general notice of interest given to the Chief Executive.

Control of Officers of Local Authorities

A local authority may appoint such officers as it thinks necessary to discharge its functions. There are, however, a few appointments which local authorities are bound to make: for example, there must be a chief education officer. A person appointed by a local authority must conform to the requirements of his employment, including, as we have seen, the declaration of any direct or indirect pecuniary interest in any contract being dealt with by his authority.

The Local Government Act, 1972, has given local authorities

much greater flexibility with regard to the use of their officers than had previously been the case. The Act recognizes that skilled, experienced officers have much to contribute to the efficient running of local government. There is therefore the means available for a local authority to delegate to an officer the discharge of certain functions without having to obtain the prior consent of the council or a committee. When an officer, acting in accordance with his duties for the local authority, commits a tort the local authority will be liable for the wrong. This liability for an officer's torts will be discussed more fully later.

4

Company Law

Company Law

Companies were first formed in this country by means of Royal Charter. The Crown had the right to create companies which had a separate legal existence to the persons forming the company. Some of the companies so formed are still in existence, for example the Hudson's Bay Company. Later, in the nineteenth century, companies were formed for public utilities such as canals, gas supply and railways. These companies were formed by Act of Parliament but this method was not available to all who wished to form a company. To meet the desires of those people the Companies Act, 1844, was passed. This Act allowed the formation of companies by the registering of their documents with a government department; these companies were known as registered companies. Later Acts were passed building up the law concerning companies and the main Act now in force is the Companies Act, 1985. Most companies in existence today are registered companies.

The question may be asked, why form a company? In what way can the small builder gain by creating a company instead of running his business as a private individual? The advantages of a company in general outweigh the disadvantages. A company usually has capital provided by shareholders, this means that sufficient funds can be obtained to allow the company to expand; bigger jobs can be taken on without causing a breakdown in the financing of the job; and further capital can be obtained if expansion is such as to require this. Shareholding also allows persons to invest money without having to take part in the running of the company. From the builder's point of view the really important feature is that the liability of the company for its debts is on the company alone, it is not on him as an individual. This differs from partnership which is considered later.

The disadvantages are that the company has a board of directors controlling the management of the company, and shareholders who expect regular payment of dividends on the shares they hold. So the control is in general shared and not the immediate responsibility of the builder whose efforts initially brought about the creation of the company.

Nature of a Company

A company has a separate legal existence to its members and can act within the objects specified in the memorandum of association; it can own property, make contracts, transact business and employ people; and it can sue and be sued concerning its affairs. The members cannot be sued for the company's debts but they may in some circumstances be called upon to pay money to the company to allow it to meet its debts. The separate existence of a company is clearly illustrated in the case of *Salomon* v *Salomon & Co.* 1897. Salomon was in business on his own as a boot manufacturer. After a number of years without any financial difficulty, he formed a company with other members of his family as shareholders holding one share each. He took debentures from the company in return for the transfer of his business to the company. The company ran into financial difficulties and the creditors sought to obtain what was due to them. As the debentures ranked higher in the order of payment than the sums owed to the creditors, the creditors asked the court to set aside the debentures owned by Salomon on the ground that Salomon and the company were one and the same person. The court refused to do this stating that the company was a separate legal entity and that the debentures had to be paid before the trade creditors.

Registered Companies

As we have seen, a registered company is a company registered under the Companies Act. The documents are registered with an official, known as the Registrar of Companies, in Cardiff.

Companies are usually registered with limited liability, this is the limitation of the liability of its members. As a general rule limitation is the amount remaining unpaid on the members' shares. Until the Companies Act 1985 came into force some companies were formed where the liability was by guarantee, the members guaranteeing payment of a sum in the event of the company being wound up. This is now for private companies only.

Registered companies may be public or private companies. By Section 81 of the Companies Act, 1985, a private company must not offer, allot or agree to allot shares or debentures of the company to the public. A private company must have not less than two members. A public company is a registered company which is not subject to the above restriction. A public company must not have less than two members. The reason for the existence of these different companies is quite simple. Private companies were intended to be companies formed from family businesses with the capital provided by the families. Public companies were intended to be formed by capital obtained by means of an invitation to the public to subscribe for the debentures and shares of the companies. A number of public companies have formed private companies as subsidiary companies. This enables the subsidiary companies to operate as separate legal entities yet still to be within the overall control of the public company. In fact subsidiary companies are often formed to deal with works which are ancillary to the work of the public company. For example, a large building contracting company may form a subsidiary company which specializes in foundation works. The subsidiary company's services are always available to the building contracting company, but when not so used may be making profit by working for others.

It should not be thought that public companies in this country are necessarily the large companies and private companies the small companies; some private companies are of a size exceeding that of many public companies.

Financing of a Registered Company

The financial affairs of companies are, in general, outside the scope of this book, but a brief note may help in understanding other aspects of company law.

Preference shares are shares giving the holder priority in the payment of dividends, usually at a fixed rate. The voting rights of such shareholders are restricted.

Ordinary shares carry, in general, the right to vote at general meetings, but they come after preference shares when payment of dividends is being made. So, if the sum available for dividends is sufficient for the preference shares only, then the ordinary shares receive nothing.

Preference and ordinary shares are usually referred to as the capital of the company and detailed in the memorandum of association.

Debentures are loans made to the company. The usual practice is to give debenture holders a mortgage or charge on the company's property as security for the loan. This allows the debenture holders to have remedies against the company's property.

Memorandum of Association and Articles of Association

The memorandum of association is the company's charter defining its powers. It informs all who deal with the company what the company sets out to do. The Companies Act, 1985, Section 2, requires the memorandum of a public company to state the following:

1. The name of the company; with 'public limited company' as the last part of the title.
2. The company is to be a public company.
3. The registered office of the company is to be situated in England and Wales.
4. The objects of the company.
5. The liability of the members is limited.
6. The share capital of the company (which is to be not less than £50,000), and its division into shares and their value.

The Department of Trade can refuse to register a company in a name the Department believes in any way to be undesirable; included in this is where there is conflict with the name of an established company. A company formed to promote art, science, religion or other useful objects can, in certain circumstances, be registered with limited liability without having to use the word 'limited'. The name of a company can be changed subject to the approval of the Department of Trade.

The situation of the registered office determines the company nationality and domicile. The actual situation of the office must be notified to the Registrar within fourteen days of the company's incorporation so that the proper address for service of notices and documents is known. Further, the Act requires the company's registers of members, directors, charges on the company, debenture holders, and similar books to be kept at the registered office.

The objects of the company are usually worded in such a manner as to permit all forms of trading the company is likely to require. The objects clause sets out the company's powers and informs shareholders of the purposes to which their money may be applied. The doctrine of *ultra vires* applies to the objects clause. Any act which is not authorized by the clause is *ultra vires*. So, in *Ashbury Railway Carriage Co. Ltd.* v *Riche*, 1875, a company having as its objects the making of railway carriages and the business of mechanical engineers was held to be acting *ultra vires* when it contracted to purchase a concession to make a railway. The Companies Act, 1985, section 35 now has changed the rule in Ashbury's case, provided the person dealing with the company has had the transaction decided by the directors of the company. So a transaction by the directors even though it is outside the objects clause is binding on the company. The objects clause can be altered by special resolution of the company provided it is for one of the reasons specified in Section 4 of the Act.

The clause dealing with the capital states the amount and how it is divided. The Act allows the capital of a company to be increased or reduced provided certain requirements are satisfied.

The memorandum is concluded by the written agreement of the persons seeking to form the company and their agreement to take shares in the company.

The Article of Association is a document setting out the rules for the members and stating how the affairs of the company are to be conducted. The document deals with such matters as shares, transfer of shares, meetings, voting rights, directors and their powers, dividends, accounts, and the winding up of the company. The Companies Act, 1985, has a schedule containing a model form of articles for both public and private companies. Variations can be made to this schedule, which is known as Table A, or entirely different articles may be used. The articles are registered in the same way as the memorandum, and both are available for inspection by the public. The registration of these documents constitutes a notice to persons dealing with the company, so every person is presumed to know their content; they also form a contract between the company and members in their position as members.

Shares

We have seen that the capital of companies limited by shares is divided into different classes. Shares may be bought when the company is formed or by transfer from an existing holder. When a company is being formed and is inviting members of the public to subscribe for the shares it must give information, prescribed by the Act, in a document known as prospectus. The prospectus includes, amongst other things, an account of the company's activities, its objects and the names of its directors.

Each share holder is given a certificate which shows his holding and is evidence of his title to it. The articles control the transfer of shares and, in certain circumstances, may well give power to the directors to decline a proposed transfer.

Shares are sometimes issued with an amount still remaining to be paid, for example a £1 share may be issued for the payment of 50p, the remaining 50p is the uncalled part of the share and the company has the right to call for this amount when it wishes. It may be asked what happens if the call cannot be met. The articles usually provide for this by giving the company a lien on the member's shares, this allows the company to decline a transfer, to take the dividends or possibly to sell the shares. Any balance after a sale must be paid to the member. Another power is that of forfeiture for non-payment of the call. In this case the shares are forfeited to the company who reissue them on terms to secure payment. Should there be any balance this is not paid to the member. The usual practice is to give notice to the member that payment must be made on a stated day or the shares are forfeited.

Directors and Meetings

The appointment of directors is governed by the articles; there must be at least two for a public company and one for a private one, but it is usual to have several. The articles place the power of management in the hands of the directors who must act lawfully in accordance with their powers. They are trustees of the company and must exercise their powers for the good of the company. A director must declare any interest he has in any contract or proposed contract; failure to do so is a criminal offence. Certain persons, such as undischarged bankrupts, cannot, except with the court's consent, be appointed directors. The articles require directors to retire at stated times but they may then offer themselves for re-election. The directors receive payment for their services in accordance with the articles. A register of the directors and one of their holdings of shares and debentures must be kept at the registered office where it must be opened for inspection. Directors who act outside their powers, may be liable for breach of implied warranty – that is, they have impliedly warranted an authority which they do not possess.

Meetings are determined by the articles and by the Act. There must be an annual general meeting every year when the directors' reports, the accounts, and auditors' reports are considered. Twenty-one days' notice must be given of this meeting. Extraordinary general meetings are called to deal with business which, by the Act, cannot be dealt with at the annual general meeting; members may, subject to certain requirements, also call an extraordinary general meeting. Not less than fourteen days' notice is needed, unless some business requires a special resolution, in which case twenty-one days' notice is necessary. The articles set out the quorum needed for a meeting and who is to be the chairman.

Secretary

Every company must have a secretary. His appointment is made by the board of directors. The duties and salary of the office are usually the subject of a written agreement. His duties include filing of returns which must be made annually to the Registrar.

Accounts and Auditors

To protect the shareholders' interests the Act requires every company to keep proper books of account showing sales and purchases, sums of money received, and assets and liabilities. The books have to be so kept as to give a true and fair view of the state of affairs of the company. A further provision for protection of the shareholders and others is that every calendar year· the directors must lay before a general meeting of the company a balance-sheet and a profit and loss account. Both must give a true and fair view of the state of affairs. The balance-sheet gives details of share capital, reserves, and liabilities of the company. The profit and loss account gives details of payment for dividends and debentures, loans, income tax, depreciation and certain other expenses. The balance-sheet and the profit and loss account must be approved by the board of directors, sent to the members and debenture holders, and filed with the annual return.

Auditors must in general be professionally qualified and may not be regular employees of the company; they are required to make a report to the members of their examination of the company's balance-sheet and profit and loss account.

Investigation of the Company's Affairs

The Act requires that the Secretary of State shall appoint an inspector to make an investigation into the company's affairs if the court so orders or if the company, by special resolution, decides that an investigation is necessary. The Secretary of State may appoint an inspector if a specified membership applies for such investigation. The Secretary of State may also appoint an inspector on the board's own volition.

Winding Up

There are a number of ways in which the existence of a company can be brought to an end. The Registrar may strike the company off the register if he is satisfied the company has become defunct. The court may wind up the company compulsorily on a specified ground; to do this a petition is presented to the court and if the court is satisfied that the company ought to be wound up the necessary order will be made. The official receiver carries out, under the court's supervision, the process of winding up, getting in all the debts and finally paying off what remains, if anything, to the members.

If the company is solvent but the members wish to end the existence of the company, this can be done by means of a Members' Voluntary Winding-up. In this case a liquidator is appointed who carries out the business of paying off the company's debts, realizing its assets, and, finally, paying the surplus to the shareholders according to their rights.

If the directors of the company find that the company is insolvent they must call a meeting of the creditors. The creditors appoint a liquidator and a committee of inspection to assist him. The liquidator then carries out his duties and reports to the committee of inspection. Here the creditors are in control of the process of winding up, this may be compared with a members' winding up where the company retains control, or with a compulsory winding up where the court supervises the process.

The proceeds that have been realized are paid out in a specified order, an important feature of which is that there is a class of preferential creditors who must be paid before other creditors. The preferential creditors include those entitled to payment of rates, tax, wages, compensation, holiday pay, and the employer's contribution for National Insurance.

Partnership

Our brief consideration of company law probably suggests that running a company and complying with all the requirements of the Companies Act is too onerous for the small builder. If this is the opinion then an alternative with less onerous duties, but with certain disadvantages, is the form of association known as partnership. A large number of partnerships are in existence at present and many of them have been functioning satisfactorily for years.

A partnership, which is more properly called a 'firm', can be formed with little formality, it may arise by express agreement or agreement may be implied. A firm is a collection of individuals and has no separate legal entity, which we have seen is the case with a company. One effect of this loose structure is that the death or withdrawal of one of the parties ends that particular partnership, if the remaining partners continue the business a new partnership is implied; the introduction of a new partner creates a new partnership. Such alterations are often announced in the local papers so that all who deal with the firm are aware of the new partnership.

The Companies Act limits the number of partners to a partnership, in general, to not more than twenty. Each partner is entitled to share in the management of the firm and, by his position, is an agent who has authority, in the normal course of business, to contract on behalf of the partnership. Any such contract is binding on the partnership even though the other partners may be unaware of its existence and, in actual fact, disapprove. What is probably the major disadvantage to a partnership is that the liability is unlimited. This means that the personal assets of the partners can be got at to satisfy any default of the partnership.

The objects of the partnership are such as the partners want to make. The internal affairs of the partnership are usually governed by the deed creating the partnership.

From the above we can see that a partnership is easily formed, altered or ended. A major disadvantage is that a partnership is an association unsuited to the conducting of business on a large scale which requires sums of money to be invested over a period of years. Investors are deterred from taking partnership owing to the unlimited liability, and the fact, which is unacceptable to investors, that individual members have the right to bind in contract the association. The effect is, therefore, to restrict partnerships to the smaller businesses.

Bankruptcy

The law of bankruptcy is found in the Insolvency Act 1986. The law does not apply to registered companies but to individuals and firms. Many bankruptcies are by individuals carrying on some form of business but trading is not essential to constitute bankruptcy; an individual who becomes insolvent solely on his personal spending, without being engaged in any trading, may also be the subject of a bankruptcy action.

The aim of this branch of law is to distribute the assets of the bankrupt fairly among his creditors; to carry out this operation in an orderly and speedy manner; and finally to put the debtor in a position where he is freed of his debts and can make a fresh start in business life.

The Insolvency Act, 1986, has changed the law formerly based on the Bankruptcy Act, 1914, in a number of ways. It is no longer necessary to show that a person or firm committed one of a number of stated acts of bankruptcy. The grounds on which bankruptcy proceedings may be started are that a debt equal to the bankruptcy level, at present £750, is owed to the creditor and the debtor appears unable to pay this debt. A petition may be presented to the court by a creditor or creditors, by the individual himself, by a supervisor of a voluntary arrangement or by the Official Petitioner or other specified person where a criminal bankruptcy order has been made. A bankruptcy petition can only be presented to the court if the debtor is domiciled in England or Wales and present in England or Wales on the day the petition is presented or has lived in or carried out business in England and Wales during a period of 3 years before the day the petition is presented.

Where a debtor commits an act of bankruptcy his creditors may present a petition for him to be made bankrupt. This petition is presented to a court having jurisdiction: in London this is the High Court, outside London the county courts. The Insolvency Act requires that, for a creditor to present a petition, the creditor or creditors must be able to show that the debt or debts owed to the creditors or creditors is not less than £750; that the debt is a liquidated sum which is payable immediately or at some certain date in the future. Another requirement of the Act is that where a creditor holds some security for his debt he must, in his petition, state that he is willing to give up his security for the benefit of all the creditors or give an estimate of the value of the security. The reason for this latter requirement is that the creditor is allowed to deduct the value of the security from his debt and then to claim the balance of the debt as an unsecured creditor.

The next step in the procedure of bankruptcy is that the court, after receiving the petition from the debtor or any creditor, may make a bankruptcy order. It will refuse to make an order where, for example, the debtor has no assets and the making of the order would only waste money. The effect of the order, when made, is to place the property of the debtor in the control of a person who is qualified to act as an insolvency practitioner. Such a person would be a member of one of the professional accountancy bodies. His appointment also suspends the remedies of the creditors against the debtor's property. Where the debtor has a business it may be to the creditor's advantage to have the business continue for the time being; the Official Receiver, who is an official appointed by the Secretary of State for Trade, can therefore, by order of the Court, appoint a special manager who conducts the debtor's business. A petition, which has the effect of warning persons dealing with the land may be registered under the Land Charges Act, 1972. A bankruptcy order is registered by the Official Receiver.

Following the making of the order a number of things happen, all of which help to unravel what is often a tangled affair. First the debtor is interviewed at the office of the Official Receiver. The purpose of this interview is to instruct the debtor to prepare his statement of affairs; this contains details of his assets, debts and other relevant information. Second a creditors' meeting is held. At this meeting the creditors decide whether a composition or scheme of arrangements shall be accepted: both these measures are salvage efforts to avoid bankruptcy and to obtain the best possible payment for the creditors. Where neither of these measures is accepted the creditors appoint a trustee of the bankrupt's property. The duty of the trustee is to dispose of the bankrupt's property in the best possible way and to distribute the proceeds to the creditors. He also possesses unusual power in that he can refuse to accept ownership of property which he considers to be onerous, and may disclaim contracts which are unduly burdensome. To assist a trustee in his duties the creditors may appoint from among themselves a committee of inspection. After the order has been made the court may hold a public examination of the debtor. The purpose of this examination is to examine the debtor on oath in public regarding his conduct and affairs. Notes of the examination are taken and may be used in evidence against the debtor.

A person adjudged bankrupt is disqualified from holding certain public offices; he is also subject to a number of requirements regarding disclosure of his bankruptcy to traders. Offences against these requirements are punishable by fine or imprisonment.

The Insolvency Act, 1986, has made it considerably easier for a bankrupt to be discharged from the bankruptcy order. Formerly a bankruptcy order continued for many years, possibly for the lifetime of the bankrupt; now, in general, set periods of time apply. So a person who has not previously been made bankrupt is automatically discharged from bankruptcy 3 years after the bankruptcy began; where his estate has been administered this period is 2 years. Where a person has been made bankrupt previously the period is 15 years but application may be made to the court after 5 years and the court may grant this application.

There are various powers under the Insolvency Act, 1986, which give the court and others the means of securing information and taking action in order to carry out the provisions concerning bankruptcy.

5

Contracts

Contracts are legally binding agreements, made between two or more persons, whereby rights are acquired by one party to some act or forbearance on the part of the other party to the contract. It is probably true to say that no other branch of English law affects the general public as much as the law of contract. So many of our ordinary daily transactions create contracts, even though we may be unaware of the fact. The commonest example is paying a fare on the bus, this creates a contract between the passenger and the bus company. Another example is a purchase in a shop; it may be a newspaper or it may be a fur coat, each is a contract.

So far as the builder is concerned he contracts to construct a building. This contract is probably on a standard form of contract: that is, it has conditions set out in the contract and all possible eventualities are covered in the contract which is likely to be a fairly lengthy written document. The builder may also create contracts of service with his employees and other contracts when he orders materials from a merchant. Whether a contract is for a small inexpensive item or for a large expensive item the law regarding the contract is the same: the value of the contract is of no account. It is true to say, however, that a contract involving a large sum of money is usually drawn up by solicitors and may, in fact, have terms in it which specifically set out to exclude certain aspects of the law of contract. Many manufacturers refuse to sell their goods unless their terms of business set out in the contract are accepted; these terms of business may take away some of the legal rights of the customer.

It is a requirement of law that certain contracts shall be in writing, but most contracts may be either in writing or by word of mouth. Oral contracts, subject to the above, are binding but one difficulty that arises is that frequently each party remembers something different, usually to his advantage, about the oral contract and disputes often arise solely by reason of lapse of memory. Another difficulty arises when trying to prove the terms of the oral contract to the court. For these reasons it can be seen that written contracts, particularly for things of value, are more satisfactory than oral contracts.

A valid contract is said to require the following essentials:

1. Offer and Acceptance. This means an offer must have been made and accepted in its original terms.
2. Form or Consideration. The law requires that something, known as consideration, shall be given in return for what the other party offers. If, however, the contract is set in a particular form then consideration is not necessary.
3. Legality. A contract must have subject matter which is not contrary to law.
4. Capacity. The law has rules with regard to certain persons who are held to be without the necessary capacity of make a binding contract.
5. Genuineness of consent of the parties. This means that the parties must not have entered into the contract by fraud, mistake or certain other grounds.

The two classes of contract are:

1. Specialty Contract. This is a contract made by a deed, that is a contract signed, sealed and delivered. The commonest example of this is a conveyance.
2. Simple Contract. This is a contract created by writing, word of mouth, or implied from the conduct of the parties. This contract is not made in any special form.

Creation of Contracts

Before we consider the more detailed matters of contract law, it will probably be helpful to consider the intention to create a contract. The parties must have intended the agreement to be legally binding. A social agreement, such as a visit to stay with friends, is not a contract, so failure to keep the agreement cannot give rise to an action for damages for breach of contract. In the case of *Balfour* v *Balfour*, 1919, a husband who worked in Ceylon returned on leave to England where his wife had to stay for medical reasons. Having promised to pay her £30 a month until she went out to him in Ceylon he failed to make the payments and his wife sued for breach of contract. The court decided that there was no legal agreement so an action for breach of contract could not be brought. The agreement was a domestic matter between husband and wife. Where the parties to an agreement have intended the agreement to have no legal consequences and this is shown quite clearly, then the court will observe the fact. This was seen in the case of *Appleson* v *Littlewood (H) Ltd.*, 1939, where a competitor sent in a successful football coupon. A condition of the football pool was that business was 'in honour only' and that no legal relationship was to arise. The court had no difficulty in deciding that this transaction was not a contract.

Invitation to Treat

The preliminaries conducted before a contract is created can sometimes give rise to difficulty. The difficulty is that a statement as to the intention of a party might be confused with an offer that awaits acceptance. The best example of this is a shopkeeper placing goods in his window with prices marked on, or putting the goods on shelves in a self-service store. Here they constitute an 'invitation to treat', that is the shopkeeper is prepared to sell the goods by tender. The shopkeeper does not have to sell the goods at the marked price; he may take less or ask for more or he may decline to sell the goods at all. Invitation to treat was dealt with in the case of *Pharmaceutical Society of Great Britain* v *Boots Cash Chemists (Southern) Ltd.*, 1953, where an inspector of the Society went into a self-service store which had a system of paying for the goods at a cash desk. The inspector took some goods and attempted to pay for them at the cash desk. The sale was refused. The court said that the display of goods at marked prices was an invitation to treat and a contract was not formed until the money was taken at the cash desk.

Offer and Acceptance

We have seen that offer and acceptance is essential to a valid contract and that an invitation to treat is not an offer. The general rule with regard to an offer is that it is effective when, and not until, the offer has been communicated to the recipient. The basis of this is that if the offer is not communicated to the other party then that party has not had the opportunity to accept or reject the offer. This is seen in the case of *Taylor* v *Laird*, 1856, where Taylor was engaged to command the defendant's ship. During the journey he gave up the command of the ship but helped to work the ship home. All this was unknown to the defendant. Taylor brought a claim for his services and it was rejected on the grounds that the defendant had not had the opportunity of accepting or rejecting the offer.

It should not be thought that an offer can only be made to one particular person. An offer can, in fact, be made to persons unknown; examples of this are to be seen every day in the 'lost' columns of local newspapers where persons advertise that a reward will be paid to the person returning the advertiser's lost article. This is an offer open to all and accepted by the person who returns the lost article.

An offer will terminate for certain reasons such as the death of the person making the offer, or the passage of time; the law will not support an action on the principle that an offer should be open for an unreasonable time. A time is often stated during which the offer can be accepted; English law requires, however, that to keep an offer open some consideration must be given: this is known as acquiring an option.

Revocation of Offer

An offer may be revoked at any time before it is accepted. This revocation must, however, be communicated to the person who has received the offer. We have seen that in law it is necessary to give consideration to keep an offer open for a stated time; when this applies the offer cannot be revoked, except with the consent of the person who acquired the option. The requirement that revocation, to be effective, must actually reach the person to whom the offer was made before he accepts the offer can be best demonstrated by considering the case of *Byrne* v *Tienhoven*, 1880, where the defendant made a written offer to the plaintiff on the 1st October asking for a reply by cable. The plaintiff received this letter on the 11th October and replied immediately by cable. On the 8th October, however, the defendant posted a revocation of his offer. This letter of revocation reached the plaintiff on the 20th October. Having to decide whether the acceptance by the cable was effective when a letter of revocation was on its way the court ruled that revocation must be brought to the notice of the person receiving the offer before he accepts it.

Acceptance

The general rule in regard to acceptance may be stated to be that acceptance means communicated acceptance. In *Felthouse* v *Bindley*, 1862, Felthouse sent a letter to his nephew offering to buy his nephew's horse for £30. In the letter Felthouse said 'If I hear no more I shall consider the horse to be mine.' The nephew withdrew the horse from an auction sale but did not write to his uncle accepting the offer. Owing to a mistake of the auctioneer the horse was sold. Felthouse brought an action against the auctioneer on the basis that the horse was his. The court held that there was no contract, acceptance had never been communicated.

If acceptance is to be valid it must be made by a person in authority. In *Powell* v *Lee*, 1908, Powell was an applicant for the headship of a school; the board of managers interviewed him and passed a resolution that he be appointed. One member of the board, in a private capacity, told Powell of the resolution. Later the resolution was rescinded and Powell was not appointed. Powell sued. The court decided that there was no contract. The court ruled that as the board had not communicated its resolution to Powell there was no contract.

An offer may be made which is capable of acceptance by several people. In *Carlill* v *Carbolic Smoke Ball Co.*, 1893, the Carbolic Smoke Ball Co. made an offer in an advertisement to pay £100 to anyone who contracted influenza after using the smoke ball in the recommended way. Further, the advertisement said that £1000 had been deposited with a bank as a sign of the company's sincerity in the matter. Mrs Carlill used the smoke ball as directed and some time later caught influenza. She sued the company, which was held liable to Mrs Carlill. The purchase and use of the smoke ball as directed was acceptance of the offer. The fact that £1000 was deposited with a bank showed the company was sincere in its offer. The offer was capable of acceptance by a wide range of persons and had, in fact, been accepted by Mrs Carlill.

Another fact which is evident from this case is that acceptance need not be communicated, it can be implied by the action of the acceptor. The offerer must, in making the offer, have indicated that some particular form of acceptance would suffice; the person receiving, the offeree, must have committed some act which showed an intention to accept.

Acceptance by Post

An exception to the general rule that acceptance must be communicated is with regard to the postal service. Here the rule is that acceptance is communicated once the letter is put in the postbox, even if the letter never reaches the offerer. This matter was considered in the case of *Household Fire and Carriage Accident Insurance Co. Ltd.* v *Grant*, 1879. The defendant had offered to buy some shares from a company. The secretary of the company made out a letter of allotment of shares to the defendant and posted it to him. The letter was never received by the defendant. The company become insolvent and the defendant was held to be a shareholder on the basis of a contract made when the letter of allotment was posted. There are two reasons advanced for this exception to the general rule: that the post office is acting as agent for the offerer and so delivery to the post office is delivery to the offerer; and that if hardship arises from the loss or delay of a letter of acceptance then the hardship ought to fall on the offerer.

Qualified Acceptance

An acceptance must be in the terms of the offer. A qualified acceptance is regarded as being a rejection of the original offer and constituting a counter-offer. This rule was considered in the case of *Hyde* v *Wrench*, 1840. Wrench offered to sell his farm to Hyde for the sum of £1000. Hyde replied that he would pay £950 for the farm. Wrench rejected this, whereupon Hyde said he would pay £1000. Wrench declined. Hyde then brought an action to have the alleged contract enforced. The court said that the offer by Hyde to buy the farm for £950 was a rejection of the offer of £1000 and constituted a counter-offer. So the original offer had been rejected.

A further example which shows the importance of understanding this point of law is seen in the decision of the Court of Appeal in the case of *Butler Machine Tool Co. Ltd.* v *Ex-Cell-O Corporation (England) Ltd.*, 1979. Here Butlers were asked to give a quotation for a machine tool. Butlers quoted a price with delivery in 10 months' time. Butlers' offer was made subject to terms and conditions which would prevail over any others. One term was that if when the machine tool was delivered the price had increased that was the price to be paid. Ex-Cell-O sent their order using their own order form. This contained terms and conditions which did not include a price variation clause. With the order form was a tear-off acknowledgement of receipt of order. On it were the words 'We accept your order on the Terms and Conditions stated therein'. This was returned with a letter saying that the order was accepted in accordance with Butlers' quotation.

The machine tool was delivered and Butlers claimed payment of a higher price. A dispute then arose as to whose terms and conditions applied. The Court of Appeal decided that Ex-Cell-O, by sending the order on their own order form had rejected Butlers' quotation and made a counter-offer. This had been accepted by Butlers returning the tear-off acknowledgement. So there was no price variation clause in the contract entitling Butlers to the higher price.

Tenders

It is the practice of most local authorities, and other similar bodies, to invite tenders either for the carrying out of constructional work or the supply of materials over a period of time. Often documents are supplied to enquirers to assist them to tender a price. In law a tender is an offer by a builder or by a supplier as to what he will do or supply and the prices. There is no obligation on the person seeking the tenders to accept any offer whether it be the lowest or the only offer. Most local authority advertisements state that the lowest, or any tender, will not necessarily be accepted. There is no legal requirement for this, it is solely to inform the interested parties that they may spend time and money in preparing a tender which may not be accepted.

A tender to supply goods over a period of time, usually a year, is an undertaking to supply the required goods at the quoted price at any time during the year. Often the contract is to supply the goods at a stated price 'as and when the corporation may order from time to time'. Each transaction is an acceptance of a standing offer to supply. The supplier can end this arrangement by giving proper notice.

Capacity of Parties

To form a valid contract each party must have full capacity to enter such a contract. The law gives a certain amount of protection to some individuals with regard to their capacity to contract. When a person without full capacity to contract enters into an agreement the effect is to make the contract void or voidable.

Corporations

Corporations have to contract by means of their servants, agents, or by a resolution made by their controlling officers. Until the Corporate Bodies Contracts Act, 1960, was passed, some doubt existed as to which contracts had to be made under the corporate seal of a corporation and those contracts for which this was not necessary. Now the position is that a corporation is bound by contracts made on behalf of the corporation by a person acting under its expressed or implied authority.

An exception to this is where a corporation has its power defined by a statute or by the object clause in its memorandum of association. In this case the doctrine of *ultra vires* applies and the corporation may be held to be incapable of entering into an *ultra vires* contract. The relevant case on this point is that of *Ashbury Railway Carriage and Iron Co. v Riche*, 1875, which was considered in the last chapter, and the effect on that decision of the provisions in section 35 of the Companies Act, 1985.

Lunatics and Drunks

A contract entered into by a lunatic or a drunken person is voidable: the person under the disability has the choice of letting the contract stand or of repudiating it on the grounds of his incapacity. The party pleading the drunkenness or insanity must show that the other party knew of his condition, and that at the time of making the contract he was so insane or drunk as to be incapable of realizing the import of his action. If he wishes to repudiate liability he must do so within a reasonable time, otherwise the contract is binding on him.

Minors

Another important consideration is the capacity of a minor to enter into a binding contract. In general, a minor is not bound by any agreement into which he enters: the agreement is void. There are however exceptions to this: under the Infants Relief Act, 1874, a contract for necessaries is binding on the minor. Necessaries are defined by the Sale of Goods Act, 1979, as: goods suitable to the condition in life of such minor or other person, and to his actual requirements at the time of sale and delivery. From this definition we can see that what is a necessary for one minor may be classed as a luxury for another minor. In *Nash* v *Inman*, 1908, a tailor supplied eleven fancy waistcoats to a Cambridge undergraduate. Evidence was produced to show that at that time, even though he was an undergraduate, he was adequately provided with clothing for his position in life. The court refused to accept that these were necessaries and so the tailor lost his action. If a contract is found to be for the supply of necessaries then the minor is bound to pay a reasonable price for the goods supplied.

Other contracts that are binding on a minor are contracts of service, of apprenticeship, or contracts otherwise beneficial. A contract of service is one where a minor binds himself so as to provide for his support; such contracts bind a minor provided they are beneficial to him. A contract of apprenticeship is similar to the above, in this case the minor receives instruction or education; this contract too must be for the infant's benefit. Contracts otherwise beneficial cover medical attention and a wide range of other matters. For example, in *Doyle* v *White City Stadium Ltd.*, 1935, a minor, who was a professional boxer, entered into a contract to box at the Stadium. Since he was a professional boxer an engagement to fight at the Stadium was held to be contract for his benefit.

The courts will not allow a claim to be made against a minor in tort so that he is made liable for what is, in fact, a breach of contract which is not binding on him.

Consideration

Consideration is an essential to a simple contract and, with one exception, is not essential to a specialty contract. Consideration was defined in the case of *Currie v Misa* 1875, as some right, interest, profit or benefit accruing to the one party, or some forebearance, detriment, loss or responsibility given, suffered or undertaken by the other. This definition is sufficiently wide to include many things. The simplest, and probably the commonest form of consideration is the payment of a sum of money in return for a promise to perform some service. So, in a building contract the contractor promises to construct a building within a stated time for the consideration of the money the client pays for the building work. In its more complex form consideration may consist of a person agreeing to give up his legal right to sue another.

Consideration must not be past; by this is meant a promise made after the act and which is unconnected with the act. An example of this is where a person who has been rescued from drowning promises his rescuer a reward and later he decided not to give the reward. The rescuer cannot sue on this promise since the service was performed before the promise of a reward was made.

Consideration is sometimes referred to as executory or executed. Executory consideration is a promise to confer a benefit at some future date: a person who obtains goods on credit sale is giving executory consideration by his promise to pay later for the goods he has obtained. Executed consideration arises when one party to the contract performs his part as soon as the contract is made: the shopkeeper handing over the goods on the credit sale is an example of this; he has fulfilled his part of the contract.

Consideration must move from the promise. That is, the person who brings an action to enforce a contract must show that he has himself furnished consideration for the promise of the other party.

In the case of *Bainbridge v Firmstone*, 1838, where Bainbridge owned two boilers which Firmstone sought to borrow for a time for the purpose of weighing them. Bainbridge agreed to the loan on condition that the boilers were returned to him in the same condition as when lent. When the boilers were returned they were in pieces. Firmstone had dismantled them so that he could weigh them. Firmstone was held to be in breach of contract. Bainbridge's consideration was the parting of possession of the boilers in return for Firmstone's promise to return the boilers in proper order.

Though consideration must be real it need not necessarily be adequate; this means that the consideration must be of some value in law but need not be what most people would consider to be full value.

The principle of consideration operated without serious doubt until 1947 when the case of *Central London Property Trust Ltd.* v *High Trees House Ltd.*, was decided. The effect of this case was to create a new principle. The principle is that if a solemn promise is given and acted upon by both the parties then the court will recognize the promise. The promise is recognized even though there is no consideration. The basis of the doctrine is that a party is estopped from acting against a promise he made. The doctrine can only be used as a defence, it cannot be used as a means of attack. The facts of the case were that the plaintiff had in 1937, let a block of flats for 99 years by lease under seal for an annual rent of £2500. In 1940, after the outbreak of war, the defendant found that he could not let all the flats so the plaintiff agreed to a reduction of the rent to £1250. In 1945, when conditions became normal again, the flats were all let. The plaintiff now brought an action claiming the full rent of £2500 for the future and for part of 1945. The court granted the plaintiff's application and said that if application had been made for the period 1940 to 1945 this would have been refused on the ground that it would have been inconsistent with the promise made by the plaintiff in 1940. The important point to remember with this case is that the principle can be used as a shield but not as a sword of attack.

Contracts Under Seal

One of the peculiarities of English contract law is that if a contract is made in a particular form the courts will, in general, uphold it even though it is without consideration. Such a contract is known as a specialty contract or a deed and must be in writing or printed on parchment or paper. The parties to the contract must sign or make their mark. At one time it was the practice to seal the contract with a party's coat of arms in a wax impression, now small red wafers are used. Originally delivery of the document was necessary, today delivery may be symbolic.

The law requires that a contract under seal is necessary in certain circumstances, including the following:

1. Where a legal estate in land is to be involved. This is a requirement of the Law of Property Act, 1925, Section 52.
2. Where a promise is made in a contract for which there is no consideration. An example is where a person promises a contribution to a charity. If the promise is by deed the contract is binding even though the charity is not giving consideration for the promise.

Before the Corporate Bodies Contracts Act, 1960, it was a rule of law that corporations had to contract by affixing the corporate seal to the contract document. This is no longer the case.

Two important features of specialty contracts are that statements in such documents are conclusive evidence, while in a simple contract statements are presumptive; and that action must be brought on a specialty contract within twelve years, while action under a simple contract must be brought within six years.

Genuineness of Consent

This term means that the consent of the parties to the contract must have been freely given and that the consent has been about the same thing. The effect of this requirement is to render void or voidable contracts which have been procured by duress, undue influence, misrepresentation or mistake. The law, in effect, is saying that it will not enforce a contract the consent of which has been obtained in some doubtful manner.

Duress arises when a contract is obtained by intimidation or pressure. The effect on a contract obtained by duress is to make the contract voidable at the option of the person intimidated.

Undue influence arises when a milder form of pressure is applied than that indicated by duress: the suggestion being that one party is in a position whereby he can influence the other party. The courts recognize this situation and in certain relationships will presume that influence has been exercised and that the transaction must be set aside. This presumption can, of course, be rebutted by showing that influence was not exercised. Examples of relationships where the courts will presume undue influence include those of solicitor and client, doctor and patient, trustee and beneficiary. In these relationships a contract must be shown to have been made without influence if it is not to be set aside. A contract obtained in this manner is voidable at the option of the injured party.

Misrepresentation

Misrepresentation arises when an untrue representation is made to a person to induce that person to enter into contractual obligations. Such representations are made before the contract is formed and are not actual terms of the contract. Misrepresentation takes two forms, representations made innocently and those made fraudulently. Both innocent and fraudulent misrepresentation have the same elements which must be proved before the contract will be set aside. These are:

1. the statement has to be one of fact and not of law;
2. the statement must be made by one of the parties to the contract;
3. the aggrieved party must show that he relied and acted on the statement in entering into the contract;
4. that by reason of the representation he had suffered damages.

Failure to satisfy all these requirements will defeat the claim.

Fraudulent misrepresentation was defined in the case of *Derry* v *Peek*, 1889, as being an untrue statement which was made knowingly or without belief in its truth, or recklessly, careless whether the statement is true or false.

The facts of the case of *Derry* v *Peek* were that the defendants, who had the right given by private Act of Parliament, to run horse trams, could, with the consent of the Board of Trade, also run steam trams. The directors of the company believed that the consent of the Board of Trade would be given without any difficulty; consequently the directors issued a prospectus stating that the company had the right to run trams by steam. When the necessary consent was sought the Board of Trade refused consent and the company was wound up. Derry, who had bought shares in the company on the statement in the prospectus, sued the directors for deceit. The House of Lords held that the prospectus expressed the honest belief of the directors and that the directors had reasonable grounds for that belief and so were not liable for fraud. A duty is placed on a person who makes a statement which he subsequently finds to be false, to inform the person who is acting on that statement.

The remedies available to the injured party in fraudulent misrepresentation are that he can treat the contract as binding and sue for deceit, or that he may repudiate the contract and bring an action for damages.

As stated above innocent misrepresentation arises when the same essential elements are proved, as with fraudulent misrepresentation, but in this case it is a misrepresentation made without fraud or negligence. The remedies available to the injured party for innocent misrepresentation are contained in the Misrepresentation Act, 1967. An injured party who has suffered loss may claim damages provided the other party would have been liable to damages if the misrepresentation had been made fraudulently. There is a provision, however, that the person making the representation may avoid liability for damages provided he had reasonable ground to believe and did believe up to the time the contract was made that the facts represented were true. A further remedy available is that of rescission of the contract. In this case, however, where proceedings arise from a contract which may be or has been rescinded, the court or arbitrator may declare the contract subsisting and award damages instead of rescission. Before awarding damages the court or arbitrator must be of the opinion that it is equitable to do so, having regard to the nature of the misrepresentation, the loss that would be caused by it if the contract were upheld, and the loss that rescission would cause to the other party.

A further provision of the Act is that in any agreement which contains a provision that would exclude or restrict any liability of a party to a contract by reason of any misrepresentation made by him before the contract was made, or excludes or restricts any remedy available to the other party to the contract by reason of that misrepresentation; then such provision shall be of no effect, unless, in proceedings arising out of the contract, the court or arbitrator allow reliance on the provision as being fair and reasonable in the circumstances of the case. The effect of this provision is to render inoperative clauses found in many contracts, particularly contracts on standard forms, which seek to exclude liability for misrepresentation; where, however, the clause is fair and reasonable in the circumstances of the case it may be upheld.

If the injured party in a case of fraudulent or innocent misrepresentation intends to exercise his right to rescind the contract, he is required to take the necessary steps within a reasonable time; otherwise the right is lost.

Contracts Uberrimae Fidei

A problem somewhat similar to misrepresentation is the circumstance where a person who is a party to a contract, which is a contract of the utmost good faith, possesses material facts essential to that contract which are unknown to the other party. In such a circumstance the law will require the party having the knowledge to disclose the facts to the other party. These contracts are known as contracts *uberrimae fidei* the commonest example of which is a contract of insurance. It is right and proper that the law should require a driver seeking insurance to disclose all material facts such as convictions for driving offences, and any other matters which would affect his liability as a driver, to the insurers if they are to calculate the risk correctly.

Mistake

Mistake in a contract is another factor affecting the genuineness of consent and may render the contract void. A mistake as to the law will not render the contract void but a mistake of fact may nullify an agreement which has all the appearance of being a contract. This aspect of the law of contract has many features: it includes mistake as to the identity of the other party to the contract, mistake as to the existence of the subject matter of the contract, and mistake as to the identity of the subject matter.

Identity of Party

In many contracts the identity of the other party to the contract is important. Indeed, in many instances the status of the other party determines whether a contract is made or not. From this it can be seen that if the identity of the other party to the contract is a material fact and a mistake is made as to that identity the contract will be void. An example of this is where Smith will contract with Jones solely because Jones is a man of substance and honesty. If another represents himself to be Jones and so deceives Smith the effect will be to make the contract void.

In *Cundy* v *Lindsay* 1878, a person named Blenkarn signed an order to Lindsay & Co. so that it appeared to come from a respectable firm by the name of Blenkiron who had offices in the same street. The order, which was for handkerchiefs, was fulfilled and Blenkarn immediately sold them to Messrs. Cundy. Lindsay & Co. sued for the return of the handkerchiefs on the ground that they had not intended to contract with Blenkarn and consequently he could not sell the goods with a good title. The court decided that there was no contract between Lindsay & Co. and Blenkarn.

In *King's Norton Metal Co. Ltd.* v *Edridge Merrett & Co. Ltd.*, 1897, the plaintiffs, who were metal manufacturers, received an order from a company called 'Hallam & Co.' of Sheffield. The letter-head had a picture of a large factory and a list of depots overseas. The plaintiffs sent the goods to the company as requested. The true facts were that there was no such company and that the letter-head had been fraudulently prepared by a person called Wallis. Wallis, having acquired the goods, sold them to the defendants. The plaintiffs sued the defendants on the ground that there was no contract to sell the goods and so the goods still belonged to them. They were seeking to show that there had been mistake in that they had not intended to contract with Wallis but with a reputable company. The court decided that the plaintiffs had intended to contract with 'Hallam & Co.' and so there was a binding contract. The defendants had obtained a good title to the goods.

Existence of Subject Matter

Mistake as to the existence of the subject matter of the contract is probably the clearest example of the operation of this part of contract law. It will arise when a mistake exists common to both parties where the existence of the subject matter is essential to the formation of the contract. In *Couturier* v *Hastie*, 1856, the parties to the contract agreed to the sale of a cargo of corn on its way to

England. Unknown to either of the parties the cargo had had to be sold by the captain of the ship during the voyage owing to the corn having been affected by the voyage. The contract was held to be void.

Identity of Subject Matter

Another important form of mistake is where there is mistake as to the identity of the subject matter of the contract. It arises where one party intends to contract in respect of one thing and the other party intends to contract in respect of another totally different thing. So in *Raffles* v *Wichelhaus*, 1864, the defendant agreed to purchase from the plaintiff a consignment of cotton coming from Bombay on the s.s. *Peerless*. Neither of the parties knew that there were two ships of the same name coming from Bombay, each on a different day. The plaintiff had intended one of the ships to be the subject matter of the contract and the defendant believed the other ship was the subject matter of the contract. The court had no difficulty in deciding this was a matter of mistake and that the contract was void.

Evidential Requirements

In the consideration of contracts under seal we saw that the law required some contracts to be made under seal. Some simple contracts must be in writing or they are void or unenforceable. Included in this classification is the requirement in an agreement for hire-purchase that there must be a note or memorandum in writing signed by the hirer. The note or memorandum must contain certain information as to the agreement. Contracts of hire-purchase will be dealt with later.

Two contracts which are unenforceable unless they are in writing are:

1. contracts of guarantee;
2. contracts for the sale of land.

Guarantee

Contracts of guarantee are governed by Section 4 of the Statute of Frauds, 1677. A guarantee may be simply expressed as being a promise to pay for something if another person fails to pay. For example: 'Give the goods to X and if he does not pay you I will.' Difficulty sometimes arises in distinguishing a contract of guarantee from a contract of indemnity. The distinction is most important since a contract of indemnity does not have to be in writing; action may be brought on a contract of indemnity which would fail for absence of writing in the case of a contract of guarantee. In a contract of guarantee the guarantor's liability only arises if the debtor primarily liable fails to pay. An example of such an arrangement is X selling a motor-bike to Y and X requiring a guarantor in the case of Y's failure to pay. The guarantor Z will only pay if Y fails to pay. Y is primarily liable and Z is secondarily liable. In the case of indemnity the position is different. Here a person promises to see that payment is made whatever happens; the promisor has made himself primarily liable, that is he pays whether the person who has received the goods can or cannot pay. An example may clarify this: X gives goods to Y on Z's promise that Z will see that X is paid. Z is primarily liable. In the case of *Lakeman* v *Mountstephen*, 1874, Lakeman, who was chairman of a local Board of Health, instructed Mountstephen, a builder, to carry out work at the Board's premises. Mountstephen asked who was going to pay, to which Lakeman replied 'Go on Mountstephen and do the work and I will see that you are paid'. The Board of Health refused to pay on the ground that it had never authorized the work. Lakeman, when sued, said he was only promising to pay the debt of the Board, that it was a guarantee within the Statute of Frauds and that since there was no evidence in writing the contract was unenforceable. The House of Lords decided that there was a contract of indemnity and that Lakeman was liable.

Sale of Land

Section 40 of the Law of Property Act, 1925, requires that for an action to be enforced on an agreement for the sale of land or other interest in land there must be a note of memorandum in writing signed either by the party against whom the action is brought or by his agent. The note or memorandum has to be in existence when the action is brought, but it need not be in existence when the contract is formed. The note or memorandum must clearly identify the parties, name the land concerned and bear the signature of the party against whom the action is brought. The memorandum may consist of several documents, for example a series of letters.

Doctrine of Part Performance

It should not be thought that the inability of a party to show that he has a note or memorandum in writing signed by the other party will necessarily leave him without a remedy; the courts will see that justice is done if the case requires action. The remedy is the equitable remedy of part performance. Since equitable remedies are at the court's discretion each case is considered on its merits. Equity will consider a claim if the following conditions are satisfied:

1. there must be acts of part performance suggesting the existence of a contract;
2. the acts of performance must have been performed by the plaintiff so that it would be unfair to allow the other party to avoid his obligations;
3. the contract must be one which, if it had been in writing, would have been enforceable;
4. there must be clear evidence of the contract.

The case of *Rawlinson* v *Ames*, 1925, is an interesting case on this topic. The facts were that Ames entered into a verbal agreement to take the lease of a flat belonging to the plaintiff. The plaintiff agreed to carry out certain alterations; during the course of these alterations the defendant inspected the work in progress and suggested further alterations which were carried out. When the work was completed the defendant refused to sign a lease and repudiated the agreement. The defence was that there was no note or memorandum in writing as required by Section 40 of the Law of Property Act, 1925. The court rejected this defence and found that there was a binding contract on the grounds that the acts of the plaintiff in carrying out the alterations as the defendant directed were acts of part performance sufficient to enable the remedy to be granted.

Discharge of Contract

A contract is held to be discharged when the person who has made the promise is no longer bound by his obligations. What is probably the commonest form of discharge is where the contract has been fully performed, but there are several other ways in which a contract may be discharged; one is the substitution of a specialty contract for a simple contract; this has the effect of discharging the simple contract. A contract is discharged when the parties to the contract agree to treat it as discharged. Where one party to the contract refuses to perform his obligations the other party may treat the contract as at an end. A contract may also be discharged when the other party is in breach of contract. This last form arises when an obligation placed on a party is made a condition to the contract; so that failure to observe that obligation is a breach of condition which discharges the other party from his obligations under the contract. If a person becomes bankrupt the trustee in bankruptcy has the power to disclaim any onerous contracts. The death of a person will end the contract only if the contract was formed for personal services.

The Limitation Act, 1980, requires action to be brought within a certain time otherwise the remedy is lost.

Impossibility

The discharge of a contract by reason of impossibility has sometimes presented difficult problems. The mere fact that circumstances have altered and that performance is impossible will not necessarily end the contract. In *Davis Contractors Ltd.* v *Fareham U.D.C.*, 1956, the building company entered into a contract to build seventy-eight houses at a fixed sum of £94,424. There was an unexpected shortage of skilled labour and materials. The contract consequently took fourteen months longer to complete than expected and cost £115,000. The building company claimed that the contract had been ended because of the shortages and that they were entitled to claim on a *quantum meruit* for the true cost incurred. The House of Lords when they came to consider the case refused to accept this claim. They said the unexpected shortage of skilled labour and materials did not discharge the contract even though the contract was much more onerous to the builder than when the contract was formed.

A further problem of impossibility, or frustration as it is sometimes termed, was considered by the House of Lords in *Fibrosa* v *Fairburn Lawson Coombe Barbour Ltd.*, 1943. A sum of money had been deposited as part payment for the purchase of some machinery to be delivered in Poland. The outbreak of war made the contract impossible to perform. The decision was that the part payment must be returned. As a result of this case the Law Reform (Frustrated Contracts) Act, 1943, was passed. The Act requires sums of money paid under a frustrated contract to be returned to the person making the payment and that all future payments need not be made; the court is permitted, however, to allow the expenses of the other party. The Act does not apply, amongst other circumstances, where the contract contains special provisions to deal with frustrated contracts, or where the intention is that the contract shall be binding in any event.

Remedies for Breach of Contract

Equity and common law both provide remedies for breach of contract. Equitable remedies, it will be remembered, are at the court's discretion, whereas common law remedies are granted as a right.

Equity may give a remedy by way of an injunction which may either require the doing of some act, or prevent some act being done which would constitute a breach of contract.

Decree of Specific Performance

The equitable remedy of specific performance may be used to enforce a contract where damages would not provide a sufficient remedy. A contract to purchase a house could be enforced by this remedy, since damages for breach of contract would probably be an inadequate remedy. Contracts for the sale of houses, land and rare objects have been enforced by the application of this remedy. There are certain principles followed by the courts in deciding whether to grant this remedy. These are that if damages would be an adequate remedy then specific performance will not be granted; the contract must be fair and the person seeking the remedy must have acted justly and honestly; if supervision of the courts is required specific performance will not be granted; and the contract must be specifically enforceable against each of the parties. This last requirement means that if a specialty contract is lacking in consideration the contract will not be enforced.

The court's reluctance to supervise the carrying out of a contract by the decree of specific performance has the effect of making contracts for personal service and contracts to build, contracts for which this remedy is usually unavailable. The reasons for this are that the court would have to exercise constant supervision to see its order was being observed (equity is not intended to be used in this manner) and that to compel a person to perform a service is not in the best interests of the parties concerned. Building contracts will not be enforced by specific performance unless it can be shown that damages would not be an adequate remedy, that the building work is clearly defined in a contract, preferably by quantities and drawings, and that the builder who has contracted to perform the work is in possession of the land, so preventing another builder carrying out the work.

Rescission

Rescission is a remedy granted by the courts, the effect of which is to return the parties to their original position before the contract was signed. It follows, therefore, that if events have occurred which prevent a party being returned to his original position the remedy is not available. Since the remedy is found in equity, the right to ask the court to set the contract aside will be lost if the plaintiff delays in bringing his action. Rescission is a remedy in lieu of damages and is given when a contract was entered into by fraud, misrepresentation, where there has been misdescription of the property or where, in the case of a contract *uberrimae fidei*, there has been failure to disclose material facts.

Rectification

Rectification is an equitable remedy which allows the court to order rectification of a contract which is in writing but which, by reason of some omission, does not fully express the true intention of both parties to the contract. The court in applying this equitable remedy will correct the written document so that it expresses the correct intention of the parties. As with other equitable remedies the court will require to be satisfied on certain grounds before the remedy will be granted. The grounds are:

1. the true intention of the parties must be clear;
2. the mistake must be common to both parties;
3. the contract must have been concluded before the written document was drawn up;
4. the mistake must be clearly shown and must have been in existence at the time the document was drawn up;
5. the mistake must be a mistake of expression only.

The application of this remedy may be best seen in considering the case of *Craddock Bros.* v *Hunt*, 1923, where property was sold by contract made by word of mouth. When the written contract was drawn up, it and the conveyance included by error an adjoining yard which had been exempt from the sale. The court ordered rectification of the contract and conveyance so that the true intention of the parties, a sale without the yard, was enforced.

Damages

In common law, in most cases, damages are given as a remedy for breach of contract. The fact that damages are found in common law means that, unlike equitable remedies, the conduct of the parties is ignored by the court. Common law damages are claimed as a right and are not at the court's discretion. There are various types of damages. Exemplary damages are not often awarded since they are by their nature a form of punishment. When such damages are awarded however they are given in excess of the actual financial loss suffered by the party. The damages were given in breach of promise actions. The House of Lords in the case of *Rookes* v *Barnard*, 1964, considered the question of the award of exemplary damages. The position now appears to be that the use of this award in future will be limited. The belief is that this award puts the court in the position where it imposes a fine on the defendants for what is a civil matter requiring compensation. So far as we are concerned this award may still be made where the defendant's conduct has led to him making a profit which is likely to exceed the damages which would ordinarily be awarded. Contemptuous damages may also be awarded. These were given in breach of promise actions. The practice is to award a contemptuous sum such as a penny as an indication of the court's opinion that even though the plaintiff has succeeded, the action ought not to have been brought. Nominal damages are awarded where there has been no actual financial loss suffered but the action is one which has been properly brought. In this case the sum awarded does not in general exceed two pounds. The usual award is substantial damages. These represent the actual financial loss suffered by the injured party.

In order to see that the award is fair and just there are a number of rules the courts will apply in awarding damages. The rules are that the award is, in general, to be as compensation and not to punish the party in breach of contract. Also the injured party is required to take all reasonable steps open to him to keep the loss to a minimum; he is not allowed to stand back and allow the losses resulting from a breach of contract to mount up when he could take steps to cut down the loss. A person is allowed to sue for damages even though at the time of the action being brought he has not actually sustained the loss. The circumstance would arise when a person had made a further contract on the strength of an existing contract which is broken; he would know that he himself is in breach with the subsequent action.

Rule in Hadley v Baxendale

The damages the court will award are only those which are reasonably foreseeable to result from the breach of contract. The leading case on this matter is *Hadley* v *Baxendale*, 1854. The decision in this case gave rise to two rules:

1. that damages are recoverable if they could fairly and reasonably be considered to be the natural consequence of the breach; or
2. that the matter was something both parties could reasonably be thought to have had in contemplation at the time the contract was formed.

The facts of the case were that Hadley, the plaintiff, owned a mill a shaft of which broke and was given to the defendant, a carrier, to take to an engineer as a model for a replacement. The defendant was told that the replacement was needed urgently but not that work had stopped because of the breakage. The delivery of the shaft was negligently delayed with the result that the plaintiff suffered loss of profits. The plaintiff in the action sought to claim for this loss of profit. The court would not allow this claim on the grounds that the carrier was not aware that this loss of profit would result from his delay. In *Victoria Laundry (Windsor) Ltd.* v *Newman Industries Ltd.*, 1949, the court decided that loss of profit, without any intimation, must be held to be foreseeable by any reasonable person when there is failure to deliver a part to a profit making plant. The second rule in *Hadley* v *Baxendale* may be said to be that where there are special circumstances, such as a peculiar risk, then any loss resulting from this peculiar risk will not be recoverable unless the parties knew of the risk when the contract was formed.

Quantum Meruit

Quantum meruit is a claim for a reasonable remuneration for work done or services by one person for another in circumstances which entitle the person performing the work or service to such remuneration. This claim will arise when there is no agreement as to the sum to be paid or where the action of the other party prevents the contract being completed. Another circumstance which may give rise to a claim for *quantum meruit* is where there is a breach of contract and the work executed is of a greater value than the contract sum. The case of *Planche* v *Colburn*, 1831, provides an example of the first application of *quantum meruit*. The plaintiff signed a contract to write a volume for the defendant's publication 'The Juvenile Library'. The payment for this work was to be £100. After the plaintiff had completed half the projected publication, the defendant decided to abandon the proposed 'Juvenile Library'. The court agreed to the claim for *quantum meruit* and awarded the sum of £50 for the plaintiff's labour.

Unfair Contract Terms Act 1977

There has been considerable concern in recent time at the practice of contracts being made which placed one of the parties to the contract at a substantial disadvantage. It had become increasingly common for those who provided goods or services to insert terms in the contract which excluded or limited liability for any fault on the contractor's part. It had been a clear case of the strong party to a contract dictating the terms and these were either accepted or no contract was made. Although the courts made efforts to reduce the severity of these contract terms their efforts were not in themselves sufficient. The Unfair Contract Terms Act 1977 has been passed to deal with this situation.

Section 2 of the Act contains two important provisions with regard to contract terms. Before considering these provisions it should be noted that Section 2 only applies to business liability, that is from things done in the course of business or from the occupation of premises used for the business purposes of the occupier. The expression business in this sense includes a profession and the activities of any government department or local or public authority. So architects, surveyors and builders come within this definition with regard to their professional work.

The first provision in Section 2 is that a person cannot by a contract term exclude or restrict his liability for death or personal injury resulting from his negligence.

This provision brought to an end a practice which has existed for years of a person carrying out a contract without being liable for death or personal injury resulting from his negligence to the other party to the contract.

The other provision is that a person cannot by a contract term exclude or restrict his liability for other loss or damage for his negligence except where the term satisfies the requirement of reasonableness.

This provision also brings to an end the common practice of persons providing goods or services under a contract which contains a term limiting their liability for their negligence to a small sum of compensation.

The only circumstance in which such a term will still be enforceable will be where the term satisfies the requirement of reasonableness.

The requirement of reasonableness is set out in Section 11. This states that the term shall have been a fair and reasonable one to be included having regard to the circumstances which were, or ought reasonably to have been, known to or in the contemplation of the parties when the contract was made.

Section 11 also states that where a contract term restricts the liability to a specified sum the requirement of reasonableness shall be assessed with regard being paid to the resources the person would expect to be available to him to meet his liability, and how far it was open to him to cover himself by insurance. These provisions apply in addition to the other matters to be considered in deciding whether a contract term was fair and reasonable in the circumstances.

An example of when a person might need to limit his liability to a specified sum would be where a structural engineer was commissioned to produce a design of an entirely new and untested kind. In this case the structural engineer might have difficulty in obtaining insurance cover or adequate insurance cover for the work he had undertaken. In this circumstance a court might decide that it was reasonable for him to have a contract term which limited his liability to a specified sum. The risk of an unusual design and the inability to obtain satisfactory insurance cover making the term a reasonable one to use in the contract.

Another common practice in commerce and industry is for parties to a contract to make their contract using written standard terms of business. In the construction industry this practice has been followed in two ways. The first has been to have a contract for a construction project on one of the standard forms of contract used in the industry; these standard forms are prepared by joint committees representing all the interested parties in the industry. The second is the use of a written form of contract which has been prepared by some particular company.

The first form of written contract has not given rise to too much difficulty since it has been produced only after there has been full consultation and discussion with all the parties in the industry who will be using the contract form.

The second form of contract has given rise to difficulty and ill-feeling since the document has been prepared by a person who may be a sole supplier of goods or services and who is unwilling to conduct business otherwise than by the use of his own form of contract. That form of contract having been prepared by him to protect his own interests only.

Section 3 of the Act now deals with the situation where a person contracts on the other party's written standard terms of business. The provisions in the section lay down that a party whose written standard terms of business form the contract cannot by any contract term exclude or restrict any liability of his when he is in breach of contract. This is however subject to the requirement of reasonableness in Section 11.

So by this provision the position now is that if a company prepares and uses its own written form of contract and will only do business by the use of that form of contract any term in that written form of contract by that company will only be effective if that term satisfies the requirement of reasonableness. That is, the court will have to decide if it was a fair and reasonable term to have been included in all the circumstances when the contract was made.

Section 3 also states that a contract term in a written form of contract which apparently entitles the person whose contract form it is to render a contract performance substantially different from that which was reasonably expected of him or to render no performance at all for either the whole or part of the contract, shall not be effective unless that term satisfies the requirement of reasonableness.

This particular provision was introduced to deal with the most extreme examples of exclusion or restriction terms. It was not unusual for some specialist supplier of goods or services to have a term in his written contract excluding or restricting his liability if he failed to perform either the whole or part of his contract. Now the position is that any such contract term will be effective only if it satisfies the requirement of reasonableness set out in Section 11.

Arbitration

We have seen that the courts have various remedies which they will grant for breach of contract. In many cases, however, the parties to a contract do not want to seek a remedy in court; when the contract is of a technical nature they often prefer to have a dispute settled by a technically qualified person. Further, there is the belief that settlement of disputes outside the courts will be less costly than a court action. Other factors are that settlement may be more speedy than a court action, and that the matter will be decided in private. It is for these reasons, amongst others, that a contract may contain a clause requiring the parties, in the event of a dispute, to appoint an arbitrator to settle the dispute. Such a clause is found in the J.C.T. (Joint Contracts Tribunal) standard form of contract. It must be made clear at this point that such a clause does not exclude the authority of the court to hear an appeal on a point of law after the arbitration award has been made or to decide a preliminary point of law before the award is made. Subject to this, an arbitration clause in a contract is valid and binding. A person may be named in the contract as an arbitrator or the means whereby an arbitrator is to be appointed in the event of a dispute may be set out in the contract.

The law relating to arbitration is found in the Arbitration Act, 1950, as amended by the Arbitration Act, 1979 and at common law. An arbitration agreement to be enforceable under the Act must be in writing. An arbitration agreement may be ended only by consent of both parties; not by the wish of one party alone, nor, for that matter, by the death of one of the parties. The court will remove an arbitrator where it has been proved that the arbitrator misconducted himself, or that he has an interest or is biased in the matter in dispute. Where the court has ordered the removal of an arbitrator it may appoint another person in his stead. The Act also gives power to the court to remove an arbitrator and make a new appointment where the original arbitrator refuses to act, is incapable of acting or is dilatory, and to appoint a new arbitrator where the one appointed under the agreement dies.

The arbitration begins by the parties informing the arbitrator of his appointment, to which he must agree. The arbitrator then completes the preliminaries, which are to confirm that he has been properly appointed and has the necessary authority to decide the dispute. Satisfied on these matters the arbitrator usually holds a preliminary meeting with the parties in dispute. The purpose of this meeting is to fix a date for the hearing, to arrange for the delivery of the claim and the defence, to settle what documents are to be produced, and to arrange for the inspection of the property by the arbitrator and the parties.

When the arbitrator has got the dispute clearly defined, with each party knowing what evidence the other will produce to substantiate his claim or defence, the hearing may take place. The hearing is under the control of the arbitrator who is under a duty to see that it is conducted properly: that is, that the rules of natural justice are applied. Though the procedure is at the discretion of the arbitrator most arbitrations follow the procedure of a civil action in the High Court. The hearing is, however, private and members of the public will not be admitted if either party objects to their presence. There is no requirement that the case for either side shall be conducted by a lawyer, if a party so elects he may conduct his own case; a solicitor or barrister may however be engaged to represent a party. Where the procedure used is that of a civil action the hearing begins by the claimant stating his case and calling his witnesses who may be cross-examined; this is followed by the defence acting likewise. Finally the respondent and claimant address the arbitrator. The arbitrator may ask any question at any stage of the hearing. The arbitrator then closes the hearing and informs the parties that his award will be announced later.

The evidence given at the hearing is governed by the law of evidence as if it were a court of law, subject however to the parties' right to agree to modify or ignore the rules of evidence. Witnesses or documents may be summoned to the hearing by the use of subpoenas. Evidence from witnesses may be given on oath if the arbitrator so requires. False evidence by such witnesses may be perjury, for which a criminal prosecution may be made.

At some point in an arbitration the arbitrator may find that he has to deal with a difficult point of law. Where this arises any of the parties to the arbitration may under section 2 of the 1979 Act apply to the High Court for the point of law to be determined. There is a right of appeal in certain circumstances to the Court of Appeal.

The award is made by the arbitrator after he has considered all the evidence. The Act allows an arbitrator to make an interim award. The time for making the final award may be fixed in the arbitration agreement; failing which the arbitrator is required to make his award with due despatch. The award itself, which usually is in writing, must be signed by the arbitrator and his signature attested by a witness. Further, the award must be certain so that no doubt can arise in its performance, and must deal fully with the issue. Two copies of the award are made, the original goes to the party raising the issue and the copy to the other party. The arbitrator has power to direct how the costs of the arbitration shall be paid. Costs include the arbitrator's own remuneration and expenses and the expenditure incurred in the case.

The enforcement of the award, which is binding only on the parties, is by application to the High Court for leave to enforce the award or leave to enter judgement in the terms of the award. The ordinary remedies of the court, previously considered, are available to enforce the award.

The Act gives the court power to remit an award. What happens in this circumstance is that the court will remit the award to the arbitrator for reconsideration together with the court's opinion on the point of law involved. The 1979 Act gives a right of appeal to the High Court on a question of law arising from the award and the court may confirm, vary or set aside the award. The court may also order the arbitrator to state his reasons for the award where either he has stated none or those stated are insufficient to enable the court to consider any point of law. The Arbitration Act 1979 has provided a system of appeals but on a point of law only. Prior to this the courts could intervene in limited circumstances only, such as where the arbitrator has misconducted himself. Even though there is this system of appeals its intention is simply to ensure that the law is upheld.

When the parties to a building contract agree in writing to settle any dispute by arbitration, that normally excludes the courts. On occasion however one of the parties will, despite the arbitration agreement, start an action in the courts. Under section 4 of the Arbitration Act, 1950, the other party can ask the court to stay the action. If this is granted the court action is stopped and the matter settled by arbitration.

The Court of Appeal in the case of *Northern Regional Health Authority* v *Derek Crouch Construction Co. Ltd.*, 1984, decided that it was possible to have a court action *and* arbitration to settle disputes which arose under the same building contract. The case arose from the construction of a hospital with a nominated sub-contractor for specialized work. Various disputes arose between the building owner and the main contractor and between the building owner and a nominated sub-contractor. An action was started in the High Court to which the sub-contractor was not a party but which could affect him. The sub-contractor wished to have his dispute settled by arbitration. The Court of Appeal agreed to this even though other disputes connected with the building work were before the High Court. The court said that in the event of any possible conflict arising between himself and the court, the arbitrator could always come to the court for directions on that matter.

Agency

Agency in the law of contract is the relationship which exists between two persons whereby one person, known as the principal, appoints another person, known as the agent, to enter into contractual obligations with a third party on the principal's behalf. Examples of agents in building work are the architect, who acts as the client's agent in connection with the construction of a building; the site foreman, who is the agent for the builder who employs him so far as the actions are within his normal duties; the partners in a partnership of builders who have the right to act as agents for the business of the partnership. The forms of agency we are concerned with may be classed as express or implied authority, apparent authority, usual authority, and ratification. It should be noted that the capacity of an agent to enter into contractual obligations is immaterial, the contractual capacity of the principal is the important feature. So a child can enter into a contract as an agent which he could not enter into on his own.

Express authority arises by the principal giving authority in writing or by word of mouth. If, however, the contract is to be a contract under seal then the authority of the agent must be under seal. So, a lease for more than three years which has to be by deed may only be made by an agent with authority by deed.

Implied authority is where an agent acts on behalf of his principal in the normal custom of a trade or business. So, such an agent is deemed to have authority to act in all matters which are the normal course of business in that trade.

Apparent authority is where a principal has made representations, by conduct or words, that a person had authority to act as his agent even though in fact that person has not authority, and that such representation deceived a third party.

Usual authority is the authority an agent possesses necessary for him to carry on any particular trade, business or profession, and that which is necessary and incidental to the execution of some express authority. An example of this authority is found in the leading case of *Watteau* v *Fenwick*, 1893, where the manager of a public house had not been given authority by the brewery company to purchase goods for the business other than bottled beer and mineral water; the brewery company was to supply other goods such as cigars and cigarettes. Contrary to this agreement the manager bought cigars from another supplier and failed to pay. The brewery company was sued as principal for an agent's action. The court decided that the company was liable since it was the normal practice for managers to buy cigars as agents for brewery companies, and so the manager was acting within his usual authority.

To relate these types of authority to building work we can see that an architect will have express and implied authority to act for his client in connection with the commissioned project. That a site foreman will have the usual authority such persons have to order goods, and to engage and dismiss labour. Apparent authority would arise where an employer, by conduct or words, represented his agent to have authority to act for him when that is not the case and when the intention was for the words or conduct to deceive.

Ratification is a form of authority whereby the principal confirms the action of the agent when the agent has acted without authority. Several conditions apply: ratification must be made within a reasonable time; the principal must have been in existence at that time; the agent must have acted on behalf of, though without express authority from, his principal; and the person ratifying must have full knowledge of the facts.

Relationship of Principal and Agent

The existence of the relationship of agency imposes certain duties and obligations on the principal and the agent.

The agent must exercise proper care and carry out the transaction he has undertaken to perform; he must himself perform these duties and not allow his own interests to conflict with his duty. Furthermore, the agent must not accept bribes, make a secret profit, or by his action prejudice his principal's business. We can see from this that a site foreman cannot accept commission or bribes for ordering goods from a particular supplier, nor can he give details of his employer's methods of work to any subsequent employers.

The rights an agent can claim against his principal are that the agent shall be indemnified by his principal for liabilities incurred on the principal's behalf; the agent may also claim to be remunerated at the specific rate if this has been agreed or otherwise at a reasonable rate.

Termination

The authority of an agent may be ended in many ways including by the completion of the authorized task, by the expiration of time, by death of the principal, and by the authority being expressly revoked. The important point to note here is that the termination of an agent's authority must be immediately communicated to the third parties with whom the agent has been acting on the principal's behalf. Failure to communicate the fact will mean that the agent will still be able to enter into contracts with those third parties and these contracts will be binding on the principal. The general notice of termination sometimes seen in the announcements column of a local paper is insufficient. So when a builder discharges a person who has acted as agent for him he must, in his own interests, communicate that fact of the termination to all those who have supplied goods through the agent's authority.

Debt Collection

Reference has been made to the power of the courts to award damages for breach of contract. What we are to consider now are the means available to the successful party to obtain the damages awarded when the unsuccessful party fails to pay promptly.

The judgement of the High Court may be enforced by execution. This is usually done by means of a writ of *fieri facias*, usually known as fi. fa., which commands the sheriff to obtain the sum due with interest from the debtor's goods and chattels. This writ authorizes the sheriff to enter the debtor's house and take his goods and sell them. Exceptions are wearing apparel, bedding and tools, and trade implements to the value of £250. He may also take any of the debtor's goods which are on some other person's land, and, by a writ of possession, take possession of the debtor's land for the plaintiff to have possession.

If the judgment debtor is himself owed a debt by a third party then this debt can, by the proper process, be recovered for the benefit of the judgment creditor. The procedure is that the court issues a 'Garnishee Order' which requires the third party, the 'garnishee', who owes money to the debtor, to pay that debt to the judgment creditor. The garnishee can dispute a debt at a court hearing. If he is ordered to pay the debt this will discharge his own obligation to the judgment debtor.

Another method which is frequently successful is to threaten bankruptcy by serving a notice on the judgment debtor requiring payment within a specific time and stating that if payment is not made a petition will be presented for adjudication in bankruptcy.

A judgment summons is another means for enforcement of a judgment debt. This method, which is frequently conducted in the County Court, consists of an examination of the debtor as to his means. The usual practice is for the court to order payments to be made at stated intervals. Under the Debtors Act, 1869, there is power to commit a judgment debtor to prison for six weeks if he has sufficient funds and he refuses to pay his debt. The imprisonment does not extinguish the debt, it still remains to be paid.

Debts may be assigned to another person, usually to somebody who believes that he has a better chance of securing payment. Where such assignment takes place Section 136 of the Law of Property Act, 1925, requires that three conditions are to be satisfied if the assignment is to be valid in law. These conditions are:

1. the assignment must be in writing;
2. it must be an absolute assignment;
3. the debtor must be given written notice of the assignment.

Where one of these conditions is absent the assignment is not legal and no action may be brought, but a remedy may be granted in equity.

Debt collecting agencies are sometimes used as a means of securing payment of a debt without taking the matter before the court. Such agencies do not have the debt assigned to them but ordinarily work on the basis of payment of a fee for debts recovered. As the business of these agencies is debt collection they are sometimes more successful in securing payment than the ordinary business man. The legal position of the agency in the matter is that of agent for the creditor.

6

Law and the Sale of Goods

Sale of Goods Act, 1979

This Act was passed to bring together in one statute the law relating to the sale of goods, which previously had been contained in several statutes. Some rules of common law regarding such matters were, however, left untouched by the Act and these still remain in force. The Act may be treated as an extension, by statute, of that branch of contract law dealing with the sale of goods. The general principles of the law of contract dealt with in the previous chapter – offer and acceptance capacity, mistake and misrepresentation – apply. The law relating to the sale of goods is at present the subject of efforts to secure sweeping changes in order to provide greater protection for the purchaser of goods. The importance of this branch of law to the builder will be apparent when one thinks of the numerous purchases made from a supplier, especially by sample, which are subject to the Act.

The definition of a contract of sale of goods is found in Section 2 of the Act. This states that such a contract is where the seller transfers or agrees to transfer the property in goods to the buyer for a money consideration called the price. When we consider this definition we can see that it does not include mortgages or pledges, the exchange of goods, or a contract for services. The contract is for the supply of goods and not for the supply of labour. It should also be noted that an agreement for sale is within the definition. This covers contracts where the transfer of property is to take place later or where some condition has first to be satisfied. The definition refers to property in goods, this means ownership which must be distinguished from possession. Possession is a limited right; ownership is a full legal right. Where for example, X lends his pen to Y, X has not got possession of his pen but he still has ownership; Y has possession only, which is a lesser right in the pen than ownership. The price mentioned in the definition, which must be in money, is dealt with in greater detail in Section 8 of the Act. This Section states that the price may be fixed by the contract, or it may be left to be fixed in a manner thereby agreed, or be fixed by the course of the dealings between the parties. Where the price is not fixed or determined there is a presumption that the price paid shall be a reasonable price. The Act also states that if an agreement is made and the price is left to be settled by a third party who fails to or cannot fix a price, then the agreement is void.

Subject Matter of Contract

The goods which are to be the subject matter of the contract are defined in Section 5 of the Act. These may be said to be goods in existence owned or possessed by the seller, or goods to be manufactured or acquired by the seller after the contract is made. The distinction between a contract for the sale of goods and a contract for work and labour is important since the contract for the sale of goods is subject to the requirements of the Act, whereas the contract for work and labour is not. If we consider two cases on this point we shall have a clearer picture of the problem. In the case of *Lee* v *Griffin*, 1861, a set of false teeth manufactured by a dentist were held to be goods which were the subject of a contract under the Act. The plaintiff who sought payment claimed that the contract was for work and labour. This claim the court refused to accept. In *Robinson* v *Graves*, 1935, the Court of Appeal had to consider a claim by a portrait painter that a portrait he had executed was a contract for work and labour, and not a contract for the sale of goods which would bring the matter within the Act. The court decided the contract was for work and labour and so the Act did not apply. The court said that what had to be decided in considering these matters was whether the contract was for the exercise of skill and labour with the material involved being of little importance in the production of the article. A portrait satisfied this test.

Conditions and Warranties

In this branch of contract law the difference between a condition and a warranty is most important. It will be remembered that representations are not part of the contract but are statements made to induce a person to enter into contractual obligations. Conditions and warranties, however, are part of the contract.

A condition is a term in the contract of such fundamental importance that a breach of that condition will go to the root of the whole contract and allow the injured party to repudiate the contract. The breach of condition may, however, be treated as a breach of warranty, in which case the contract is binding and the injured party will sue for damages. An example of a condition in a contract for the sale of goods may be the time of delivery. In the case of, for instance, a contract to supply window frames to a building under construction, failure on the part of the seller to deliver the goods on the agreed day would give the builder the right to end the contract and go elsewhere for the window frames, or to let the contract stand and sue for damages.

A warranty is a term in a contract which is not of such fundamental importance as a condition, so that breach of warranty does not give rise to a right to repudiate the contract. The right available is to sue for damages. A warranty is said by the Act to be an agreement which refers to the goods but is collateral to the main purpose of the contract. A warranty is sometimes said to affect the quality of the contract but not its substance. An example of a warranty is where the mileage of a car is a term of the contract of sale.

Documents in business transactions frequently contain conditions or warranties inserted by either or both parties. Once the terms are agreed these conditions or warranties form part of the contract and bind the parties. The Act, however, will imply certain conditions and warranties in contracts for the sale of goods, unless the parties expressly exclude these conditions or warranties or the circumstances show a different intention.

Section 12 of the Act makes it an implied condition of the contract that the seller has a right to sell the goods or will have a right to sell the goods. This means that a person who sells goods to which he has not got a good title has not made a binding contract. This can be illustrated by considering the case of *Rowland* v *Divall*, 1923, where the plaintiff bought a car from the defendant. Rowland used the car for four months and then discovered that it had never been owned by the defendant. The defendant had bought the car in good faith from another person who had not had a good title to the car. The Court of Appeal decided the plaintiff was entitled to the return of the full purchase price; there had been failure to satisfy the implied condition in Section 12. The use of the car for four months was disregarded. This Section also implies a warranty that the purchaser shall have quiet possession of the goods and that the goods shall be free from any charge in favour of a third party not declared or known to the buyer when the contract was made.

Section 13 is most important, dealing with sale by description. The Section states that there is an implied condition in a contract for the sale of goods by description that the goods shall correspond with the description, and that in the case of a sale by sample as well as by description the goods shall correspond with the sample and with the description. The leading case on this topic is *Varley* v *Whipp*, 1900, where the defendant agreed to purchase a reaping machine he had not seen. The machine was described as being second-hand, one year old and little used. The truth was that the machine was very old, and when he saw it the defendant refused to take the machine. The court decided that the defendant was entitled to return the machine since it did not correspond with the description. If we apply similar circumstances likely to be encountered in the building industry, we can see that the sale by description of a concrete mixer or other plant which does not correspond with the description would entitle the purchaser to return the plant. The purchaser has the right to repudiate the contract on the ground of a breach of implied condition as to description required by Section 13.

The rule in common law for the purchase of goods is *caveat emptor* which means 'buyer beware'. The buyer is warned that he will get what he bargained for, no more and no less. If he gets something which turns out to be less favourable to him than what he thought he would get then he cannot turn to common law for a remedy: he got what he bargained for. The Act, however, does give some protection to a buyer. Section 14 states that there shall be an implied condition that the goods shall be reasonably fit for their purpose when the buyer has made aware to the seller the particular purpose for which the goods are required. The effect of this is to show that the buyer is relying on the seller's skill and judgement. The goods have, however, to be of a description which it is the seller's business to supply. The effect of this Section is to place a duty on the seller to sell goods which are reasonably fit where it is made aware to the seller that is skill and judgment are being relied upon. In *Priest* v *Last*, 1903, the plaintiff went to a chemist's shop and asked for a hot water bottle. The hot water bottle subsequently burst causing damage. The court decided that Priest had relied on Last's skill and judgment in selection and that the hot water bottle was required for an obvious purpose.

Section 14 continues by implying a condition that goods shall be of a merchantable quality where the goods are sold by description by a person who deals in goods of that description. 'Merchantable quality' is defined in section 14 as goods which are fit for the purpose or purposes for which goods of that kind are commonly bought as it is reasonable to expect having regard to any description applied to them, the price (if relevant) and all the other relevant circumstances. An early case on merchantable quality was that of *Wilson* v *Rickett, Cockerell & Co. Ltd.*, 1954. The plaintiff bought a quantity of 'Coalite', a smokeless domestic fuel. This was delivered and when, some time later, it was placed on the fire an explosion occurred causing damage. The explosion was caused by a detonator which in some way had found its way into the fuel. The court said the fuel was quite suitable for use but that it contained a quality which made it unsafe and this meant that the fuel was not of merchantable quality.

Section 15 of the Act contains provisions which are most important to the builder. Knowledge of the contents of this Section will be of great assistance to those whose duty it is to order goods. The Section deals with the purchase of goods by sample. There are three implied conditions in this Section:

1. That the bulk of the goods shall correspond with the sample in quality;
2. that the buyer is to have a reasonable opportunity of comparing the bulk with the sample;
3. that the goods are free from any defect rendering them unmerchantable, which would not be apparent on reasonable examination.

Each of these conditions is a separate matter, a breach of which will enable the buyer to repudiate the contract if he so wishes. We can see the importance of this Section if we think of the representative of a supplier calling at a builder's office to show his samples and to secure orders. Let us imagine that the samples are of door handles. On the evidence of the examination of the sample the builder gives a bulk order. When the goods arrive in bulk the door handles are found to be inferior to the sample to an extent where they can be said not to correspond with the sample. The position now is that the builder, because of the breach of the implied condition, may repudiate the contract if he wishes or he may treat the matter as a breach of warranty and sue for damages.

Delivery

Delivery of the goods is the seller's duty and the buyer is under a duty to accept and pay for the goods according to the terms of the contract. Delivery according to the Act does not mean delivery at the buyer's premises. It means transfer of possession which the Act states takes place at the premises of the seller when the sale is completed. The effect of this is to mean that the delivery of the goods by post is at the risk of the buyer. The Act also requires that, unless the parties agree to the contrary, delivery of the goods shall not be by instalments. Where delivery by instalments is agreed then each instalment must be satisfactory as to quality, description and any other term in the contract.

Exemption Clauses

Until recently it has been the practice for suppliers to have clauses in their contracts which exempted them from the provisions of the Act. Now this right has been substantially modified. The Unfair Contract Terms Act 1977, states that in the case of a contract made by a person who is dealing as a consumer any term in the contract limiting liability for a breach of the provisions in sections 13, 14 and 15 is void. In any other contract any term which seeks to limit liability must satisfy the test of reasonableness set out in the 1977 Act.

There is therefore a different approach between a consumer sale and a non-consumer sale. The test of reasonableness under the Act was considered earlier (page 70). If the seller of goods can show that the exemption provision in his terms and conditions satisfies the test of reasonableness then they will be upheld by the court. Two cases need to be noted on the application of the test of reasonableness. The first is a decision of the House of Lords in *George Mitchell (Chesterhall) Ltd.* v *Finney Lock Seeds Ltd.*, 1983. In this case a seed merchants sold cabbage seed to farmers. The purchase price of the seed was £200 and it was sold subject to terms and conditions in the suppliers' invoice. These included a clause limiting the suppliers' liability, should the seed prove to be defective, to replacing it or refunding the purchase price. Any other loss or damage was excluded. The seed was a failure and the farmers suffered a loss of some £61,000. A claim for this sum, together with interest, was rejected by the suppliers. The House of Lords decided that section 55 of the Sale of Goods Act, 1979, which allows exclusion or limitation of liability if this is fair and reasonable, applied. The Law Lords were of the opinion that the limitation clause was not fair and reasonable. The reasons for this were that in previous cases of seed failure the suppliers had not relied on the limitation clause but had negotiated settlements with farmers; the supply of the seed was due to the suppliers' negligence; and the suppliers could have insured against that loss.

This decision was applied in the case of *Rees Hough Ltd.* v *Redland Reinforced Plastics Ltd.*, 1984. Here Redland supplied concrete pre-cast jacking pipes to a tunnelling and pipe jacking contractors. The pipes were supplied under Redland's terms and conditions which, in the event of the pipes being found to be defective, limited liability to repairing or replacing the defective pipes. Some pipes were defective and when sued Redland used as a defence the limitation clause. The High Court refused to accept this. The court decided the terms were not ones which satisfied the test of reasonableness under the Unfair Contract Terms Act, 1977, and so Rees Hough were successful in their claim.

Consumer Credit Act 1974

The practice has been common for a number of years to have a means whereby a person can have possession of goods with the intention of paying for them by instalments. Such a system enables a person who does not have the purchase sum immediately available to him to use the goods but to pay for them over a period of time. A number of abuses of this system, both by seller and buyer, became apparent and to give proper protection the above Act was passed. A word of explanation as to the position of finance companies in these transactions may be helpful. Most traders are themselves unable to provide the finance needed for hire purchase. So, after the purchase has been completed, the finance company buys the goods from the trader, paying the trader the purchase sum, and makes a hire-purchase agreement with the purchaser. The arrangement sometimes is such that the purchaser makes his payment to the trader who then sends the money to the finance company. The trader is acting as a collector for the finance company. It should not be thought that hire purchase is something confined to the purchase of household goods or cars. It is a system allowing a small builder to purchase a plant which he could not, because of lack of capital, buy outright at that time.

Nature of Hire Purchase

As the term implies, the goods are acquired by a system of hire with a right given to the hirer to purchase the goods if he so wishes. The usual arrangement is that the hirer has the use of the goods, that he pays for the use of them, and that at the end of the hire period he has the right to purchase the goods, usually for a nominal sum such as 5 pence. The hirer need not necessarily buy the goods. When that final sum is paid and not until then are the goods owned by the purchaser. So the hirer has not a good title to the goods enabling him to sell the goods to another. The Act dealing with such agreements restricts the application of the provisions of the Act to transactions to the value of £5000 or less. Further, the Act does not apply to corporate bodies. This means that the builder is covered by the Act if he works on his own or as a partnership but not if a company has been formed.

The Contract Terms

It is now a requirement that the actual agreement has to be signed by the hirer and a copy sent or delivered to the hirer within seven days of signature. The agreement is subject to certain implied conditions and warranties. The conditions are that the goods are of merchantable quality; that the goods are reasonably fit for the purpose required if the hirer has made that purpose known; and that the seller has a good title to the goods which he can transfer. The warranties are that the goods are free from a charge and that the hirer shall have quiet possession of the goods. The seller is also under a duty to set out in the agreement the purchase price, the instalments to be paid, when they are to be paid, and the cash price of the goods.

Seller's Rights

The seller has the right in the event of failure to pay the instalments to retake the goods. It should be noted that if the hirer has paid or offered to pay one-third of the hire-purchase price, the hirer can only retake the goods with the leave of the County Court in the area where the hirer lives or carries on business. The County Court, which is given jurisdiction to deal with claims of this extent, has power to make different orders in the matter. The court may order the goods to be returned immediately, or it may order return of the goods with postponement of the order so long as the hirer makes stated payments.

Hirer's Rights

The hirer can refuse to purchase the goods at the end of the hire period if he so wishes, in which case the goods are returned. He may at any time during the hire period, end the agreement by giving notice in writing and paying any money due so that that sum, together with money already paid, does not exceed one-half of the hire-purchase sum. The goods are, of course, returned. If more than one half of the hire-purchase sum has been paid no further payment need be made after giving written notice. An important feature in this connection is that the court has power to make an order for payment of a sum less than one-half of the hire-purchase price if the court believes the payment of a smaller sum would be equal to the owner's loss.

Credit Sale

We have seen with hire purchase that the ownership of the goods does not pass until payment at the end of the hire period of a stated sum. With credit sale the arrangement is different: the ownership of the goods usually passes when the contract is made. Credit sale is defined by the Consumer Credit Act 1974, as an agreement for the sale of goods where the purchase price is to be paid by five or more instalments. The purchaser is bound contractually to buy the goods; the hirer, it will be remembered, is not so bound. If the credit sale is for more than £30 but less than £5000 there must be a written agreement similar to that in hire purchase. The conditions and warranties mentioned in considering the Sale of Goods Act, 1979, apply to a credit sale.

7

Law and Land

Land

Land occupies, in English law, a somewhat privileged position; the reasons for this are historical. The extent of a person's holding of land was an indication of his wealth and standing. Many years ago it was not possible to invest money in stocks and shares and then to live off the proceeds of the investment; the wealthy had to buy land and rent it out to others, in this way securing an income for themselves. Nor should it be forgotten that the person having the greatest interest in land was the King who in earlier times ruled the country by his wishes, with little regard to Parliament. It was, therefore, in his own interests to keep land in a privileged position.

It was possible until a short while ago for a person to use his land in any way whatsoever, no regard had to be paid to the effect on others. There was no form of control for the social benefits of the public; the law regarded land as being something a person could use as he wished, an offensive factory could be erected on land without any permission from the local authority, or from any other body. The right of the owner of the land was such that the law could not interfere.

The needs of the public became so pressing that the law had to be amended so as to provide, for the benefit of the public, control over the use of land. The erection of buildings became subject to building bye-laws, and legislation was made to secure the removal of dwellings unfit for human habitation. These measures all took time, sweeping changes were not made overnight, the privileged position of land had to be gradually whittled away, and indeed is still being whittled away today.

We now have the position where land is treated in law as being not just for the benefit of the owner or occupier, but for the public too. Development of land is controlled, buildings may not be erected which will detract from the enjoyment of the land by the public, nor may land be used other than in a permitted manner. Buildings have to comply with certain standards. The legislation dealing with all these measures of control have means of enforcement including, if necessary, criminal prosecution.

Estates

In 1066, William the Conqueror took the whole of the land for himself, not for the benefit of the Normans, nor for any other race but for himself alone. This is the reason why in this country nobody other than the Crown owns land. William the Conqueror gave the use of the land to others as a reward; they were in fact tenants of his. In return for the use of the land the tenants had to perform some service, in some cases this was the provision of a certain number of armed horsemen for the use of the Crown for so many days in a year. This was known as 'tenure' and indicated the manner of holding the land. If the services were not performed the land went back to the Crown. The length of time a person was entitled to hold land was known as an 'estate'. He held the land as an 'estate' from the Crown. The person having the estate of the Crown could in turn grant an estate to another person, but the ownership still remained with the Crown.

The position today is that most of the tenures have been abolished either by statute or by falling into disuse. The position of holding an estate of the Crown still exists, but is of such little practical importance that a freehold estate may be treated as absolute ownership.

An interesting form of tenure was that of copyhold land, this was known as unfree tenure. Unfree tenure was when the tenants, who before the fifteenth century were little more than slaves, held land of the lord of the manor. The tenant held the land in return for services rendered to the lord. The tenant's rights were very few and in the event of a dispute the matter had to be decided in the lord's court; he had no right to go the King's court. The lord originally had the right to eject the tenant when he so wished, and was not obliged to grant the land to the tenant's son on the death of the tenant.

Certain customs became recognized in the manors so that the position of the tenant improved; the King's courts came to recognize the rights of the tenant and were willing to enforce those rights.

Copyhold land was, by the Law of Property Act, 1922, converted to freehold land. The name copyhold was given to it because of the way in which the land was conveyed. Since the land was subject to such strict control by the lord, the transfer of the land had to be recorded on the court rolls of the manor. The tenant was given a copy of this entry on the court record to show his right to hold the land.

Freehold land existed before 1925, the term freehold coming from the estate; it was held by free tenants. Free tenants were tenants of land who, in return for fixed services, held an estate of land from the Crown or from the lord. The fixed services ranged from agricultural services to the lord, to the performance of a service to the King. Most of these services had fallen into disuse by 1925 or were abolished by statute.

Section 1 of the Law of Property Act, 1925, stated that after 1925 there should be only two legal estates in land. These are:

1. an estate in fee simple absolute in possession;
2. a term of years absolute.

The definition fee simple absolute in possession means the following: 'fee' means that the estate is capable of inheritance; 'simple' means that the estate is not restricted to a particular class of person, for example the male descendants of a person; 'absolute' means that the estate is one which is not restricted to enjoyment for a limited period of time; 'possession' means that the owner of the estate must be entitled to possession.

The term of years absolute is used for a lease of land and may be granted for a number of years, such as 999 years, or for a short period such as a week. The ordinary weekly tenancy of a house is a legal estate. The land need not be in possession for a legal estate to exist, it may well be restricted so as to arise in the future.

Rights and Duties of Owners and Occupiers of Land

As we have seen, the holder of the fee simple absolute in possession is for all practical purposes the absolute owner, and formerly could use the land in any manner he wished. In theory the fee simple holder owns the surface of the land, the air space above and the earth below down to the centre of the earth. To allow these rights to exist without restriction would impose an intolerable burden on society; the social and economic needs of the society could not be met in these circumstances. There have been, therefore, restrictions imposed on the holder of the fee simple. The more important of these are the following:

1. Treasure Trove; this is the right of the Crown to claim as treasure trove all gold or silver, in any manufactured form, which has been deliberately hidden, the owner of which is unknown. If the coins or objects have been lost and not deliberately hidden they are not treasure trove. It is the practice of the Crown to pay a sum of money, as compensation to the finder of treasure trove.

2. Minerals; the Crown claims the right to all gold or silver produced from a mine. The Petroleum (Production) Act, 1982, vests in the Crown petroleum in its natural condition found in a stratum. Coal is now vested in the National Coal Board.

3. Air Space; this is regulated by the Civil Aviation Act, 1982, which states that no action may be brought for trespass or nuisance for an aircraft flying at a reasonable height above the land.

4. Water; the owner of land adjoining a river, shares with the other owners certain rights. If the river forms the boundary between two properties, the centre of the river is the boundary. The rights of the owner of land adjoining a river are known as riparian rights. Such an owner may take water from the river in unrestricted quantity if it is for the ordinary purposes connected with the land, e.g. for domestic purposes. The owner may take water for extraordinary purposes connected with his land, e.g. irrigation, provided water of the same quality is returned to the river in substantially the same quantity. The riparian owner cannot take water for purposes not connected with the land.

5. Use of the Land; the use of the land is governed by both

common law and statute. At common law a landowner must use his land in such a manner as not to harm others; at statute the Town and Country Planning Act, 1971, restricts the use of the land to a purpose best suited to the needs of the public.

These, then, are the restrictions imposed on an owner of land; subject to these he may deal with the land as he wishes, it is his to enjoy, to destroy and to pass to any person he selects.

Leases

The leasing of land creates a position in law between the parties, who are known as the lessor and the lessee, or landlord and tenant in the case of short leases, whereby certain rights and duties are implied between the parties, even if no mention has been made of these matters in the terms of the lease. It is of course the usual practice to have a lease drawn up by a solicitor so that his client's interests are properly protected, these are made terms of the lease, they are covenants and if the lessee is in breach of covenant the lessor may sue for forfeiture.

Essential Elements

There are two essential elements of a lease, these are:

1. The lease must be for a definite term. It does not matter how short the period is but it must still be a definite period. In *Lace v Chantler*, 1944, where an agreement was created 'for the duration of the war', the court decided that it was not a definite period and so was not a lease: the commencement of the lease was known but not its end. A weekly or monthly tenancy continues from week to week or month to month, the term is automatically renewed until there is contrary action by one of the parties. This type of tenancy is known as a periodic tenancy.
2. The lease must give exclusive possession of the land. This means that a person who lodges in a house and has exclusive possession of his bedroom, or possibly of several rooms in the house, but shares some other room with the others in the house, does not have exclusive possession of the house and so is not a lessee but a licensee. The house as a whole is still controlled by the owner.

Creation of a Lease

The Law of Property Act, 1925, Section 52, requires that, with one exception, a lease which creates a legal estate must be by deed. The exception is that Section 54 of the same Act allows a lease to be created either verbally or in writing provided it is:

1. for a term not exceeding three years;
2. to take effect in possession, that is the lease is to start forthwith;
3. for the best rent obtainable without taking a sum of money for granting the lease.

If these three conditions are satisfied then the lease may be created verbally or in writing.

The question of the position of the parties to an agreement for a lease was dealt with in the case of *Walsh* v *Lonsdale*, 1882, here the parties had signed an agreement to create a lease by deed. The land was occupied for some time without a deed being executed, a dispute arose and the occupier of the land attempted to show that a lease did not exist since there was no deed. The court said that in equity the parties who had acted as if the agreement was binding would be held to it, and that it would be treated as binding as a deed.

The effect of this is to make an enforceable agreement to create a lease almost as good as the lease itself. The difference is that the agreement is not sufficient to pass certain easements and other interests in land, which would pass if a lease had been created.

A further danger with an agreement for a lease is to third parties. An agreement for a lease is an equitable interest and, as such, subject to the general rule in equity that equitable interests are void against a *bona fide* purchaser for value of the legal estate without notice of the equitable interest. What this means in simple terms is that where a person, acting honestly, purchases a legal estate which is subject to equitable interests and he has no notice of these interests then those interests do not bind him. A most important point in this matter is that of notice. What is notice? Notice in equity is of three kinds. The first is actual notice; this means the circumstances where a person has in some way or other obtained actual knowledge of all the facts. Secondly there is constructive notice; this means the circumstance where a person would have had possession of all the facts in the matter if he had made those enquiries a reasonable man would have made. So a person who suspects the existence of equitable interests in a legal estate he is purchasing and, therefore, hoping to avoid their consequence, omits to make enquiries is deemed to have knowledge of them if reasonable enquiries would have revealed their existence. Thirdly there is imputed notice; this arises where a person employs an agent who has received actual or constructive notice of an equitable interest. Notice to the agent is imputed to the purchaser. Notice of agreements for leases is now governed by the Law of Property Act, 1925. This Act requires agreements for leases made after 1925 to be registered as land charges in the register set up under the Land Charges Act, 1972. Only if this is done will there be notice of the agreements.

If a lessor wishes to assign his lease to someone else this assignment must be by deed, even if the lease has been created by an oral agreement.

Leasehold Reform Act, 1967

This Act was introduced to deal with the problem of certain leasehold houses whose leases were about to expire or would expire within a short time. The expiration of the lease of a house means that the land, together with the house on the land, would revert to the landlord and the owner occupier of the house would be dispossessed. The Act has introduced a radical measure in the law concerning certain leasehold houses which are owner occupied. The measure is that the owner occupiers of certain leasehold houses are to have the right to purchase from landlords the freehold of the property or to have the lease extended for a further period fifty years. It should be noted that the Act applies to owner occupied leasehold houses only and does not apply to flats, maisonettes or business premises.

To come within the provisions of the Act the following conditions must be satisfied:

1. the lease of the house must originally have been granted for a term of more than twenty-one years;
2. the lease must be of the whole of the house;
3. the lease must have an annual rent less than two-thirds of the rateable value of the house. The rateable value is that as assessed

on the 23rd March 1965 or the first day of the term where the lease commenced after that date;

4. the house must have a rateable value on the 23 March 1965, of not more than £400 in Greater London or £200 elsewhere. If the house was not in the valuation list on the 23 March 1965 but is entered on or after the 1 April 1973, then the rateable value must not exceed £1500 in Greater London or £750 elsewhere.

5. the house must be occupied as the main or only residence and have been occupied as such for the last three years or for a total of three years in the last ten years.

A person who can satisfy all these requirements may, if he so wishes, exercise the right given to him under the Act. The right to purchase the freehold or to have the lease extended for fifty years is a discretionary matter for the owner occupier of the house. Where a lease is extended, a new rent is fixed which is based on the value of the site in its present use. The purchase of the freehold is to be at the market value of the freehold interest of the site with the right of the leaseholder to extend the lease for a further period of fifty years taken into account. Where the site has some redevelopment value, this must also be taken into account in fixing the price to be paid. No account is to be made of the value of the house which is standing on the land. Any dispute concerning the price to be paid for the freehold or the extension of the lease may be determined by the Lands Tribunal.

A landlord has a right to object to the purchase of the freehold or the extension of the lease. This right is available where the landlord claims that he wants the house for his own occupation or for occupation by a member of his family when the lease expires. The landlord must show that if he is denied possession of the house when the lease expires he will be caused greater hardship than would be caused to the leaseholder in having to leave the house. Compensation for the loss of the fifty-year extension to the lease must be paid by the landlord to the leaseholder.

Leases frequently contain covenants, the purpose of which is to protect the landlord's interests in other property. To permit the freehold to be acquired without the covenants continuing to have effect, would be unfair to the landlord. To deal with this circumstance the Act allows the landlord to insist that the freehold shall be subject to any restrictive covenants in the lease which benefit other property in which he has an interest.

The procedure to be followed in exercising the right to extend the lease or to purchase the freehold is that notice in the prescribed form has to be served on the landlord stating the leaseholder's intention to exercise his right under the Act. Any delay by the landlord in dealing with the notice may be dealt with by the County Court. The price is then agreed or, in the case of dispute, determined by the Lands Tribunal.

Obligations Under a Lease

We can now look at the obligations of the parties to a lease. As we have seen, it is the usual practice to have the lease drawn up by a solicitor so that any matter of importance is properly dealt with.

If the lease deals with nothing more than the description of the property, the length of the lease, the names of the parties and the rent, then the law will imply certain things from the relationship of lessor and lessee that has been created. These are:

1. That the lessor is subject to an implied covenant for quiet enjoyment. This means that the lessor and those claiming under him are under an obligation not to disturb or interfere with the lessee's enjoyment of the land. A breach of this covenant makes the lessor liable to an action for damages. The covenant for quiet enjoyment is implied when the word 'demise' is used in the lease, and it seems that it will be implied in an oral lease from the relationship of lessor and lessee.

2. There is also an implied covenant that the lessor will not derogate from his grant. This means that the lessor must not act in such a manner as to prevent the land, which had been leased for a particular purpose, being used for that particular purpose. An example of this is *Aldin* v *Latimer Clark*, 1894, where land had been leased for the storage of timber. The lessor erected a building on adjoining land and it was found that this building obstructed the flow of air to the drying sheds of the timber yard. This act was held to be derogation of grant by the lessor and compensation had to be paid to the lessee.

3. There is an implied covenant of fitness for habitation where a

house is let furnished or where a house is let as a 'low rent'. This 'low rent', or rent limit, is set out in the Landlord and Tenant Act, 1985, as not more than £52 outside London and £80 in London. In this case it is implied that it is fit for human habitation and will be kept fit throughout the tenancy. This implied covenant does not apply in the case of a lease for three years or more when the parties have agreed that the lessee will put the house in a fit condition. The Landlord and Tenant Act, 1985, imposed certain obligations for the repair of houses where the lease is for less than seven years.

The lessee is under implied obligations when a lease is made with only the bare essentials. These are:

1. to pay rent and taxes, the taxes do not include the landlord's income tax;
2. not to commit waste. Waste which is dealt with in more detail later, means the destruction or neglect of property;
3. to permit the lessor to enter and view the state of repair. This arises if the lessor has covenanted to carry out the repairs or is under a statutory obligation to carry out repairs.

A lease may be created and provide that the 'usual covenants' shall apply. This means that the implied covenants previously mentioned apply with the exceptions that the lessor is given an unconditional right to enter and view the state of repair and that he has a right to re-enter on non-payment of rent. Other covenants may be usual in certain parts of the country.

A lease having expressed covenants usually contains the following:

1. Covenant to repair; the exact liability of the lease is set out in the lease. The Landlord and Tenant Act, 1985, Section 11, imposes on the lessor of a dwelling house let after 24th October, 1961, for a lease of less than seven years, an obligation to keep the structure and exterior in repair, and to keep in repair and working order space heating, water heating, water, gas and electricity supplies, and sanitation installations. This obligation cannot be excluded except by the consent of the county court.
2. Covenant to pay rent; the amount of rent and times of payment are stated. This obligation on the lessee continues so long as the tenancy lasts. The lessor may, in the event of non-payment

of rent, sue for the rent owing, or seize personal property on the premises and sell to recover the amount owing. This is known as distress. It is more usual to make provision in the lease for the lease to be forfeited on non–payment.

3. The lessor usually requires that the lessee shall not assign the lease or sublet the premises, except with his consent. If this is in the lease the Landlord and Tenant Act, 1927, Section 19, requires that the lessor's consent shall not be unreasonably withheld.

In the case of a breach of covenant, other than that to pay rent, the lessor, before he can forfeit the lease must serve notice on the lessee. The notice has to specify the breach, require the lessee to remedy the breach, and claim financial compensation. The notice is required by the Law of Property Act, 1925, Section 146. The time given for remedying the breach is usually three months, following which the lessor may take action to forfeit the lease. In the case of a breach of covenant to pay rent, the lessor is under a duty at common law to make a formal demand for the rent due. This is not necessary if the lease contains a provision that the lease may be forfeited if the rent is a specified number of days in arrears. The lessee may, at the court's discretion, avoid forfeiture or even be restored after forfeiture, if he pays the rent due, the lessor's expenses, and if it is just and equitable that he should be granted this relief.

The question of the enforcement of covenants in leases is important particularly when the lease is assigned, either by the lessor or by the lessee. A covenant is a promise made under seal. How far is this enforceable by or against a person who was not a party to the original deed? We shall see that the law views this matter in two ways, from the viewpoint of the benefit of the covenant, and from the viewpoint of the burden.

If the parties to the original deed are still the same all the covenants will be enforceable between them for as long as the lease exists. This is, of course, privity of contract since the lessor and lessee are bound by the terms of their contract. If, however, the lessor assigns his interest in the lease, or the lessee assigns the lease, the law will enforce certain covenants in the lease if it can be shown that the parties to the action are in the position of landlord and tenant, or, as it is termed in law, 'privity of estate' exists. We can take as an example to clarify this point a lease made between A the lessor, and B the lessee, in which certain covenants are made. As long as neither A nor B assigns his interest in the lease there is privity of contract and the covenants can be enforced between the parties. If B assigns the lease to C there is not privity of contract between A and C since C was not a party to the original deed creating the lease; there is however privity of estate since C will be paying rent to A; the position of landlord and tenant exists. If C sub-leases the land to D there is privity of contract between C and D as they are the parties to the deed creating the sub-lease, and there is of course privity of estate, C is D's landlord. A in this situation, has neither privity of contract nor privity of estate with D, he was not a party to the deed creating the sub-lease and he is not receiving rent from D.

The importance of the difference in privity of contract and privity of estate is that where privity of estate only exists not all the covenants are enforceable. With privity of estate only those covenants which 'touch and concern the land' are enforceable. Covenants which do not touch and concern the land are enforceable only if there is privity of contract. Covenants that 'touch and concern the land' are those that concern the lessor in his position as lessor of the land, and the lessee in his position as lessee of the land. Any covenant which is of a personal nature not concerning the land does not 'touch and concern' it and so cannot be enforced if there is solely privity of estate; it can be enforced if there is privity of contract. Examples of these covenants which touch and concern the land are: on the part of the lessor, to renew the lease, not to build on adjoining land; on the part of the lessee, to pay rent, to repair, to use the premises as a private dwelling house only. The court decides in each case whether the covenants do touch and concern the land. If there is neither privity of estate nor privity of contract then, with the exception of restrictive covenants which are dealt with later, the covenant cannot be enforced.

The enforcement of a covenant where there has been an assignment would appear to present difficulties. Against whom is the action commenced? The answer is that the lessor can bring his action against the original lessee if he wishes, or against the assignee of the lessee. If action is brought against the original lessee he may claim indemnity for the breach of covenant from the assignee. In any assignment for value made after 1925 such an indemnity is implied by the Law of Property Act, 1925, Section 77. In the case of a sub-lease the lessor of the sub-lease will have inserted covenants in that sub-lease so that he is protected. In this way the person who has actually committed the breach of covenants is held responsible.

Control of Land

Town and Country Planning Act, 1971

The 1971 Act is the latest in a series of statutes dealing with the control of land and buildings. The earlier statutes, which were in the main ineffective, date from the Housing, Town Planning, etc., Act, 1909. The subsequent statutes tried to provide more power for authorities to deal effectively with the mis-use of land and buildings; our national characteristic of 'a man's home is his castle' hindered both the passage of effective statutes and the implementation of the statutes which were eventually passed. The Town and Country Planning Act of 1947 was a major step forward, creating new principles in planning law. Other amending statutes followed and eventually the provisions of these were gathered into the Town and Country Planning Act, 1962, which has been replaced by the 1971 Act. This Act has itself been amended by later Acts.

Administration

The Act gives the Secretary of State for the Environment central authority for administration of the Act in England and Wales.

Local planning authorities administer the ordinary duties of the Act. These authorities are county councils and district councils. Most of the functions are carried out by the district council but the major matters such as the preparation of the structure plan, where a wider view than that of a single district council is needed, are dealt with by county councils. Applications for planning permission are almost all dealt with by the district councils, since these tend to be straight-forward matters. More complex matters, for example a proposed housing estate in a local beauty spot, would be dealt with after consultation with the county council.

There is also provision in the Act for joint planning boards to be formed by two or more local planning authorities.

In an attempt to deal more efficiently with applications for planning permission some local planning authorities have used the power under the Local Government Act 1972, and delegated to a committee or officer the power to deal with certain planning matters.

Development Plan

It will be readily appreciated that planning the development of the district is of importance to many. Financial considerations and building development require that planning proposals must be known. This requirement is dealt with in the Act by the duty placed on a local planning authority to submit to the Secretary of State a development plan for its area, showing amongst other things areas allocated to residential and industrial use, open spaces, and land subject to compulsory purchase. There is also a requirement that a development plan shall be kept under review and the review sent to the Secretary of State. A development plan shows how the local planning authority proposes the land shall be used and the stages by which such development will be carried out. If a local planning authority has not prepared a development plan or carried out a review as required by the Act, the Secretary of State may take the necessary action to prepare the development plan. The expenses incurred in preparing the plan may be recovered from the local planning authority in default. The development plan must be approved by the Secretary of State with or without modifications. Since the plan is of such importance there are provisions allowing interested parties to object to the plan. The Secretary of State may then hold a public local inquiry to hear the objections, following which he makes his decision.

The 1971 Act introduced a new form of development plan known as a 'structure plan'. This differs from the old type of development plan in that it expresses planning policy in a written statement without the use of detailed maps. The structure plan has to be approved by the Secretary of State after interested parties have had the opportunity of making representation before the plan is prepared, and of objecting to the plan when it is prepared. Any area within the structure plan which requires comprehensive treatment within a short time is referred to as an 'action area', and for such an area a 'local plan' must be prepared. The 'local plan' states in detail, by the use of maps, diagrams, illustrations and descriptive matter, the local planning authority's proposals for the development and use of the area. Adequate publicity has to be given to the proposed plan so that interested parties may make representations, which must be considered. When the plan has been prepared but before it is adopted the public are to be made aware of its provisions and the time within which objections may be made to the local planning authority. The authority have to hold a private hearing or public local inquiry into the objections. A 'local plan' may also be made for areas other than 'action areas' but this is at the discretion of the authority. There is power given to the Minister to require that the plan shall not be operative until he has approved it.

Development

What is meant by development which comes within the Act? No single definition is sufficiently comprehensive to deal with all the circumstances Parliament intended should be controlled by the Act. General definitions are found in Sections 22 and 29. These are that the carrying out of building operations, engineering operations, mining operations or other operations in, on, over or under land, or the making of any material change in the use of any buildings or other land is development. Some other circumstances are specifically mentioned so as to bring those circumstances within the Act. The expression 'material change of use' has caused some difficulty in application. To remove some of this difficulty the Secretary of State, in Circular 67/49, said that in his view, for a change of use to be a material change of use, the new use must be substantially different from the old use. Where a person has doubts concerning his proposed work and the application of the Act, Section 53 of the Act gives that person the right to apply to the local planning authority for their determination. When the local planning authority has determined the issue, the applicant, if aggrieved by the decision, may appeal to the Secretary of State. A further appeal is possible against the Secretary of State's decision but this is on a point of law only and is made to the High Court.

The Act allows certain developments to be carried out without permission. These developments are set out in classes in the Act and are known as 'permitted development'. One such class is Class IV which authorizes the erection of buildings and plant needed temporarily on that land to carry out the development which is the subject of planning permission; this class covers the erection of builders' huts and plant on a building site.

Planning Permission

Where development is sought for which planning permission is necessary, application has to be made on the prescribed form to the appropriate local planning authority. An interesting and useful feature of the Act is that application may be made for planning permission by a person who has not got a legal interest in the land. Any person may make an application known as an 'outline application'. This form of application does not deal with all the details of the normal application. Where permission is granted to an outline application, the local planning authority will make the consent subject to what are referred to in the Town and Country Planning General Development Order 1977 as amended as 'reserved matters'. These cover such things as design, layout, external appearance and road access. Approval of all these matters is necessary before the development can be started.

The local planning authority must, in general, give a decision to an application within two months of the application being made. Where a decision is not given to the applicant within this time the applicant may proceed as if his application has been refused and appeal to the Secretary of State. Section 29 of the Act allows the local planning authority to decide:

1. to grant permission unconditionally;
2. to grant permission subject to conditions 'as it thinks fit';
3. to refuse permission.

Conditions attached to planning permission must be sensible conditions which are related to the facts of the case. A usual condition is to require that the buildings shall be removed at the end of the specified period.

An appeal may be made against the decision of the local planning authority within six months of receipt of the decision. Appeal is to the Secretary of State. The usual practice is for the Secretary of

State to arrange for a public local enquiry to be held, this enquiry is conducted by one of his inspectors. These inspectors are trained and experienced town planners, civil engineers or surveyors. The Secretary of State may allow the appeal, dismiss it or grant it subject to modification. The Secretary of State, in deciding an appeal, considers the whole of the decision of the local planning authority, and so he may alter some part which the appellant was willing to accept. The decision of the Secretary of State is final, but it is possible within six weeks of his decision to object to the decision, on a point of law only, to the High Court.

Originally the Secretary of State made the decision based on the report and recommendations of his inspector who had heard the appeal. Now the position is that an inspector can decide almost any appeal. This power, however, is subject to the Secretary of State having the right to reserve to himself the determination of any appeal. Other than this the inspector makes the decision in the name of the Secretary of State. The appeal is dealt with by public local inquiry, written representation or private hearing.

Enforcement

Where after the end of 1963 development is carried out which has not received the necessary planning permission, or where development does not comply with conditions in the planning permission, the local planning authority is empowered by the Acts to remedy the matter. The local planning authority may serve an enforcement notice on the owner and occupier of the land. Notice may also be served on other persons whose interest in the land is affected. The enforcement notice must in general be served within four years of the development being carried out. Dates must be specified when the notice will have effect, which must be not less than 28 days, and within which any specified steps must be taken. There is a right of appeal to the Secretary of State against the enforcement notice. Where an enforcement notice becomes effective the local planning authority may enter the land, carry out the necessary measures to comply with the notice, and recover their expenses for so doing.

In practice it was found that the service of an enforcement notice was not fully effective, since an appeal against an enforcement notice suspends the enforcement notice so that the operation or change of use could be continued without penalty. To remedy this procedural defect the 1971 Act introduced a stop notice procedure. This allows a local planning authority, when an enforcement notice has been served, to prohibit the carrying on of the operation which is a breach of planning control by issuing a stop notice. There is no appeal against a stop notice but if the enforcement notice is quashed or withdrawn the local planning authority may be liable to pay compensation.

Conservation Areas

The Civic Amenities Act, 1967, introduced a new measure into planning law when it required every local planning authority to determine which parts of its area are of special architectural or historic interest the character or appearance of which it is desirable to preserve or enhance. Any such areas are to be designated 'Conservation Areas'. The Secretary of State is given power to require local planning authorities to determine any such areas and is required to consult with a local planning authority before issuing a direction to determine 'Conservation Areas'.

The aim of this provision is to define areas, which may be town centres or terraces of buildings, where conservation measures are needed to preserve the character. New development in a conservation area will be examined critically to make sure that it accords with the special qualities of the area and planning approval will only be given after the most careful examination of the proposal.

Buildings Listed and Tree Preservation Orders

Section 54 of the 1971 Act empowers the Secretary of State to compile lists or to approve lists compiled by others of buildings considered to be of architectural or historic interest. The listing of a building affords a degree of protection since by section 55 of the 1971 Act it is an offence to demolish or execute works which will affect its character as a building of special architectural or historic interest without listed building consent. Where work is carried out without listed building consent an offence is committed and an enforcement notice may be served. In the event of failure to comply with an enforcement notice the local planning authority may take any steps necessary to secure compliance and they may recover the expense incurred.

A further measure introduced by the 1971 Act is that of the service of a building preservation notice to protect a building which is of special architectural or historic interest but which has not yet been listed. The notice remains in force for six months during which the building is protected as if it were listed. In the event of the building not being listed during this period the local planning authority are liable to pay compensation for loss or damage arising from the making of the building preservation notice.

A Tree Preservation Order is made to preserve the amenity value of an area. The effect of the Order is to prohibit cutting down or other work to the trees, except with the consent of the local planning authority. The Order is confirmed by the Secretary of State when objection has been made. The Order may be made so as to have immediate effect but does not extend beyond six months unless it is confirmed by the Secretary of State. The penalty for contravention is a fine up to £2000.

Fixtures

The term 'fixtures' includes anything which has been so attached to the land that it must be treated as forming part of the land. This is of importance in deciding such matters as whether a garage or greenhouse can be removed on the sale of a house, or the termination of a lease. In deciding whether or not an object is a fixture there are two tests to be applied, these are:

1. the purpose of annexation;
2. the degree of annexation.

The purpose of annexation test is to show whether or not the object was fixed with the intention that it should become part of the land or merely to allow its fuller use. Some objects are of such size or form as to require fixing to the building so that they may be properly displayed. In the case of *Leigh* v *Taylor*, 1902, a tapestry owned by the tenant was fixed by tacks to wooden strips which were fastened by nails to the wall. A dispute arose as to whether or not it was a fixture. The House of Lords held that it had been so fixed to allow enjoyment as an object of beauty and was not meant to pass with the building. It was, therefore, not a fixture.

The degree of annexation test is applied to show how permanently the object has been attached to the land. The more permanent the fixing the stronger the presumption that it was intended to become part of the land.

Thus it can be seen that buildings which are resting on the ground by their own weight, for example some types of greenhouses, are not fixtures. In some cases however, where the object is to form part of the architectural layout of a building this has been held to be different. Statues in a garden put there permanently as part of the architectural layout are fixtures even though attached solely by their own weight.

From the above we can see that when land is sold any object on it which is not a fixture may be removed. In certain cases, however, where a lease has come to an end the law allows the lessee to remove fixtures. These are fixtures attached by the lessee in connection with his trade or business, ornamental or domestic fixtures, and agricultural fixtures. The lessee may remove agricultural fixtures, after giving proper notice, up to two months after the ending of the lease; trade, ornamental or domestic fixtures must be removed before the lease ends.

Dilapidations

The term 'dilapidations' is used to describe the legal liability arising from the defective or dangerous condition of buildings and land. The liability is found at common law and in statute law. It includes the liability at law between the lessor and lessee, to persons lawfully using the building, and to passers-by who might be injured by reason of the defective condition of a building. We shall see in dealing with the law of torts how nuisance, negligence, and liability for spread of fire impose liability in the use of land.

The Occupier's Liability Act, 1957, places certain duties on the occupier of a building regarding lawful visitors. The Act imposes on the occupier the common duty of care to all his lawful visitors. There is power for the occupier to restrict, modify or exclude this duty of care, but this is subject to the provisions of the Unfair Contract Terms Act 1977, considered earlier. The common duty of care is that duty to take such care as is in all the circumstances reasonable to see that the visitor is reasonably safe; regard is to be had to visitors who are children and so likely to be less careful than adults. The occupier may expect a workman who is carrying out his work to be prepared for any risk normally found in carrying out his trade. A warning of danger will not free the occupier of liability unless it is adequate warning in the circumstances. The Act states that an occupier shall not be liable for danger created by his independent contractor, unless it can be shown that he did not act reasonably in his selection of the contractor. In *O'Connor v Swan and Edgar*, 1963, the plaintiff was lawfully on Swan's premises when he was injured by a fall of plaster from a ceiling plastered by Swan's independent contractor. The court held that Swan had not failed in his duty under the Act and so was not liable for the independent contractor's work.

At one time the position was that a trespasser took premises as he found them, subject to the occupier not creating any danger knowing that the trespasser was on the land. Now by the provisions in the Occupier's Liability Act, 1984, a duty is owed to trespassers in certain circumstances.

We have seen that the position regarding repairs is often expressed in the terms of a lease. Frequently this is that the premises shall be kept in good repair, fair wear and tear excepted. In *Regis Property Co.* v *Dudley*, 1959, the House of Lords had to consider the precise meaning of the exception 'fair wear and tear'. They decided that it excused the lessee from a repair which was due to wear and tear, the lessee's reasonable conduct being assumed. But a limitation was placed on the exception, the lessee being under a duty to take the necessary steps to prevent further damage being caused from the defect which was due to fair wear and tear. One of the law lords, Lord Denning, said, as an example, that if a slate came off the roof by fair wear and tear then the lessee is not under a duty to replace it, but if it should let rain in then he should replace it to prevent further damage.

An important aspect of the law of dilapidations is that of waste. Waste, to give it its proper meaning, is the change in the nature of land for its improvement or to its detriment. It tends in practice to be restricted to acts of neglect or of destruction. Permissive waste is the failure to carry out an act which ought to be carried out, for example, the failure to repair a building. Voluntary waste is the committing of an act of destruction to a building or land: the cutting of timber on an estate has been held to be voluntary waste.

Equitable waste was said in one case to be that which a prudent man would not do in the management of his own property. In *Vane* v *Lord Barnard*, 1716, a relative of the plaintiff occupied, under a trust, a house which he stripped of its lead and other fittings by acts of wanton destruction. This was held to be equitable waste. The term equitable waste is used to denote that it is a remedy granted in equity.

A lessee for a fixed term of years is held in law to be liable for voluntary and permissive waste. If the lease is yearly the same applies, but the permissive waste is restricted to keeping the premises wind and water tight. A lease for a shorter period does not make the lessee liable for permissive waste.

Easements and Profits

An easement is the right to use the land of another person or to restrict that other person from using his land in a particular way. This interest in another person's land includes such matters as rights of way, the right to light, the right to support of a building and the right to take water; it does not include a right to take natural produce from the land, with the exception of water. In order to establish a valid easement four essentials must be shown to exist, these are:

1. These must be a dominant and servient tenement. This means that the land which has the easement over the other land is the dominant tenement, the land which is subject to the easement is the servient tenement. From this we can see that an easement may only arise in connection with land. Where, for example, the owner of a plot of land allows X to walk over it, and X does not own any adjoining land, this is not an easement since there is a servient tenement but no dominant tenement.

2. The easement must accommodate the dominant tenement. This means that the right must make the dominant tenement a better place, increasing its value in some way.

3. The dominant and servient tenements must be in different ownership and occupation. Since an easement is a right to use another person's land in some way there cannot be an easement over one's own land provided the two pieces of land are in the same occupation.

4. The right must be capable of forming the subject matter of a
   grant. This means that there must be a capable grantor and
   grantee; the person who gives the right and the person who
   receives it must have this capacity. An easement cannot be
   claimed by the inhabitants of a village since this is a changing
   body of persons, but as we have seen some rights are recognized
   as forming a custom. The right must come within the general
   classification of easements. This classification is not a closed
   one. In *Miller* v *Emcer Products Ltd.*, 1956, the right to use the
   lavatory of a neighbour was recognized as an easement. In
   Copeland v *Greenhalf*, 1952, however, the court refused to recognize as an easement a right to park and repair vehicles on a
   piece of land; it was said that this was too extensive to permit
   of its inclusion in the classification of easements. A more recent
   case was that of *Phipps* v *Pears*, 1964, where an attempt was
   made to establish an easement of protection against the weather.
   The facts of this case were that a terrace house was demolished
   and a new house built in its place; the gable wall of the new
   house was close to the wall of the existing house, but not built
   into it. Subsequently the other house was demolished leaving
   the gable wall of the new house exposed to the weather. This
   wall had not been rendered or given any other form of protection against the weather, it relied on the other house for protection. The claim for an easement of protection against the weather failed, the Master of the Rolls, Lord Denning, saying that
   this was no more an easement than a right to a view. If such
   an easement were granted it would unduly restrict a person's
   use of his land, it would prevent him demolishing his house if
   he so wished.

Some rights which appear to be easements are not and should
be carefully distinguished. These are:

1. Natural right to support; that is the right to support of land an
   owner possesses from his neighbour – this relates to land only
   and not to buildings. If a person excavates on his land and this
   removes the support to his neighbour's land an action may be
   brought.
2. Quasi-easements; these are rights a person exercises over his
   own land, which, if he were not the owner, would be classed
   as easements.

3. Licences; these are rights given by a person concerning his land, they are described later.
4. Restrictive covenants; these are equitable rights in land and are described later.
5. Public rights; these are rights exercised over land by members of the public who do not have to own land to exercise the right. Public rights of way are the most usual of these rights which may be acquired by statute, or by dedication and acceptance. The statute creating the right will set out all the relevant authority. If the right is by dedication and acceptance at common law it is necessary to show that the owner of the land dedicated the way to the public and that the dedication was accepted by the public. Dedication may be inferred from long usage.

Easements may be created in the following ways:

1. By statute. The easement and details concerning it will be specifically mentioned in the statute.
2. By express grant or reservation. Here a deed of grant will specify the easement. An express reservation arises when some land is sold and the vendor reserves for himself, in connection with the land retained by him, an easement over the land sold.
3. By implied grant or reservation. An implied grant is where land is sold and the law implies that the purchaser, the grantee, acquires all easements and quasi-easements which are continuous and apparent, reasonably necessary to the enjoyment of the land granted and were previously enjoyed as quasi-easements. Implied reservation is where land is sold and part is retained which is entirely surrounded by the land sold, in this circumstance the law will imply that an easement of access will be reserved to the land retained; this is sometimes known as an easement of necessity.
4. By presumed grant or prescription. This is that where there has been long enjoyment of an easement, the court will uphold the easement on the presumption that the long enjoyment shows that the long enjoyment shows that there once was a grant. This presumption comes under three headings: prescription at common law; prescription by lost modern grant; and prescription under the Prescription Act, 1832. But first it is necessary to consider the three conditions

which in general must be complied with to establish an easement by prescription. These are the following:

(a) User of the enjoyment must be 'as of right'; that is it must have been used without force, secrecy or permission. If a right has been used by force, secrecy or permission it cannot create an easement by prescription. Thus in the case of *Liverpool Corporation* v *H. Coghill & Son Ltd.*, 1918, where there had been secret and intermittent discharges of injurious chemicals to a public sewer no easement could be established.

(b) The user must be by or on behalf of the fee simple owner of the dominant tenement. This limits, in general, the acquisition by prescription to fee simple holders or persons on their behalf.

(c) The user must be continuous. This means that the easement must have been used continuously (it does not mean that it should be used every day, for by the very nature of some easements, e.g. right of way, this is not possible).

We can now consider the three types of prescription.

Prescription at Common Law. This requires that the right must have continued from time immemorial, which we saw in Chapter 1 was fixed at 1189. The task of proving that a right has existed since 1189 is almost impossible so the courts have ruled that use for twenty years or more will be presumed, in the absence of other explanation, to have existed since 1189. Difficulties in proving some of these matters, especially with regard to buildings and to the right to light, led to the creation of a legal fiction called the lost modern grant.

Lost Modern Grant. The law recognized that in many cases where it was not possible to show prescription at common law it was unjust to refuse recognition to a right that had existed for years. The court overcame this difficulty by the legal fiction of presuming that a grant of the right had been made subsequent to 1189 but had been lost. A use of twenty years was sufficient to create this presumption.

Prescription Act, 1832. The Act was passed to deal with the difficulties encountered in the application of the lost modern grant and prescription at common law. The Act makes separate provisions for easements of light and for other easements. An easement, other than that of light, cannot be defeated by showing that it must have come into existence after 1189, provided it has been enjoyed without interruption for twenty years. If it can be shown that the right has been enjoyed without interruption for forty years the claim cannot be defeated unless permission was given by deed or writing. From this we can see that a claim based on the twenty-year period will be defeated if it can be shown it was enjoyed by oral permission; this is not so with the forty-year period, unless it is shown that oral permission was given from time to time. It is necessary, in order to succeed, to show that the right has not been interrupted and that the period of user was immediately before the action was brought. But Section 4 of the Act states that an interruption shall be disregarded unless it has been submitted to or acquiesced in for not less than a year after the party interrupted had notice of the interruption and of the person responsible for the interruption.

The Act makes further provision where the servient tenement has been held by a person under a disability (a lunatic or an infant) or where the land is held on a lease for more than three years or for a life interest. Section 7 of the Act states that any period when the servient tenement has been owned by a person under a disability shall be deducted from the twenty years' period but not the forty years' period. Section 8 of the Act states that where a servient tenement has been held under a life interest or under a term for more than three years then that period may be deducted from the period of forty years.

As stated above the Act deals with easements of light separately from other easements. Section 3 of the Act provides that the enjoyment of access of light to a dwelling-house, workshop or other building for a period of twenty years without interruption is an absolute right, unless the right has been enjoyed by written consent or agreement. It can be seen, therefore, that only the one period of twenty years is applicable and that this can be defeated by written agreement only, oral agreement is not sufficient. The provisions in Sections 7 and 8 of the Act noted above do not apply.

An alteration to the law regarding easements of light became necessary by reason of the bombing in World War II and the subsequent control of building work. The effect of the war and building control was to place the owner of a bombed site in the position that another tenement would acquire a right of light from it unless he could, in some way, prevent this happening. The Rights of Light Act, 1959, gave power to such owners to protect their rights. As a temporary measure the period of time was extended from twenty years to twenty-seven years. This allowed a person to bring an action to protect his right. This provision has now ended. The Act makes a permanent change, however, in that it allows a servient owner to register a notice as a local land charge, subject to satisfying the Lands Tribunal that proper notice has been served on the persons likely to be affected. The effect of this notice is to act as an obstruction of the right of light, the notice remains in force for one year.

The amount of light a dominant owner may claim was the subject of so many disputes and actions, that a rule of thumb method evolved; an obstruction of a line drawn upwards and outwards from a window at an angle of 45 degrees was held to be actionable. The matter was finally settled in the case of *Colls* v *Home & Colonial Stores Ltd.*, 1904, where the court said there was no '45 degrees' rule; the test was whether sufficient light had been left to enable the servient tenement to be used for ordinary purposes. The fact that there had been a substantial reduction in the amount of light was not relevant, the test was how much light remained.

Extinguishment of easements may be by an Act of Parliament; by a deed being executed to release the servient tenement; by the law implying a release, which it will do in the event of failure to use the easement for a long period; or by the dominant and servient tenements being united in the same ownership and possession.

Profits

These, to give them their correct title, *profits à prendre*, resemble easements but differ in that a profit gives the right to take natural produce from the land of another person. Another difference is that it is not necessary to show ownership of land to claim a profit.

Profits are found as either:

1. profits of common, that is rights enjoyed in common with other persons; or
2. several profits, that is rights enjoyed by one person alone.

Profits are of many kinds, the commonest being those where a person has the right to take cattle on land; the right to dig turves or peat for fuel; the right to cut wood for repairs to fences and houses; and the right to catch and take away fish.

Profits are created in the same ways as easements, under the Prescription Act, 1832; however, the periods of time for profits are thirty years and sixty years, instead of twenty years and forty years.

Extinguishment of profits is similar to the extinguishing of easements; by statute, by release, or by the uniting in the same person of ownership and possession of the land over which the profit is enjoyed.

Licences

In dealings with land a transaction sometimes takes place which is not a lease but bears a likeness to it; this is a licence. A licence is permission given by the occupier to a person to go on his land; without this permission that act would be a trespass. This transaction does not create an interest in the land; while a lease gives exclusive possession of the land, a licence does not. The commonest example of a licence is that of a lodger; he does not have exclusive possession and is there by permission of the occupier.

Licences are found in the following classifications:

1. A bare licence; this is a licence given by the occupier to a person without payment being made. An example is permission granted to a village cricket team to play a match in a field. Such a licence can be revoked without giving notice, and cannot give rise to an action for damages for the revocation.
2. A licence coupled with an interest. This is where a licence is granted with a right to take something away from the land. An example of this is the granting of permission to enter and take wood from land. Such a licence cannot be revoked and an injunction will be granted to prevent revocation.
3. A licence for value. This is a licence granted on the payment of some value. An example of this is the licence granted by the occupier of a cinema to the members of the audience to see the show on the payment of the appropriate charge. In the case of *Hurst* v *Picture Theatres Ltd.*, 1915, it was held that the licence granted could not be revoked, so that when a member of the

audience was removed forcibly he was able to recover damages for the assault.

It has been common practice for many years for owners of dwellings to allow their use by means of a licence. This put the letting outside the provisions of the Rent Act, 1977. The occupier therefore lost the protection of rent control and security of tenure. The House of Lords in the case of *Street* v *Mountford*, 1985, stated that a licence which gave the occupier exclusive possession of the dwelling was, in fact, a lease. This decision has altered the legal position substantially. Many licence agreements made in the past would now be classed as leases. This is so even though the parties to the agreement state specifically that it is a licence.

Restrictive Covenants

In dealing with covenants in leases we saw that they depended on privity of contract or privity of estate. And we saw too that difficulties arose in the covenants in that at common law for an assignee to enforce the covenant it was necessary to show that the covenant touched and concerned the land; that the covenantee had to have a legal estate in the land intended to benefit by the covenant; and that the covenantee's assignee possessed the same estate in the land as had the assignor.

Where the benefit of any covenant is passed to his assignee by the covenantee in equity the position is the same as at common law, but in the enforcement of the burden of the covenant equity differs from common law. Subject to satisfying certain conditions, the burden of a restrictive covenant will be enforced against a person having an interest in the land. A *bona fide* purchaser for value of the legal estate without notice of the restrictive covenant is not, however, bound. Notice includes not only actual notice but notice which would have been available had proper investigation been made, or notice which could be imputed to an agent. And this is the same whether the burden of the restrictive covenant is in a lease or is a condition of the sale of the fee simple of land.

This equitable doctrine was dealt with in the case of *Tulk* v *Moxhay*, 1848. The facts of the case were that the plaintiff, the owner in fee of the vacant centre of Leicester Square, London, sold it to X, X covenanting for himself, his heirs, and assigns, that he would keep the land uncovered by any building. The land eventually came into the hands of Moxhay who had notice of the original covenant but had not himself covenanted to the same effect. Moxhay intended to build on the land. The plaintiff, who was still the owner of several houses adjoining the Square, sought an injunction restraining the defendant from acting in breach of the covenant of which he had notice. The court granted the injunction.

The doctrine will not apply unless the following conditions are satisfied:

1. The covenant must be negative in nature. This means that the covenant must be one which does not require the expenditure of money. If it does require the expenditure of money it is a positive easement.
2. The covenantee must retain the land for the benefit of which the covenant was made. From this we can see that if the covenant is one which does not touch and concern the land it will be a personal covenant and the benefit cannot be assigned. The problem of creating a restrictive covenant for the benefit of a large estate is one the court has had to deal with. Can a restrictive covenant be annexed for an estate extending to thousands of acres? In *Re Ballard's Conveyance*, 1937, a restrictive covenant purported to be for the benefit of an estate of some two thousand acres, not all of which could benefit from the covenant. The court said that the estate could not benefit from the covenant, and it furthermore refused to separate those acres of the estate which could benefit from the covenant and declare the covenant applicable to that land. This problem seems to have been solved by the decision in the case of *Zetland* v *Driver*, 1939, when it was held that the use of the word 'for the whole or any part of the estate' would be sufficient to enforce the covenant.
3. An assignee of the land having the benefit of the covenant must prove that the benefit of the covenant has passed to him. This is done in one of three ways:
   (a) By showing that the covenant is expressly annexed to the land he has acquired. This means that the covenant must have been created for the benefit of the land and not for the personal benefit of the covenantee. The fact that a person was not a party to a deed creating a restrictive covenant

does not prevent him enforcing it; Section 56 of the Law of Property Act, 1925, allows this provided it can be shown that it was intended he should so benefit.

(b) By showing that the benefit of the covenant had been assigned to him by express terms. This means that if the covenantee sells the land, for the benefit of which the covenant was created, without assigning the benefit of the covenant, the covenant is no longer effective.

(c) If there is a building scheme in force. It often happens that a land-owner develops his land as a residential estate and wishes to keep the land for residential purposes only. This he can do by selling the plots of land to the purchasers and obtaining from each a restrictive covenant in the same terms. The effect of a building scheme is to bind the purchasers each to the other for their mutual benefit. In *Elliston* v *Reacher*, 1908, the essential conditions of a building scheme were stated to be the following:

(i) The plaintiff and defendant in the action must both have derived title from a common vendor.

(ii) Before the plots were purchased by the plaintiff and defendant the estate must have been laid out in plots subject to restrictions showing a general scheme of development.

(iii) It should have been the intention of the common vendor that the plots of land should all benefit from the restrictions.

(iv) The plaintiff and defendant must both have bought their plots of land on the understanding that restrictions were for the benefit of all the plots.

In the case of *Reid* v *Bickerstaff*, 1909, it was held that the area of a building scheme must be clearly ascertainable.

To show that a building scheme is in existence it is not essential to prove that an express undertaking has been given; it will be sufficient if it can be proved that before the purchase the purchaser was shown a plan of the estate with the restrictions marked on it.

As we shall see in more detail later a restrictive covenant made after 1925, other than one in a lease, must be registered as a land charge. Restrictive covenants made before 1926 and those in leases, whenever made, are not registerable and the purchaser must have notice of them if he is to be bound by them.

The conditions existing when many restrictive covenants were made have altered so much that it is often pointless to continue to enforce them; in fact in some circumstances they will prevent the development of an area of land in a particular way. Provision is found in Section 84 of the Law of Property Act, 1925, for an application to be made to court for a declaration as to whether a restrictive covenant is still applicable to a plot of freehold land. The same Section authorizes applications to be made to the Lands Tribunal for a restrictive covenant to be modified or discharged; compensation may be ordered to be paid.

To succeed in an application to the Lands Tribunal the applicant must be able to show that one of the following exists:

1. That by reason of changes in the character of the land subject to the restrictive covenant, or in the neighbourhood, or of other material changes, the restriction is obsolete and its continued enforcement will prevent the reasonable use of the land.
2. That the persons of full age and capacity entitled to the benefit of the restrictive covenant have agreed by express terms or by implication that there should be a modification or discharge of the restrictive covenant.
3. That the proposed discharge or modification would not cause injury to the persons who are entitled to the benefit of the restriction.
4. That the continued existence of the covenant would impede some reasonable use of the land for private or public purposes. In considering this matter regard must be had to the development plan under the Town and Country Planning Act 1971, and the pattern of decisions on applications for planning permission.

The Housing Act, 1985, Section 610, authorizes the county court to disregard any restrictive covenant and permit the conversion of a house into two or more tenements. It has to be proved that owing to changes in the character of the neighbourhood the house can no longer be let as a single tenement.

Land Charges Act, 1972

We have seen in dealing with rights in or over land, how important they are and how they may affect land to a substantial extent. A knowledge of these rights in connection with a particular piece of land is essential in deciding whether to purchase it, or whether it is worth purchasing at the price asked. This knowledge is so essential that in 1972 an Act of Parliament was passed forming a system whereby this information can be registered, and so be available for inspection by any member of the public. The Land Charges Act, 1972, did this; information is entered on five registers, with, where necessary, sub-divisions, according to its particular classification. The information is entered on the appropriate register against the name of the owner or owners concerned. The registers are kept in Plymouth at the Land Registry Office. If X is buying a house from Y, X or his solicitor will have a search made of the registers to see if anything is registered against Y. Registration under the Act constitutes actual notice to all persons of the matter entered on the register. In general it may be said that failure to register an interest which is capable of registration is void against a purchaser for value of any interest in the land.

When an official search is made of the registers a certificate is given showing what, if anything, is entered in the registers. This certificate is conclusive proof, even if a mistake has been made. The State will pay compensation for the default of the official who has conducted the search.

In addition to those mentioned there are other registers kept concerning charges against land; these are known as local land charges and are kept by local authorities. They differ in that the charges are registered against the land and not against the owner. The information entered in these registers includes such matters as restrictions on the use of land under planning law, building lines, and financial charges incurred by the local authority in such things as road improvements. An official search can be made of this register as with the land charges register. Failure to enter a local land charge makes it void against a purchaser for money, or money's worth, of the legal estate.

8

The Law of Torts

The word tort comes from Latin and French and describes actions
which are civil wrongs. To the builder some of these torts, such
as negligence, nuisance, and breach of statutory duty, are of great
importance. As we shall see later, the contract of service between
the employer and employee places duties in tort on the employer
to safeguard his employee, so far as is reasonably foreseeable,
against risks and injuries in his employment. In the carrying out
of constructional work the builder may well be involved in torts
when he infringes some person's rights in property or when he
causes injury to property or to an individual. The use of noisy
machinery at unreasonable hours could possibly involve the builder
in a claim for damages for the tort of nuisance from occupiers of
adjoining property affected by that noise.

The law of torts covers many features of ordinary life which do
not concern us in our consideration of building law. Many torts
are found in common law, but as the law has developed so legislation has intervened to alter and strengthen the law. Since much
of this law is common law the decisions of courts and judges are
of major importance. Some parts of the law have in fact their basis
in one decided case, such as, for example, the rule in *Rylands* v
Fletcher.

The Nature of Torts

Many attempts have been made to define a tort. Some definitions
are more satisfactory than others but no definition is completely
acceptable. The definition by Lord Denning in the *Law Quarterly*

Review 63, page 517, is simple and conveys much, this is that 'The province of tort is to allocate responsibility for injurious conduct.' To be certain as to what we mean we must separate a tort from a contractual obligation which only arises as a result of an agreement between parties; from a trust which is a situation where a person is a trustee of property on behalf of another; and from a criminal action where the state will be involved. A tort is actionable by the injured person; the state plays no part in the matter.

A tort may arise from circumstances which are also a breach of contract. An example of such a situation would be the negligence of an architect in his professional capacity to his client; there would be a breach of an implied term of the contract for the architect to perform his services with proper care, and there would also be liability for the negligence of the architect. Similarly with circumstances involving a breach of criminal law, such as dangerous driving which caused personal injury. Here there would be a criminal prosecution by the state for the dangerous driving, followed by an action for negligence by the person who was injured as a result of the dangerous driving.

It must not be thought that it is always necessary to show that damage has been suffered by some person before a claim may be brought in this branch of law. Some torts are actionable without proof of damage. Trespass to land is one such tort. The mere fact of trespassing on another's land, without causing damage to the land, gives rise to a right to sue; the law allows an action to be brought because there has been an infringement of a person's legal rights.

Other torts, however, require that there shall be proof of damage before an action can succeed. The tort of negligence requires that there shall be proof of damage from a breach of duty of care.

The fact that damage has been suffered by reason of another's action does not necessarily give rise to a right to sue; some actions which cause damage to another are considered to be lawful and so the injured party has no remedy. An example is found in the case of *Bradford Corporation* v *Pickles*, 1895, where Bradford Corporation had bought land for purposes connected with their reservoir but had not purchased land from Pickles. The defendant, who wanted the Corporation to purchase his land, started to abstract water which ran in undefined channels underneath his land. This water would, but for his action, have found its way into the Corporation's reservoir. The defendant had acted with a bad motive and in doing so had deprived the plaintiffs of water they otherwise expected to receive. What the House of Lords had to decide was whether the defendant's action was a tort so allowing the Corporation to sue for damages. The decision was that the defendant was exercising a legal right in abstracting the water even though he had a bad motive, and so the action failed.

The fact that a person acted with malice will not necessarily make some happening actionable, as we have just seen, but the absence of malice in a tort will not in general act as a defence; trespass may be committed innocently and without malice but this fact will not be a defence in any subsequent action.

Nuisance

Nuisance in law is divided into two categories: Public Nuisance and Private Nuisance.

Public Nuisance

This is not a tort, it is a criminal offence. A public nuisance is a matter affecting the Queen's subjects in general, and so it is considered best to deal with the matter as a criminal matter and not to have numerous individuals bringing separate actions. Included in this branch of nuisance is the obstruction of highways. If the circumstances should be such that an individual, by reason of the public nuisance, suffers injury above that suffered by other members of the public, he is allowed to bring an action to recover for his injuries.

Private Nuisance

This is a tort for which an action is brought by an individual. The essential feature to the tort of nuisance is some interference with the enjoyment of land or rights in connection with land.

The occupier of property who claims interference with his land must show that the interference is of a substantial nature; that is to say the land cannot be enjoyed to its full extent. Proof of physical injury to health need not be shown; it is sufficient to be able to show reduction in the enjoyment of the land. The courts expect members of society to live peaceably together; for this reason there is an assumption that there must be some 'give and take'. Trivial matters are not accepted by the courts as constituting nuisances.

Interference with the Enjoyment of Land

This interference may take various forms: noise, smell, dust, damp or smoke; the list is wide. The interference need not be for a prolonged period to give rise to a right to sue. In *Matania v National Provincial Bank Ltd. and Elevenist Syndicate Ltd.*, 1936, it was decided, on the particular circumstances of the case before the court, that dust and noise of a temporary nature from building alterations could be a nuisance.

In deciding whether there has been substantial interference regard has to be paid to the locality where the land is situated. In *Sturges v Bridgman*, 1879, a confectioner had for some twenty years operated machinery in his premises which adjoined the garden of a doctor's house. No complaint was made during this time. When the doctor then built a consulting room in his garden near the confectioner's premises he found that noise and vibrations from the premises of the confectioner affected his work in his consulting room. He sought an injunction to restrain the confectioner in the use of machinery; this was granted. The court took into account the fact that the locality was used mainly by doctors with consulting rooms. Where, however, there is actual damage caused, the fact that the locality is of a particular nature is no defence. In *St. Helens Smelting Co. v Tipping*, 1865, the House of Lords had to consider a case where fumes from a factory had caused damage to vegetation on Tipping's land and reduced the value of his land. The fact that the factory was situated in an industrial locality did not provide an adequate defence.

Where the plaintiff or his goods are of an abnormally sensitive nature, nuisance will not arise when injury is caused to the plaintiff or his goods solely because of that abnormal sensitivity. This rule was seen in *Robinson v Kilvert*, 1889, where the defendant manufactured paper boxes in the basement of a building. Hot air was used in the process and some of it found its way to a floor above where the plaintiff manufactured brown paper which was extremely sensitive to hot air. The court decided that since the discharge of hot air would not have caused injury to ordinary paper there was no remedy for injury to the sensitive goods.

A nuisance which occurs unknown to the occupier of premises is still actionable even though it arises by natural forces; this is provided the occupier ought to have known of the tort. Trees have been the subject of several cases under this rule. An interesting case is that of *Davey* v *Harrow Corporation*, 1958, where the occupier allowed trees to grow to such an extent that the root system caused damage to the foundations of an adjoining house. This was held to be nuisance and damages were awarded.

What, we may ask, is the position when a trespasser causes the nuisance? The answer is that if the occupier knows or ought to know of the existence of the circumstances causing the nuisance then he is liable. If, however, he could not know of the circumstances he is not liable. In *Sedleigh-Denfield* v *O'Callaghan*, 1940, a trespasser carried out work to the defendant's ditch, the result of which was to cause the ditch to become choked and so flood land belonging to the plaintiff. The House of Lords said the defendant was liable since he had a servant who knew, or ought to have known, of the trespasser's work and to have realized its dangers.

Landlord and Tenant

Where the damage is caused by reason of the dangerous condition of premises, the liability of the landlord and of the tenant has to be considered. Neither the landlord nor the tenant will be liable if the nuisance arose from the action of a trespasser, provided neither makes use of the action. In general, liability for any nuisance arising from the condition of the premises falls on the occupier of the premises. The fact that another person owns the premises will not make that person liable, unless of course the owner has created the nuisance.

As we have already seen, the landlord often covenants in a lease to carry out repairs, or he may reserve the right to carry out repairs. Where either of these applies the landlord will be liable for any nuisance resulting from failure to repair the premises. This rule may be seen in the case of *Wringe* v *Cohen*, 1940, where the defendant was the owner of a building which he had let. In the lease he had covenanted to repair the premises. Owing to his failure to keep the premises in good repair the gable wall of the building fell and caused damage to the premises of the plaintiff. The court decided the defendant was liable even though he was unaware of the condition of the building. He had covenanted to repair and had failed to honour his obligation. The courts have also decided that if the landlord has an implied right at law to enter and carry out repairs, which is usual with the letting of small houses, then the liability for nuisance arising from disrepair of the premises is that of the landlord. In *Mint* v *Good*, 1951, the defendant, the landlord of the premises, had not reserved the right to enter and carry out repairs to the house he had let on a weekly tenancy. A wall collapsed and injured the plaintiff. The decision of the court was that a right to enter and execute repairs must be implied and so the defendant was liable.

Nuisance and the Enjoyment of Rights in Land

What we have been considering have been principles and cases concerning the enjoyment of land; the definition of nuisance however included interference with rights to land. These rights include rights to light, to support of buildings, and to take water from rivers. Interference with such rights is actionable under this part of the law of tort.

Who can Sue and be Sued

The person who has suffered the injury, which means the person who is in actual possession of the land, is the person who can sue for nuisance. But if the nuisance is of such a nature as to be likely to affect the interest of the landlord, where the property is leased, then he too may bring an action.

The person who can be sued for nuisance is the person who has brought about the circumstances causing the nuisance. This means that a builder whose work creates a nuisance is liable even though he is not in occupation of the premises where the circumstances giving rise to the nuisance exist.

A person is responsible for the torts of his servants; including nuisance, if the torts have been created in the course of the servant's normal course of employment.

The creation of a nuisance by an independent contractor engaged by an occupier to carry out work of special danger will make the occupier liable. The reason for this is that the law places, in the circumstances where a person requires work of special danger to be carried out, a duty on that person to see that the work is properly carried out. The occupier cannot divest himself of this duty, even by the appointment of a competent independent contractor. This does not mean that the builder, if building work has created the nuisance, will escape from the matter without any liability. It is probable the occupier will sue him for breach of contract for failing to comply with an implied term of the contract to execute the work in a competent and workmanlike manner. An example of the occupier being held liable for his independent contractor's tort is seen in the case of *Bower* v *Peate*, 1876. A person engaged a builder to carry out work on his premises; during the course of this work the builder withdrew support from the building of Bower. In the subsequent action Peate was held liable for his independent contractor's action. The judge, Chief Justice Cockburn, said that Peate was under a duty to see that no mischief resulted from the carrying out of the building work and that he could not have avoided this responsibility by employing someone else.

Trespass to Land

Trespass, another tort concerning the occupation of land, is some direct interference with the possession of land. It differs from nuisance, however, in a number of respects. These are:

1. That trespass is actionable without proof of any damage, whereas nuisance in general must be accompanied by proof of damage to be actionable.
2. Trespass is a wrongful entry on to the land of another whereas nuisance may arise on the land of the defendant; for example, creating foul smells which pass from the defendant's land to that occupied by others may cause nuisance.
3. Trespass is a direct action, such as driving piles into some other person's land. Nuisance however need not be a direct action. Trees growing over the boundary of another's land may be nuisance but it is not trespass, the action is not direct.

Nature of Trespass

Trespass to land does not mean just trespass to the surface of the land, it also includes trespass to land beneath the surface of the soil, and in the air space above the land. A further example of trespass is where a person remains on land after the licence authorizing his presence on the land has expired.

Since trespass to land is a tort for which a civil action is the remedy it follows that many of the notice-boards erected with the warning that trespassers will be prosecuted have no basis in law. Prosecution is for a criminal offence so it cannot be used for a civil wrong. It is for this reason notice-boards of this nature are sometimes referred to as 'wooden lies'. To overcome the difficulty of having to bring a civil action for trespass many statutory bodies, for example the Railways, are given power in statutes to prosecute for trespass on their premises.

Trespass to the surface of the land and to buildings on the land may consist of a person walking on land or of things being fixed to land.

Trespass to land below the surface may consist of driving a tunnel below the surface of the land of another person without his consent. Mining operations are now generally dealt with by statutes which have vested the minerals in the nation and made their removal lawful.

Trespass to air space is a matter which still has some doubts attached to it. How far, it may be asked, does this area of space extend above the surface? It is acknowledged that an aircraft may fly at a reasonable height without causing trespass. The case of *Kelson* v *Imperial Tobacco Co. Ltd.*, 1957, provided some guidance on this point after earlier cases had unsuccessfully tried to settle the matter. The facts were that the defendants erected an advertising sign on a building and the sign projected into the air space above the shop of the plaintiff. The court decided that this was trespass. A case which decided that there could be trespass to air space even though it was of a temporary nature only was *Woollerton & Wilson Ltd.* v *Richard Costain Ltd.* 1970. In this case Costains were erecting a building on a restricted town site. They made use of a tower crane to swing materials from delivery lorries on the adjoining highway on to the site and for moving materials on the site itself. In the course of these operations the jib of the crane swung over the roof of the premises of Woollerton & Wilson. This action caused no damage or nuisance but it did pass through the air space about fifty feet above the roof. Woollerton & Wilson objected to this and despite offers of insurance cover, indemnity and a lump sum payment they sued Costains claiming damages for the acts of trespass that had occurred and seeking an injunction to restrain any further acts of trespass. The application for the injunction was dealt with first and this was granted. The judge however suspended the operation of the injunction until the contract date for completion of the building. He justified this action on the grounds that it was the first legal action of its kind and that Costains had acted innocently in the matter. The judge's action in suspending the injunction has been criticized and it is a course of action which is unlikely to be taken by a judge again.

This in fact was the approach of the judge in the case of *Anchor Brewhouse Developments Ltd.* v *Berkley House (Docklands Developments) Ltd.*, 1987. Here contractors were using several tower cranes on a London dockland development. The occupiers of adjoining land objected to the free-swinging booms swinging over their land when in use. This, they said, was trespass to their air space and they sought an injunction to restrain the use of the cranes in passing over their land. The judge agreed on the basis of Woollerton and Wilson's case and granted an immediate injunction. He was aware of the consequence of the injunction on the building operations and observed that this was a matter for some kind of action by Parliament.

Who can Sue?

The person in possession of the land, and only that person, can sue for trespass. If, however, damage is caused by the trespass which affects the property then the owner can sue to protect his interest in the property. It would seem that the law is such that where a builder has taken exclusive possession of a site in order to carry out building work under a contract, the builder is entitled to sue for any trespass to the land or buildings on the site. A person who is in possession, even if without legal right, can maintain an action for trespass against anyone except the person with a lawful right to possession or entry. An owner out of possession may also sue when he subsequently recovers possession: his possession of the land is, in law, related back to the time he had a right to possession.

The Rule in Rylands v Fletcher

The rule in *Rylands* v *Fletcher* is a particularly good example of how the law of tort has been built up by case law. The rule has its origin in a case decided in 1868 which placed a duty on an occupier of land to take care that things on his land do not escape and cause damage. The tort is one of strict liability: that is to say the defendant is liable for damage under the tort without proof of negligence on his part or the necessity to show some wrongful intent. The rule was stated by Mr. Justice Blackburn to be: 'A person who for his own purposes brings on his lands and collects and keeps there anything likely to do mischief if it escapes must keep it at his peril, and, if he does not do so, is prima facie answerable for all the damage which is the natural consequence of its escape.'

The facts of the case were that Fletcher employed an independent contractor to construct a reservoir on his land. During the course of the work the contractor discovered disused shafts and passages which, unknown to him, communicated with the plaintiff's mine. The contractor failed to seal off these shafts so that when the reservoir was filled, water escaped down the shafts and flooded the plaintiff's mine. The House of Lords decided that Fletcher was liable for the damage resulting from the escape of water.

There are a number of important points to note when considering the rule. These are the following:

1. That there must be an escape which causes damage.
2. That the thing must have been brought on the land.
3. That the thing in question must be non-natural user of the land.

If we consider some cases the importance of these points will be seen. In *Charing Cross Electricity Supply Co.* v *Hydraulic Power Co.*, 1914, a water main, laid by the defendants by statutory authority in a highway, leaked causing damage to the plaintiff's electric cables which were in the same highway. The court decided that there had been an escape within the rule and the plaintiff could recover damages. In *Ponting* v *Noakes*, 1894, a yew tree was growing on the land of the defendant. A horse belonging to the plaintiff was poisoned by reaching over the boundary and eating leaves of the tree. The court decided that since there had been no escape from the land of the defendant the rule did not apply. In *Giles* v *Walker*, 1890, there was a large collection of thistles growing on the land of the defendant. Seeds from the thistles blew on to the land of the plaintiff. The rule was held not to apply since the occupier had not brought the thistles on his land: their presence there was by reason of natural forces. This case dealt with two of the elements of the rule; the thistles had not been brought on the land, and the thistles growing on the land were natural users of the land.

Read v Lyons

The rule, after it was established in 1868, was used in cases dealing with a wide range of events. As time went on the rule became extended; so much so that in one case it was held to apply to gypsies on land who went on neighbouring land and caused damage. The application of the rule was considered by the House of Lords in the case of *Read* v *J. Lyons & Co Ltd*. 1947. The facts were that a claim was made for personal injury suffered by the plaintiff as a result of an explosion occurring in the defendant's factory where munitions were produced during the war. The plaintiff did not allege that the defendants had been negligent. The decision was that the claim under *Rylands* v *Fletcher* failed. The following points were made in the judgements:

1. that there had not been an escape within the rule;
2. the manufacture of munitions in wartime may well be natural user of a factory;
3. that the strict liability of the rule may well not apply to personal injuries;
4. that the strict liability under the rule, so far as it concerned hazardous work, meant that a high degree of care was sufficient.

The effect of this decision was to restrict any further extension of the rule. And in fact it must be said that this decision means that many cases decided before 1948 would, if they were to be decided today, be possibly held to be outside the rule.

Defences to the Rule

There are a number of defences available to the defendant in an action for this tort. The main defences are the following:

1. That the defendant acted by statutory authority in bringing the thing on his land which later escaped.
2. That the thing had escaped from the defendant's land because of the plaintiff's own default.
3. That the escape arose by reason of some wrongful act of a stranger over whom the defendant had no control. In *Rickards* v *Lothian*, 1913, the House of Lords decided that where there had been an escape of water to a lower floor of a building caused by a stranger's malicious interference with the waste pipe to a wash basin, this fact was a complete defence for the defendant.
4. That the plaintiff had consented to the dangerous thing being brought on to the defendant's land. So when in *Peters* v *Prince of Wales Theatre (Birmingham) Ltd.*, 1943, the bursting by frost of a sprinkler fire extinguishing device caused flooding to the shop of the plaintiff on a lower floor, the case was held to come within this defence. The plaintiff had taken the premises knowing a sprinkler system was fitted and so had consented to the risk.
5. By Act of God. The rule does not place a duty on the defendant to guard against a happening no reasonable man could have expected. In *Nichols* v *Marsland*, 1876, a weir erected by the defendant on a natural stream burst during an exceptional storm and caused flooding. It was held that no reasonable man could have foreseen a storm of such severity and so Act of God was a defence.

Negligence

The word negligence in tort is used in two ways:

1. To show the state of mind of a person when some torts are committed. For example, the tort of nuisance may be committed because of some careless or negligent action.
2. As an independent tort.

It is with this last meaning we are concerned.

The tort of negligence was said by Lord Wright in *Lochgelly Iron Co.* v *M'Mullan*, 1934, to mean not just careless conduct but a complex concept of duty, breach of that duty, and damage suffered by the person to whom that duty was owed.

No action can succeed for the tort of negligence unless each of these elements is satisfied: duty, breach of that duty, and damage resulting from that breach.

Duty of Care

There is no liability unless it can be shown that a duty of care exists. Such a duty of care may be required by statute, as we saw when we considered the Occupier's Liability Act, 1957. In other cases the duty will be implied by law or have its origin in a decided case. To whom is this duty owed? Lord Atkin, in *Donoghue* v *Stevenson*, 1932 said 'You must take reasonable care to avoid acts or omissions which you can reasonably foresee would be likely to injure your neighbour. Who then is my neighbour? The answer seems to be – persons who are so closely and directly affected by my act that I ought reasonably to have them in contemplation as being so affected when I am directing my mind to the acts or omissions which are called in question.' This definition is a general guide which may be used to determine to whom a duty is owed. It is not, however, a rule which can be applied in every circumstance. It has been said that negligence is a tort whose categories are still open; and for this reason, if for no other, this definition must be used as a guide.

There are numerous situations where a duty is owed. Possibly the commonest is the duty placed on all users of a highway not to cause harm to others or to their property. Builders owe a duty of care to those persons likely to be injured by careless building work. An examination of some cases will demonstrate the duty on a builder. In *Haley* v *London Electricity Board*, 1964, the House of Lords decided that when an excavation in a pavement was made, by statutory authority, the defendants owed a duty of care to blind persons. The facts of the case were that the excavation was guarded in a manner which was reasonably safe for a sighted person but, as the facts showed, not for a blind person. The Lords said that blind persons going unaccompanied on the highway were not uncommon and so they ought to be taken into account when protecting excavations. The duty is to make the excavation reasonably safe for those who might be expected to use the highway. In *Sharpe* v *E. T. Sweeting & Son Ltd.*, 1963, a local authority employed a building company, as independent contractors, to build a housing estate. The erection of the houses was not directly supervised by the local authority. After one of the houses had been occupied for some time, the concrete canopy over the front door fell and injured the tenant. Investigation revealed that the construction of the canopy was faulty. The building company were sued and held to be liable; they owed a duty of care to the tenant. There had been a breach of that duty of care from which damage had resulted. The House of Lords in *A. C. Billing & Son Ltd.* v *Riden*, 1958, considered the circumstances where a building company carried out work at a house and as a result a visitor to the house was injured. What had happened was that work at the front of the house prevented the front path being used. The visitor used the only practicable route, a path in the next garden, and in the darkness fell in to the sunken area and suffered injury. The visitor successfully sued the building company for negligence. The Lords said that the builder owed a duty of care to all persons who might be expected to visit the house; there had been failure to take reasonable care to protect such persons.

An interesting case which dealt with the respective duties of the architect, builder and demolition contractor was that of *Clay* v *A. J. Crump & Sons Ltd.*, 1964. Buildings were being demolished on a site. One wall of a building was left standing. The architect, without carrying out an inspection himself, accepted the opinion of the demolition contractor that this could be done with safety. Inspection would, however, have revealed that the wall was in an unsafe condition. Later the building contractor commenced work without carrying out an inspection of the wall. Several days later the wall fell injuring the plaintiff, a workman of the building contractor. The decision of the court was that the architect, the demolition contractor, and the building contractor owed a duty of care, to varying extents, to the injured workman.

A recent development with regard to the duty of care in the tort of negligence of particular importance to the building industry has been that relating to defective building work. This development is in fact an extension of the principle of law created by the decision in *Donoghue* v *Stevenson*, 1932. Until this development it was thought that neither a local authority nor its building control officer owed a duty of care when discharging their statutory duty in administering the building regulations.

The first case in this new development of law was *Dutton* v *Bognor Regis Urban District Council*, 1972. In this case the local authority approved plans for the erection of a house on land which had previously been used as a rubbish tip. The foundations for the house shown on the plan were the usual type for that area. When the foundation trenches were dug the true nature of the land was discovered. As a result of this the builder dug the foundations to a greater depth than normal and made use of steel reinforcement. This was done to the external walls only. The building control officer inspected and approved the foundations. Within two years serious cracking occurred to the walls which was traced to the inadequate foundations to the inner walls.

Mrs Dutton sued both the builder and the local authority for negligence. The builder settled the action with Mrs Dutton by making a payment to her. The local authority however resisted her claim and the matter came before the Court of Appeal. The court decided that the local authority were liable for negligence in that their building control officer had negligently approved the foundations.

A somewhat similar case came before the House of Lords in *Anns* v *London Borough of Merton*, 1977. In this case plans were approved for the erection of a two storey block of maisonettes. The plans showed the foundations to be three foot or more in depth. The foundations were apparently inspected and approved by the local authority's building control officer. When serious cracking to the walls was noted, examination showed the foundations to be two feet six inches deep only. The local authority were sued for negligence and the House of Lords held them to be liable. The Law Lords said that liability arose when 'there was a present or imminent danger to the health or safety of the occupants'.

This decision of the House of Lords confirmed the decision of the Court of Appeal in *Dutton* v *Bognor Regis Urban District Council*. The House of Lords said that a local authority had to exercise reasonable care in administering the building regulations with regard to foundations and if they failed to do so they would be liable in damages to the owner of the building; that the builder responsible for the faulty work was not immune from liability because the local authority had approved his work; and that the damages awarded by the court to a successful house owner included personal injury and damage to the property.

An extension of this new principle of law came quickly in the case of *Batty* v *Metropolitan Property Realizations Ltd.*, 1978. Here a house had been built in a hilly area. The house was built on a plateau, from which the ground fell steeply to a stream in the valley. Before the decision to build was made the developer and builder had inspected the land on which the house was to be built to ensure that it was safe to build on. On being satisfied on this matter plans were submitted to the local authority for the necessary approval which was given.

Two years or so after Mr Batty moved into the house part of the back garden on the edge of the plateau slipped down the side of the steep slope. This did not cause any damage to the house or foundations. Examination of the slipped portion of ground showed that it was due to a layer of clay and that within ten years there would be further movement which would make the foundations move down the slope and ruin the house.

Mr Batty sued the local authority, the builder and the developer. The local authority were held not to be liable since the house foundations were properly constructed. The builder and developer were however found liable and ordered to pay damages of £13,000, the full value of the house which was now unsaleable, and £250 to Mr Batty's wife for the distress of the matter.

This case, which was decided by the Court of Appeal, extended the principle of law by holding the builder and developer to be liable for negligence in not ensuring that there was adequate support to the land before building on it; by failing to use reasonable care in examining and investigating, by subsoil investigation as well as other means, the land; and that liability existed even though the damage was limited to the garden of the house.

As a result of the decision in Ann's case numerous claims were made against authorities for the failure of their building control officers to detect faulty work. Builders successfully sued local authorities for negligence even though they themselves had been responsible for the work which did not meet the standard of the building regulations. Many cases were settled out of court once the local authorities, and their insurers, realized there had been negligence by their building control officers. It was apparent that the courts were unhappy with the situation of a builder responsible for faulty work being able to sue the local authority because the building control officer had not detected the faulty work. The House of Lords therefore in the case of *Governors of the Peabody Donation Fund* v *Sir Lindsay Parkinson and Co.*, 1984, ruled that, in general, a builder would not be able to sue for his own faulty work. The rule affects developers as well as builders, and now the position is that the original building owner has little chance of success if he sues the local authority. The case arose from a large housing development which was carried out on land where ground movement was likely. For this reason the drainage systems were designed and approved by the local authority with non-rigid pipes and joints. When the work had started the resident architect agreed with the local authority's drainage inspector that the drainage systems would be rigid pipes and joints. This was done. A few months later, whilst work was still proceeding with the development, the drainage systems to the houses now occupied became obstructed. Investigation revealed that pipes had broken and moved because of ground conditions. The developers, the Peabody Fund, sued the architects, the contractors and local authority. The architects paid a substantial sum to the Fund in settlement of the claim against them. The local authority disputed liability. The Law Lords decided that they owed no duty of care to the Fund. They ruled that an original building owner, in general, has no right against a local authority when the faulty work was done by the original building owner or his contractor. This decision was applied by the Court of Appeal in the case of *Investors in Industry Ltd.* v *South Bedfordshire District Council*, 1986. From this decision it appears that where an owner has made use of an architect, structural engineer or other professional the courts will expect the owner to look to him, and not local authority, for compensation for the faulty work.

As will be appreciated, this development of liability of the builder and architect has caused considerable worry to them. There have been many cases where architects were sued years after the work was completed, and some where an architect had retired from practice and was no longer insured for professional negligence. To be balanced against this is the need to protect a house owner who has probably taken a mortgage to buy the house and then finds it has been badly built. In an attempt to deal with these conflicting interests Parliament passed the Latent Damage Act, 1986, which amended the Limitation Act, 1980. The provisions in the 1986 Act apply only to latent negligence; that is such actions as constructing faulty foundations to a building, with the fault not being immediately apparent but becoming apparent later. The Act maintains the six year period for suing for negligence. After this has expired a claim may be made within a three year period from when the damage was discovered or ought to have been discovered. This is referred to as the 'starting date'. It means that an owner who discovers negligent work ten years after it was done has three years from then to bring his action. The protection for the architect and builder is given by the provision, referred to as the 'longstop', which states that no action may be brought after fifteen years have expired from the negligent work being done.

A further development with the tort of negligence and building work needs to be noted. This is the House of Lords decision in the case of *Junior Books Ltd.* v *Veitchi Co. Ltd.*, 1982. Here the Law Lords ruled that a nominated sub-contractor owed a duty of care to a building owner for the work he did. The facts, briefly, are that a flooring sub-contractor was selected to lay a floor on which was to stand printing machinery. The main contractor was told to enter into a sub-contract with the nominated sub-contractor, which was done. When the floor was found to be defective the building owner did not sue the main contractor, with whom he had his contract, for breach of contract. Instead he sued the nominated sub-contractor, with whom he did not have a contract, for the tort of negligence. The Law Lords decided that the sub-contractor was liable; a duty of care existed which had been breached and the building owner had suffered injury. They said that the close proximity of the building owner and the nominated sub-contractor was almost a contractual relationship and so a duty of care existed. This decision is one which courts are now somewhat reluctant to apply. There seems to be a belief that a claim for what was basically financial loss ought not to have been allowed.

This belief is to be seen particularly in the decision of the House of Lords in the case of *D and F Estates and Others* v *Church Commissioners for England and Others*, 1988. Here the Law Lords declined to apply the principle in Junior Books and threw doubt on other earlier decisions on liability for economic loss arising from defective building work. It does seem as if the present Law Lords are of the opinion that the widening of the application of negligence already considered was a departure from a principle of law which was incorrect and ought therefore to be put right.

The facts in the case were that the Church Commissioners owned land in London on which they decided to build a block of flats. Wates were the main contractors and they engaged sub-contractors to carry out the plastering work. The flats were completed in 1965 and shortly afterwards the Church Commissioners granted a 98 year lease for flat 37 to D and F Estates. D and F Estates was one of a number of companies controlled by a Mr and Mrs Tillman and they occupied the flat.

In August 1980 when the Tillmans were away on holiday the flat was being redecorated. The decorators found some ceiling plaster and plaster on one wall to be loose. Some plaster fell off. The affected areas were replastered and then decorated. The cost of this was £10,676 and a claim for this was started in 1980 by D and F Estates. In 1983 however an expert investigation revealed that further defective plastering to ceilings and walls existed and required attention. When the claim of D and F Estates came before the court in 1985 it included an estimated cost of the further work necessary to remedy the defective plaster and for prospective loss of rent which would arise from the flat being unavailable whilst the work was being carried out.

D and F Estates were successful in the High Court but this decision was reversed in the Court of Appeal. The Court of Appeal came to this decision on two grounds. The first was that Wates, the main contractors, were not liable since they had employed an apparently competent sub-contractor, and that the cost of replacing the defective plaster could not be recovered since it was pure economic loss. D and F Estates appealed from this decision to the House of Lords.

The House of Lords agreed that the main contractors were not liable for the defective plastering since they had employed an apparently competent sub-contractor. This was an application of the rule that if a person makes use of an independent contractor then he is not liable, provided he has employed a competent person, for the wrongs committed by that person. The Law Lords did observe, however, that a main contractor would be liable if in supervising a sub-contractor he became aware of and condoned negligence on the part of the sub-contractor. In this circumstance both would be liable.

The Law Lords also agreed with the decision of the Court of Appeal that the claim for the cost of replastering and redecoration failed because it was pure economic loss. In the absence of a contractual relationship between the parties and where there was no evidence of personal injury or physical damage to other property, a claim of negligence must fail since it would be for economic loss on its own and this was a claim the law did not recognize.

As has been noted the earlier decisions on liability for defective building work which have been based on the tort of negligence now appear to be of doubtful authority. It would seem probable therefore that those who wish to have building work carried out will pay greater regard to contractual provisions and will exercise closer supervision on the work during its execution.

At the time Dutton's case was being considered in 1972 Parliament was passing the Defective Premises Act 1972. This Act, which came into force in 1974, has some provisions of considerable importance to the building industry. Section 1 of the Act states: 'A person taking on work for or in connection with the provision of a dwelling (whether the dwelling is provided by the erection or by the conversion or enlargement of a building) owes a duty – (a) if the dwelling is provided to the order of any person, to that person; and (b) without prejudice to paragraph (a) above to every person who acquires an interest (whether legal or equitable) in the dwelling; to see that the work which he takes on is done in a workmanlike or, as the case may be, professional manner, with proper materials and so that as regards that work the dwelling will be fit for human habitation when completed.'

The provisions of this section are extremely wide but it can be seen that a duty is imposed on a professional man, such as an architect, to see that his work in connection with the dwelling is done in a proper manner so that the dwelling will be fit for human habitation. The duty on the builder is to use proper materials and workmanship to see that the dwelling is fit for human habitation. This duty extends not only to the first owner but to subsequent owners. Section 1 also states that the duty of care extends for six years from the date the dwelling was completed, but if remedial work is done the six year period runs from the date the remedial work was done.

Chattels

The duty of care extends to chattels. That is to say a duty of care is owed by a person who produces or puts into circulation a chattel which is of a dangerous nature. If, however, he knew of its dangerous nature and gave adequate warning as to the dangerous state of the chattel, this warning may be an adequate defence.

Negligent Mis-statements

It was thought until recently that the law with regard to statements which were made, and subsequently found to be incorrect, was that there was no liability on the maker unless he was contractually bound to the other party. The House of Lords decided in *Hedley Byrne & Co. Ltd.* v *Heller & Partners Ltd.*, 1964, that where a person made a statement knowing that the person seeking the information relied on the other person's skill or ability, then a special relationship exists. The effect of this special relationship is that the maker of the statement owes the other person a duty of care. This decision places professional men, such as architects and surveyors, in a position whereby they owe a duty of care, in the circumstances described, to those to whom they offer advice. This is the position even if the advice is being given free. The advice can of course be given with the qualification that the statement is made without responsibility. If such a course is followed no liability will arise.

Standard of Care

The law does not set an impossible standard of care for the tort of negligence. The requirement is that the standard of care is that of the ordinary reasonable man; what he would do in the circumstances is the test. For example, building work being carried out at a school would require more care to protect the children than the same work being carried out at a warehouse. A requirement under this heading is that person who claims special skill, such as an architect, must exercise the skill usually found in a member of that profession.

Res Ipsa Loquitur

The general rule is that the person alleging negligence must prove it to the satisfaction of the court. In certain circumstances, however, this is not the case. Where an accident happens which in ordinary circumstances would not have happened unless there had been negligence, the doctrine of *res ipsa loquitur*, applies. *Res ipsa loquitur* means 'the fact speaks for itself'. The effect of the doctrine is to make the defendant bring evidence to rebut the presumption of negligence. Thus the plaintiff will succeed unless the defendant can rebut this presumption or show that he personally was not negligent./An example of the application of this doctrine is seen in the case of *Walsh* v *Holst & Co. Ltd.*, 1958, where the plaintiff was walking on a road by the side of which was a building which was being demolished. He was hit on the head by a brick. *Res ipsa loquitur* applied and so the burden was on the defendants to prove that they were not negligent. The defendants were, however, able to show that they had exercised care to prevent harm and so they were not liable.

Remoteness of Damage

The damages, which may be awarded to a successful party in an action for negligence, are restricted to the damages resulting from injury which was reasonably foreseeable. Where damage is caused which is different from the damage which was reasonably foreseeable then the defendant is not liable for that damage. This principle is known as the Wagon Mound case, which is a short way of referring to the case of *Overseas Tankship (U.K.) Ltd.* v *Morts Dock & Engineering Co. Ltd.*, 1961.

Contributory Negligence

Many accidents which happen are torts of negligence. Often in these accidents the plaintiff is in some way, however slight, to blame. Before the passing of the Law Reform (Contributory Negligence) Act, 1945, the negligence of the plaintiff would have defeated his claim entirely. Now, by reason of the above Act, a person can bring an action for negligence even though he is himself partly to blame for his own injury. The Act requires that in these circumstances the plaintiff's claim shall not fail, but that the damages awarded shall be reduced to the extent the court thinks right having regard to the plaintiff's own negligence.

Breach of Statutory Duty

A number of statutes impose duties on people and provide that fines may be imposed if there is a breach of that duty. The imposition of a fine under such a statute is a criminal matter for which the body responsible for bringing the matter before the court is the state. In addition to this penalty, however, some statutes are interpreted as giving an injured person a right to sue for damages. This right to sue, which is for the tort known as breach of statutory duty, only arises where the statute was intended to give the right in addition to the fine imposed by the criminal court. Not only must the Act be one which allows the injured person to sue, it must be intended to protect the plaintiff and protect him against the injury he has suffered.

The Factories Act, 1961, is an Act which allows the injured person to sue in tort. If, for example, a person cuts his hand on a power saw because the saw was not fenced as required by the Act, the employer will be prosecuted in a criminal court. The injured employee may then bring an action for breach of statutory duty against the employer.

The advantage gained in bringing this action instead of suing for the tort of negligence is that there is no necessity to prove lack of reasonable care on the part of the employer.

The tort does not, however, provide a remedy in every case. In *Close* v *Steel Co. of Wales Ltd.*, 1962, Lord Morton in the House of Lords said that a requirement in the Factories Act to keep machinery 'securely fenced' was to keep the worker out and not the machine in. If, therefore, a piece of the machine breaks and flies out it is not breach of statutory duty.

Liability for Spread of Fire

There are a number of ways whereby liability for the spread of fire arises. One tort, of course, is that of *Rylands* v *Fletcher* (see p. 132). The escape of fire from land has been held to come within that rule. The rule will not apply if the fire has spread from a normal fire on the land, such as a fire in a domestic grate, for this would be natural user of the land.

A statute, the Fires Prevention (Metropolis) Act, 1774, which applies throughout the land requires that no action shall be brought against a person on whose land fire started by accident. The Act does not exempt a person from his negligence. Further, if the fire started accidentally but later spreads by negligence the Act will not apply. So in *Musgrove* v *Pandelis*, 1919, a fire started accidentally in a car engine when the engine was started. The servant, who had started the car engine, failed to turn off the petrol supply with the result the fire was fed with petrol and spread to the adjoining property. The court decided that the failure to turn off the petrol supply was negligence which removed the protection given by the Act to the defendant when the fire had originally started accidentally.

Another case of negligence was that of *Balfour* v *Barty-King*, 1957, where a plumber, an independent contractor, had been engaged by the defendent to thaw out frozen pipes in the loft of the defendant's house. The plumber applied a blowlamp to the pipes and felt lagging caught fire. The fire spread to the property of the plaintiff and caused damage. The court decided that this was a negligent way of thawing pipes but that the occupier was liable for the spread of fire from his premises even though caused by an independent contractor.

Vicarious Liability and Independent Contractors

Vicarious Liability

In considering the law of tort mention has been made of employers being sued for wrongs committed by their employees. The reason for employers being held liable for the employee's wrongful acts is the principle in law that, in general, the employer is responsible for his employee's wrongs when committed in the course of the employee's employment. This is so even if the wrong is something not authorized by the employer. The reason for this principle is simple: all the employees are agents for the employer performing the work on his behalf, and so the employer is responsible. The employee is also liable for his wrong but since he will have little money there is no point in suing him; it is usual to sue the employer who has money or is insured against this kind of risk.

Who is an employee or, as he is usually referred to in law, a servant? Such a person is one whose work is under the control of another, not only as to what is to be done but how the work is to be done. The important point here is the employer's control over the manner of work.

As we have noted above an employer is liable for his employee's torts even if they are not authorized acts. Provided the wrong is committed in the course of his employment the employer is liable even if he expressly forbade the employee to do that particular thing. So, if an employee does his work negligently and causes injury the employer is liable. In *Century Insurance Co. v Northern Ireland Road Transport Board*, 1942, a driver of a petrol tanker was filling an underground tank at a filling station. During this work he lit a cigarette and threw the match on the ground. An explosion resulted causing considerable damage. The employer was held liable for the employee's negligent performance of his work.

The position is different, however, if the employee causes injury by an act which is outside the course of his normal employment. In these circumstances, which are sometimes referred to as being 'a frolic of his own', the employee alone is liable.

Independent Contractors

The general rule is that a person who engages an independent contractor is not liable for the torts of the independent contractor.

How does an independent contractor differ from an employee? The difference is important. In defining an employee control of the way the work was to be done was the important factor; with an independent contractor there is an undertaking by a person to produce a given result. The control of the work, how it is to be done, is in the hands of the independent contractor and nobody else. An example may help to clarify this point: a handyman employed by a factory is an employee since the factory owner can tell him what to do and how to do his work. If, however, the factory owner engages a building firm to carry out alterations he can tell them what to do, that is the alterations required, but not how to do the work; the factory owner has, therefore, less control of the building contractor than he has of his handyman. The extent of the control exercised is the deciding factor in determining whether a person is an employee or an independent contractor; and of course whether the employer is liable for the torts committed or not.

The general rule is that an independent contractor is liable for his own torts; this is, however, subject to a number of exceptions. The main exceptions are:

1. Where the plaintiff was negligent in selecting an independent contractor for the work in hand. For example, engaging a plumbing contractor to repair a mechanical lift, work not normally performed by the plumbing contractor.
2. Where there is a duty placed on the employer to prevent wrongs arising from his actions. The employer is liable for the torts of the independent contractor if the torts are wrongs which the employer was under a duty to guard against. There are numerous matters coming under this heading: the rule in *Rylands* v *Fletcher*; liability for spread of fire; liability imposed by statute, such as the Factory Act; and work of a hazardous nature which was considered when *Bower* v *Peate* was dealt with earlier.

Defences and Remedies

In an action for tort there will generally be a defence or defences which the defendant may use to avoid liability or to reduce liability. Both the defences, some of which have been mentioned already, and the remedies the court will grant, vary with the torts.

Defences

There are a number of defences available to a defendant in an action for tort; the principal ones are the following:

1. Act of God; this is a defence to an action for a breach of the rule in *Rylands* v *Fletcher*. It is, however, of limited application. It may be used in those circumstances where a person could not reasonably be expected to guard against an event of exceptional severity.
2. Statutory Authority; this claim is made on the ground that an Act of Parliament has authorized the doing of something and that the tort complained of was part of the authorized work.

In deciding whether this is a valid defence the court will look most carefully at the statute in question. The statute may give absolute power to do something, in which case the power will act as an indemnity. It may, on the other hand, give a conditional power; that is, authority to do something provided the doing of that thing will not interfere with private rights. Should there be interference with private rights the statute will not provide an indemnity.

3. Necessity; this will be a defence provided the action taken which caused the damage was done to prevent loss of life or some great damage; the threat to life or property must be shown to be real and further, the action has to be reasonable having regard to the circumstances. This defence was considered in the case of *Esso Petroleum Co. Ltd.* v *Southport Corporation*, 1956, where an oil tanker in a river estuary was in difficulties and likely to break her back, with possible loss of life. Oil was discharged in an attempt to save the ship. The oil was washed ashore on to the beach of Southport Corporation. The Corporation sued for damages for trespass and nuisance. The House of Lords held that the discharge of oil in an attempt to save the ship and the lives of her crew was a necessary act and thus a complete defence.

4. *Volenti Non Fit Injuria*; this is a special form of defence frequently used in actions for negligence. The principle of the defence is that a person who has undertaken to run a risk cannot succeed in an action if he suffered damage as a result of accepting the risk. For the defence to apply it must be clearly shown that the person knew of the risk and fully consented to the risk; the mere fact that he knew there was a risk will not be sufficient. Circumstances may frequently arise during the course of building operations where an employee is injured and it appears that the defence of *volenti non fit injuria* applies. The courts are, however, reluctant to apply *volenti non fit injuria* in employer and employee actions. To do so could well mean that employees forced to work in dangerous situations might lose their legal rights. If they have clearly accepted the risk then of course the defence applies. An example of the possible application of maxim is in the case of *Smith* v *Baker & Sons*, 1891. A workman was engaged in his work in a rock cutting. At intervals a crane swung stones over the heads of the men who were working in

the cutting. A stone fell while it was being swung and injured Smith who was busy with his own work at the time; Smith sued for damages. The House of Lords decided that the maxim *volenti non fit injuria* did not apply and so Smith was successful in his claim.

Remedies

There are two forms of remedy available to a person injured by a tort. The first is only available in certain torts and consists of actions by the injured party to prevent the tort continuing or to reduce its effects. These actions are authorized by law but are not remedies the court grants. The second form of remedy is that granted by the court. This may be an order for damages, the granting of an injunction, an order for specific restitution, or a combination of these.

Extrajudical Remedies

An occupier who is wronged by an act of trespass may forcibly defend his property. The degree of force he uses, however, must not go beyond that needed to defend his property with the minimum amount of harm. A trespasser may also be ejected by the lawful occupier, but here again the force used, if any, must be reasonable in the circumstances.

With private nuisance the injured party has a right to take action to abate the nuisance. In abatement no unnecessary action is permitted. Notice should be given if entry is to be made on to land, unless the urgency of the nuisance is such that it is reasonable to act without giving notice.

Judicial Remedies

Before proceeding to consider these remedies attention must be drawn to the Limitation Act, 1980. This Act requires in general, that an action for tort must be brought within six years of the date when the right of action arose. In the case of personal injuries the period of time is three years, but with leave of the court this period of time may, in certain circumstances, be extended.

A conflict arose in the courts as to when the cause of action arose with negligent building work. Was it when the negligent work was done or was it when the negligence was discovered? For some time the courts applied the rule that the cause of action arose when the damage was discovered or ought with reasonable diligence to have been discovered. This approach however was overruled by the House of Lords in the case of *Pirelli General Cable Co. Ltd.* v *Oscar Faber and Partners*, 1983. Here a defect in the construction of a chimney was not discovered until seven years after it occurred. A claim that the consulting engineers had been negligent was held to be out of time. It was made more than six years after the damage occurred. The rule, therefore, now is that the time for bringing an action starts from when the damage occurred and not when it was discovered. The harshness of this rule is softened by the provisions in the Latent Damage Act, 1986, referred to earlier.

Damages

This is the usual remedy sought by the plaintiff. A payment of money is ordered by the court to compensate the plaintiff for the injury he has suffered, whether it be personal injury or injury to his legal rights.

Nominal damages are awarded, usually a sum up to two pounds, where the plaintiff's legal rights have been infringed but he has suffered no actual loss. In some cases if the court believes that the action should never have been brought an award of a 'contemptuous' sum, such as a penny, may be made.

Substantial damages are to compensate the injured person for the loss he has suffered. It is under this heading an award of several thousands of pounds may be made as compensation for personal injury.

Exemplary damages may be awarded where the tort not only involved a legal right but also caused loss of dignity to the plaintiff. An award of exemplary damages is a punishment of the plaintiff by the court.

In considering an award the court will have regard to the decision in the Wagon Mound case regarding remoteness of damage. If, therefore, some damage was not reasonably foreseeable then that will be excluded in considering the award.

Injunction

In some matters, such as nuisance, the payment of damages may not in itself be an adequate remedy. An order of the court may, therefore, be sought restraining the defendant from repeating the tort. An injunction can in fact be obtained against the commission, continuance or repetition of a tort. Injunctions are discretionary remedies which the court will grant in those circumstances where the court is satisfied no other remedy is adequate; it is not possible to claim an injunction as a right. The value of an injunction is that if there is an infringement the court will deal with the matter as contempt of court, which may well mean imprisonment.

Injunctions are of three kinds, mandatory, prohibitory and *quia timet*. A mandatory injunction is a court order to the defendant ordering him to correct some wrong he has done. A prohibitory injunction is a court order requiring the defendant not to commit a wrongful act. These injunctions may be obtained either as perpetuity or interlocutory. A perpetual injunction is a court order made after the matter has been determined by the court. An interlocutory injunction on the other hand is obtained before the matter is brought before the court; the purpose being to maintain things as they were before the acts which are the subject of complaint; for example, to prevent work being done which it is alleged constitutes a nuisance. This injunction has a limited life and ceases to be effective when the matter is finally settled by a court. The third injunction is *quia timet*. This is an injunction granted when no act has taken place which constitutes a wrong but where there is evidence to suggest that a wrong is likely to occur. It may be used by, for example, a person whose land adjoins a building site where the work is such that there is a strong likelihood of trespass being committed to his land. He does not have to wait for his legal rights to be infringed provided there is sufficient evidence to justify his fears.

Specific Restitution

This is a remedy of the court ordering the return of land or chattels. A person who has wrongfully been deprived of possession of his land would seek this remedy to recover possession.

9

Industrial Law and Trade Unions

Industrial Law

In English law we do not have a separate body of law dealing solely with employer and employee as is the case in some countries. The law that is applied in our country, in such matters as employer and employee relationship and the regulation of working conditions, is a hotchpotch of statute law and common law.

An examination of the history of industrial law in this country is really an examination of social history. To have reached the present position of legal control in industrial affairs has meant hard work and some bitter disappointments for those who, over almost a century of time, have been concerned by bad .conditions and unfair treatment of workers. The sustained efforts of these people have resulted in the improved conditions enjoyed at the present time.

Since early in the nineteenth century numerous statutes have been passed dealing with trade unions and the combination of workers who tried to secure better working conditions; others include Factories Acts which eventually secured improved conditions in factories.

A feature of this development was the reluctance of judges to interpret the new statutes in a manner which would lead to improvement in the conditions of employment in spite of the fact that this was the purpose of the statutes. It is difficult in these times to appreciate that judges would act in this manner and so prevent the improvement of conditions; but this in fact was what happened. When a judicial decision was made which invalidated the real purpose of the statute, another statute would have to be passed to overcome the effects of that judicial decision. So it became, during the nineteenth century, a slow and hard process of improving industrial conditions by statutory measures. The common law too was held back in its development so that help for the workers was not readily forthcoming from that source either. The judges, it seems, acted in this manner because they believed that their interpretation of the law was the correct and proper one. If this all appears to be particularly harsh, too much criticism should not be made of the attitude and conduct of the judges. What they did was, in their opinion, right and proper. The belief that existed in the country at that time, that affairs between employer and employee were no concern of the state, undoubtedly influenced them. The judges came from the wealthy and ruling class and so had not, in general, great sympathy with the efforts of the workers to improve their lot.

After the turn of the century the social conscience was such that the nation recognized that workers must be given better conditions and means for improving their conditions. Statutes were passed therefore which brought about this change; national insurance, trade unions, welfare, safety in factories, control of hours of employment, all eventually were the subject of legislation. In more recent times statutes have been passed to strengthen earlier statutes which have been found to be ineffective in some matters and to keep up with changing social circumstances. At present we have a statute such as the Employment Protection (Consolidation) Act 1978 in force imposing conditions in employment which would have been fantasies some sixty or seventy years ago.

What of the future? Has the development of industrial law now come to an end? Are the workers, by reason of trade unions and different social climate, in a position where no further legal changes are needed? All these questions, and many others, are matters to be dealt with in the future. It seems, however, to be a reasonable assumption that further legislative control of the worker and his conditions will occur. Modern industry requires certain assurances from the worker who, in turn, is entitled to expect improvements in his conditions. The position of the state should not be forgotten in these matters; the prosperity of the country depends on the best use of labour, and this will be achieved by controlling the conditions and terms of employment.

Statutory and Common Law Position of Master and Servant

Under this heading is the backbone of industrial law. Some of the law is common law, the use of which brought about the earlier controls. Later, part of the common law was amended by statute and new measures were introduced by statute. It will probably be better to consider the position of master and servant, or employer and employee as it is more usually known, by dealing with the common law and statute law separately. It must not be forgotten, however, that these two mingle to form the industrial law we are considering.

Common Law

The first feature to consider under this heading is the contract of employment.

Contract of Employment

The usual principles of contract law apply to a contract of employment. There must be offer and acceptance: there may be a written contract as for instance in the engaging of a building manager; or there may, on the other hand, be a contract formed by word of mouth, for example a building foreman on a site engaging a workman. In the case of a minor it will be remembered that a contract for his benefit, such as a contract of apprenticeship, will, until the contrary is proved, be held to be binding. In the building industry it is the practice to have contracts of apprenticeship made by deed, in which case the parent or guardian must sign.

Terms of the Contract

When the contract has been formed its terms will, subject to certain legal requirements, govern the future relationship of the parties. Where the terms are expressed little difficulty should arise; matters such as pay, holidays, sickness, and the duties to be undertaken by the employee will be defined in the contract. If, later, changes occur by reason say of salary increases or alterations in holiday entitlement then these will be incorporated in the contract of service. Incorporation may be by fresh agreement, new offer and acceptance or by implication that the contract is to continue subject to the altered terms.

What is the position where a contract of service has been formed without express terms? In the case of the building industry the law will imply, in the absence of any evidence to the contrary, that the terms of the contract are those customary in the industry. So the rate of pay would be that customarily paid in that part of the country according to the skill of the person employed. Other matters would be those that are customary in the industry. It should be noted that these are terms implied by law.

The termination of the contract of service will be in accordance with any terms expressed in the contract. Failing such terms the notice to end the contract will be that customary in the industry. In trades where the practice is to pay wages at a weekly rate, the notice to end the contract will be one week; where there is no stipulation or custom the requirement is that the notice of termination shall be of a reasonable time. Each party may treat the contract as discharged by breach, without notice being given, when the other party has shown by an act of sufficient gravity that he is treating the contract as at an end. Unreasonable refusal by the employee to carry out his duties may be treated as breach of contract. A prolonged period of sickness by the employee may entitle the employer to treat the contract as ended. Other reasons may also be considered to be breach of contract. The employee can treat the contract as at an end when the employer acts in a manner which indicates the employer regards the contract as ended. All these acts, however, must be of sufficient gravity to go the root of the contract.

The Employer's Duty

At common law the employer must discharge his obligations under the contract and take reasonable steps to ensure that the employee has safe working conditions. He must, as we saw in considering the law of tort, indemnify his employee for damages which occur in carrying out the employer's orders. The employer, it should be noted, is not under any duty at common law to provide a testimonial or act as a referee for an employee.

The Employee's Duty

At common law the employee is subject to the following duties:

1. To obey his employer's lawful orders.

Under this duty come such matters as performance of service and absence of an employee from his work without proper reason. A particularly important feature is that of a strike by the worker. A strike, whether it be official or unofficial, is a breach of contract since it is absence from employment without the employer's consent. Most employers do not exercise their right to treat the contract as ended and discharge the worker, for to do this would mean loss of their labour force; the normal practice is to treat the contract of service as suspended during a strike. This suspension of the contract of service has, of course, no basis in law; where an employer treats the contract as still existing this operates as an acknowledgement that he is ignoring the breach of contract by the worker.

2. To give faithful and honest service

There are under this duty a number of far-reaching requirements. An obvious requirement is that the employee shall not, in performing his service, allow other matters to conflict with the discharge of his duty. He must not divulge his employer's trade secrets to trade rivals, spend his spare time working for a rival firm, take bribes or collect lists of names and addresses of customers or details of trade processes for use against the employer. A building manager who left his employer and took another appointment with a rival firm and then used knowledge gained at his previous employment, which was of a secret nature, would be liable for breach of his implied obligation to his previous employer.

The development of an invention by an employee in the course of his employment does not give the employee any right to the invention; the invention belongs to the employer. In fact, if the employee perfects an invention in his spare time the invention may be claimed by the employer if it can be shown that the knowledge, or possibly some part of the knowledge, was acquired in the course of the employee's duties. The case of *British Syphon Co. Ltd.* v *Homewood*, 1956, demonstrates the extent to which the courts will go in these matters. The facts of the case were that a chief technician of a company which manufactured soda syphons was employed to give advice on technical matters. Acting without any request from the employer the technician invented a new soda syphon. He left the company's service and later tried to patent the invention. The company asked the court to declare the patent to be the property of the company and not of the technician. This the court did.

3. To perform his service with proper care.

The requirement here is that in performing the duties for which he was engaged the employee must exercise reasonable skill and care. The duty is that performance shall be that which could reasonably be expected from a person of average skill and prudence. A person who claims skill must give service consistent with that skill. So a skilled joiner must carry out his work in the manner of an average skilled joiner.

This duty raises an interesting and little-known point of law. This is that if an employee fails to discharge his services with reasonable care and skill then he must indemnify the employer for any resulting damage. In *Lister* v *Romford Ice and Cold Storage Co. Ltd.*, 1957, the House of Lords considered this particular point of law. Lister was a lorry-driver for the company. One day on the premises he negligently drove a lorry and injured another employee. The injured employee sued the company who were of course vicariously liable for their servant's torts. An insurance company paid the damages awarded by the court. Then the insurance company, exercising a right in the policy, sued in the employer's name the lorry-driver for breach of his duty of care. The House of Lords agreed with the claim and ordered the employee to pay a sum of money equal to the damages awarded to the injured party.

Numerous examples probably come to mind when this duty of care of the employee is considered: damaging a lorry by careless driving, damaging a lifting hoist by inattention, damage to goods or tools; there seems to be a long list which could be quoted. Why, it may be asked, have employers not taken advantage of this decision and sued employees for negligent performance of their duties? The answer is that to do so would create bad feeling between employer and employee; the employer would probably lose his labour force if he chose to exercise this right.

Agreement in Restraint of Trade

A not uncommon feature in a contract of service is the employer's requirement that when the employee leaves he will not take a job of a similar nature within the area for a specified period of time. The aim of such an agreement is to protect the interests of the employer who may well train a worker in some secret process or give him special training which he does not wish to see used against him at some later date. After some earlier doubts the House of Lords decided in *Nordenfelt* v *Maxim Nordenfelt Guns and Ammunition Co. Ltd.*, 1894, that such restraints were unenforceable. If, however, it could be shown that the restraint was reasonable then it would be enforced. The test of reasonableness was determined by applying two principles of law:

1. That the restraint must be shown not to be unreasonable in the public interest.
2. That the restraint was reasonable between the parties having regard to their interests.

Each of these is a matter of law for the court to decide. The first is based on public policy. That is, will it be contrary to the best interests of the public to allow the restraint to be enforced; here the matter is examined in its widest sense, the parties are not considered. In the second the interests of the parties are considered. The restraint will be upheld if it can be shown to be something which was necessary for both parties in order to protect their interests. The courts are increasingly reluctant to enforce restraints of trade since they accept that the employee may have little option in the matter: if he wants the job he must agree to the restraint, otherwise someone else will get the job. Further, he may well not appreciate fully the consequences of such a restraint if it is enforceable. Each case is considered by the court on its own circumstances. The more senior an employee is in the organization of a company the more harm he might do to his previous employer. It follows that it is more likely a restraint will be upheld in these circumstances.

A consideration of two cases may help to explain this point of law. In *Fitch* v *Dewes*, 1921, a solicitor's clerk at Tamworth entered into an agreement which included a condition that he would not, after leaving his employment, go into practice within a radius of seven miles from the Town Hall of Tamworth. No period of time was specified. This restraint was considered by the House of Lords who decided that, on the facts of that particular case, the restraint was reasonable and so enforceable. What influenced the Law Lords in their decision was the fact that in a small town a solicitor's clerk would have knowledge of the affairs of the solicitor's clients; a fact which could well prove to be an embarrassment if the clerk had set up in practice in the area. In *Sir W. C. Lang & Co. Ltd.* v *Andrews*, 1909, however, the, court decided a restraint was unreasonable where it tried to prevent a junior reporter from working for another newspaper within twenty miles of Sheffield after his employment with the plaintiff had ended. In support of the plaintiff the claim was made that such a restraint was necessary to protect the plaintiff's newspaper organization and sources of information. The court refused to accept this.

The position with regard to agreements in restraint between traders to avoid competition and to regulate trade affairs is now dealt with by the Restrictive Practices Court which was set up to administer the Restrictive Trade Practices Act, 1956. This Act requires registration of agreements of restraint between traders. Such agreements are, by the Act, void unless they can be shown to be for the public interest.

Discharge of Contract of Employment

There are a number of ways in which the contract of employment may be ended.

1. By Breach. This has already been mentioned and, it will be remembered, is when either party commits an act which is so fundamental as to go to the root of the contract. The effect is to put the injured party in a position where he can treat the contract as discharged by breach.
2. By Death. Since a contract of employment is, like any other contract, formed between two parties, the death of one of the parties brings the contract to an end. If, therefore, a builder who is not a company or member of a partnership employs staff, his death will discharge all their contracts of employment. The staff have a right to sue the builder's personal representatives for their wages up to the discharge of the contract. Should

the personal representatives continue the business then a new contract of employment will arise.

3. By Notice. If a contract has, as part of its terms and conditions, a clause which deals with the notice to be given to end the contract, then this will apply. Otherwise the term of notice will be implied from the contract and from the custom in a trade. The common law position with regard to notice has been altered substantially by the Employment Protection (Consolidation) Act, 1978, which is considered later.

4. By Performance. If a contract is formed for a definite period of time or to carry out some stated task, the passage of that time or the completion of that task automatically discharges the contract.

Common Law Duty of Care by Employer to the Employee

In considering the tort of negligence we found that a duty of care exists in certain circumstances. One such circumstance is the common law duty on an employer to guard his employee against harm. This duty of care requires the employer to exercise reasonable care and skill, he is not under a duty to guard against any unforeseeable happening. The defences available to the employer in an action under this part of the common law are those for negligence. Contributory negligence plays an important part in these actions.

There have been a number of cases on this matter which give guidance to the employer. The duty of care has been held to place the following obligations on the employer:

1. to provide a competent staff;
2. to provide proper premises and plants;
3. to provide a safe system of work.

Each of these obligations is of importance and to understand this importance we must consider each separately.

Competent Staff

This is an obligation on the employer to employ men who are trained or experienced in the work they are to perform. A possible failure would be the employment in a team of scaffolders of an inexperienced man whose inexperience caused some injury to a fellow worker. In *Hudson* v *Ridge Manufacturing Co. Ltd.*, 1957, an employer who continued to employ a workman who was known constantly to play practical jokes, one of which injured a fellow-worker, was held to have failed to satisfy the duty of care to provide a competent staff.

Proper Premises and Plant

An employer must, at common law, provide premises and plant which ensure the safety of the worker. Failure to provide either of these requirements will be breach of duty. Not only must proper premises and plant be provided, they must also be adequately maintained to satisfy the law. The duty on the employer covers not only his own premises but those to which he sends his men to work. Lord Pearce in *Wilson* v *Tyneside Window Cleaning Co.*, 1958, said 'Whether the servant is working on the premises of the master or on those of a stranger that duty is still the same; but its performance and discharge will probably be vastly different in the two cases'. His Lordship went on to say 'If, however, a master sends his plumber to mend a leak in a respectable private house, no one could hold him negligent for not visiting the house himself to see if the carpet in the hall creates a trap'. The importance to the builder of this duty cannot be over stated. Consider Lord Pearce's statement in the circumstances normally found in repair and alteration work at premises belonging to some one other than the employer. The builder must see that premises at which his men are to work will be safe. Where a builder suspected that some premises at which his men were to work were unsafe, his failure to inspect and make proper provision for his staff would be lack of care under this heading. As Lord Pearce said, however, this duty must not be construed to mean that in every case an inspection must be made.

Safe System of Work

This is the arrangement of work so that the task to be undertaken is satisfactorily carried out. Since each job differs so the system of work must differ. Some jobs are of a simple nature and normal instructions to the workers are adequate. Others are more complex and possibly more dangerous, here special instructions will be needed; more thought must be given to the work; and modification of existing systems may be needed. It must be remembered however that though the duty on the employer is to provide a safe system of work, that is to guard against known risks, he is not expected to guard against every eventuality.

The experience of workers does not necessarily free the employer from liability; the law places the duty on his shoulders not on the shoulders of his employees. In *General Cleaning Contractors Ltd.* v *Christmas*, 1953, the House of Lords had to deal with a case brought under this duty. The facts of the case were that an experienced window cleaner was employed by a firm of window cleaners. He was working at a building where ladders could not be used and where there was no provision for fixing safety belts. The practice was to stand on the sill and to hold on to the sash but there was no provision for wedging the sash open so as to ensure an adequate handhold. The window cleaner was using this system when the sash fell catching his hand with the result that he fell and suffered injury. The employee was held to be entitled to recover damages from the window cleaning firm for failure to provide a safe system of working.

When considering work at premises not under the control of the employer, it should not be forgotten that the injured employee may well have a claim against the occupier of the premises for failure to exercise the common duty of care under the Occupier's Liability Act, 1957.

A safe system of work must take into account the physical defects of the employees. If an employee is known to have some physical defect, which ought to be taken into account when considering a proper system of work, then if that fact is ignored the employer has not taken reasonable care. In *Paris* v *Stepney Borough Council*, 1951, a workman who had only one good eye and was, therefore, a known risk of total blindness if he lost the sight of his good eye, was working without goggles. A piece of flying metal took the sight of his good eye. His employers were held liable: he was a known risk and should have been provided with protective goggles.

In considering this duty many questions spring to mind. What happens if an employer provides safety equipment which is not used? What is the position when a builder provides safety helmets on a building site and puts a notice in a position where it can be read by all the workmen that the helmets shall be used, but injury results from failure to use a helmet? What about the man who rides in a hoist contrary to written notices displayed in prominent positions? The answer to all these questions is that the duty on the employer is to take reasonable care. He is not required to take elaborate measures to discharge this duty of care. If the proper plant is provided and clear instructions are given for its use with warning given of possible consequences if the plant is not used in the correct manner, then the employer has discharged his duty of care.

Breach of Statutory Duty

The tort of breach of statutory duty applies in industrial affairs, particularly with regard to the Factories Act, 1961. The same principles apply in the application of breach of statutory duty in industry as elsewhere. The statute in question must give the right to sue in addition to any penalty which may be imposed. That right must be given to a class of person of which the plaintiff is a member. The defence of *volenti not fit injuria* is not available to the defendant who is an employer being sued by an employee for breach of statutory duty. The reason is that the law will not allow these parties to make agreements that statutes shall not bind them. Otherwise many employees would have to agree to forgo the protection of statutory duty in order to secure a job, which would of course defeat the purpose of many statutes introduced to protect the worker. The maxim *res ipsa loquitur* does not apply in an action for breach of statutory duty. In its place is a presumption that if a requirement of a statute designed to prevent an accident has been ignored, and an accident of the type the statute set out to prevent has occurred, then until there is some evidence proving otherwise, that accident has been caused by this omission.

Statutory Law

Over a period of time it became apparent that there were gaps in the common law which needed to be filled if workers were to be given the protection society believed they ought to have. These gaps were filled by Parliament passing legislation. Some of this legislation dates back to the nineteenth century, such as the Truck Act 1831, but the most substantial and important pieces of legislation are found in recent Acts of Parliament. The Contracts of Employment Act 1963, the Redundancy Payments Act 1965 and the Employment Protection Act 1975 were legislative measures which strengthened considerably the position of the employee in his contract of employment.

Payment of Wages

There is a long history of judicial decisions concerning this matter and of statutes introduced to regulate the payment of wages. Many abuses such as paying wages in public houses, giving instead of wages vouchers which could be exchanged for goods in the employer's shop, and deductions from wages for faulty work, have been removed by statutes.

The Truck Act, 1831, was the first statute to require that certain workers should be paid their wages in coin of the realm and further statutes were passed to strengthen the law on this point; the Truck Amendment Act, 1887, finally included all workers engaged in manual labour as coming within this requirement. Payment by coin of the realm prevents payment by cheque. The position now is governed by the Wages Act, 1986. The Act provides that an employer shall not make any deduction from an employee's wages unless the deduction is one which is required or authorized by a statutory provision; it is allowed by a provision in the employee's contract or the employee has given his consent in writing to the deduction. An employer is however allowed to make deduction from an employee's wages with regard to any overpayment of wages or expenses. Payment of the wages may be by cheque, cash or some other means.

Employment Protection (Consolidation) Act 1978

This was introduced in 1978 as an Act to consolidate into a single Act of Parliament a number of Acts which related to employment matters. Before the Act was introduced it was necessary to consult a number of Acts, such as the Contracts of Employment Act 1972, the Redundancy Payments Act 1965 and the Trade Union and Labour Relations Act 1974 in order to find out the legal requirements concerning employment. Even so, certain provisions in the Act do not apply to specified employment since those employees, dock workers and seamen, have their employment matters regulated by other statutory provisions.

Written Statement

Section 1 of the Act requires that not later than thirteen weeks after an employee starts work his employer is to give to him a written statement containing specified information about his employment. In this statement the employer must identify the parties, state the date when the employment began and state whether any employment with a previous employer is to count as part of the employee's continuous period of employment. The purpose of these provisions is to state essential facts of the employment at the beginning of the employment and in this way avoid confusion arising later, possibly when a dispute has arisen on some matter of employment.

The main provisions in the written statement relate to the terms of employment, and these provisions must state the position not more than one week before the statement is given. These written particulars must give the rate of pay or the method of calculating the pay, the intervals at which payment is to be made, the hours of work, the entitlement to holidays and holiday pay, payment, if any, during sickness, pensions and pension schemes, the length of notice the employee is required to give and entitled to receive to end his employment, and the title of the job he is employed to do.

The written statement must also include a note setting out any disciplinary rules applying to the employee, or where a document setting out those rules may be consulted, the person to whom an aggrieved employee may apply if he is dissatisfied with any disciplinary action relating to him, and the person to whom the employee can apply for redress of any employment grievance. Information as to any further steps in a disciplinary matter must also be made known to the employee.

With the provision of this detail of the particulars of employment there is much less likelihood of an employment dispute arising.

There are supplementary provisions concerning the written

statement which are found in sections 2, 3, and 4 of the Act. These state that if there are no particulars to be entered with regard to such matters as sick pay and a sickness scheme this fact must be stated. If the contract of employment is for a fixed term its date of expiry must be stated. If an employee leaves his employment and returns within six months with the terms of the employment remaining the same no further written statement need be issued. If, however, there is during the course of employment a change in the terms of employment the employer must within one month inform the employee of this change. An employer may, however, refer to future changes in the initial statement, in which case there is no need to inform the employee of those changes when they do occur. A written statement of the particulars of employment is not, in general, needed where the hours of employment are normally less than sixteen each week. If an employee's contract of employment changes from more than sixteen hours a week to less than sixteen but more than eight hours a week then for a period of twenty-six weeks he is entitled to a written statement and notices of any change in the terms of employment. Finally, an employee whose hours of work are normally less than sixteen but more than eight and who has been continuously employed for five years or more is entitled to a written statement under section 1 of the Act.

Employers discharge this duty of providing a written statement in a number of ways. Some set out the details in the letter of appointment to the employee; others use specially printed forms or loose leaf booklets which allow for subsequent changes with a minimum of cost. All these methods are permissible under Section 5 of the Act. That section also allows the practice of referring the employee to the details provided in a document which must be readily accessible to the employee.

It is inevitable that some employers will fail to provide the written statement or will fail to provide in the written statement all the details required by Section 1 of the Act. In this circumstance Section 11 of the Act allows an employee to require a reference to be made to an industrial tribunal.

Industrial tribunals are set up under the Industrial Training Act 1982 and they sit in different parts of the country. Each tribunal has a legally qualified chairman, who may be full-time or part-time, and two other members who are selected from employers' and employees' panels. The decision of an industrial tribunal may be the subject of an appeal on a point of law to the Employment Appeal Tribunal.

The industrial tribunal decides what, if any, particulars should be inserted in a written statement and that decision is deemed to constitute the written statement given by the employer under the Act.

The Act gives power to the Secretary of State to make an order to require further particulars to be included in the written statement, and to vary the number of hours worked each week from sixteen to some smaller number.

One further point to note with regard to the provision of information to employees as to their terms of employment is that in Section 8 which requires an employer to give his employee an itemized pay statement showing the gross pay, the deductions from that gross pay and the net sum payable.

Termination of Employment

The 1978 Act has made a number of provisions which are to apply when a contract of employment is ended. Before considering these provisions, however, it must be noted that these are minimum requirements at law and so certain employees may at common law be entitled to longer periods of notice. A number of employees, usually senior employees, have individual contracts of employment which require both the employer and the employee to give, say, three months notice to end the employment. This in a number of cases will be longer than the Act requires an employer to give an employee whose period of employment has been short. Even if a contract of employment does not stipulate a period of notice the common law will imply that the period of notice must be a reasonable period. What is a reasonable period depends mainly on the standing of the employee. In the case of *Hill v C. A. Parsons & Co.* 1971 the Master of the Rolls, Lord Denning, when dealing with the case of the dismissal of a senior engineer who had worked for his employer for 35 years, said: 'In order to terminate his employment they would have to give reasonable notice. I should have thought that, for a professional man of his standing and, I may add, his length of service, reasonable notice would be at least six months and may be 12 months. At any rate one month is far too short.'

The provisions concerning minimum periods of notice under the 1978 Act do not apply to certain employees: Crown servants, dock workers, merchant seamen, employees working abroad and those employees who normally work less than eight hours a week.

Section 49 of the Act requires an employer to give to an employee who has been continuously employed for one month or more the following periods of notice:

(a) one week's notice if the period of continuous employment is less than two years;

(b) not less than one week's notice for each year of continuous employment if the period of continuous employment is two years or more but less than twelve years;

(c) not less than twelve weeks' notice if the period of continuous employment is twelve years or more.

This means, for example, that an employee who does work of an ordinary kind with eight years' continuous employment is entitled to eight weeks' notice even though his contract of employment probably states that he is entitled to one week's notice only.

The section states that an employee who has been continuously employed for four weeks or more need give one week's notice only to end his employment. This is so even though he might have worked for his employer for a number of years.

The rights, which existed at common law before the passing of the Act, for either party to treat the contract as ended are not affected. The purpose of this is to preserve the right to end the contract without notice in the case of some serious misconduct or some similar act.

The section allows a party to a contract of employment to waive his right to the period of notice or to accept a payment in lieu of notice. These provisions allow an employer to permit an employee who wishes to leave to leave without working his notice, and for an employee to accept a payment and leave immediately instead of working, say, a three month period of notice.

Section 51 states that if an employer fails to give the required period of notice, this fact shall be taken into account in assessing his liability for his breach of contract.

Section 53 states that where an employee is given notice by his employer, or is dismissed without being given notice, or is employed on a fixed term contract which expires without being renewed, then the employee is entitled if he so requests, within fourteen days of that request, to a written statement giving particulars of the reasons for his dismissal. Where an employer has unreasonably failed to provide such written statement or the particulars in the statement were untrue or inadequate, a complaint may be made to an industrial tribunal. The tribunal may, if it is satisfied the complaint was justified, make a declaration as to the employer's reasons for the dismissal and shall award the employee two weeks' pay. Complaint must be made to the tribunal within three months of the dismissal, and may only be made by an employee who has been continuously employed for at least twenty-six weeks.

The purpose of this provision is to enable an employee to have in writing his employer's reasons for dismissing him. From this he can decide whether the Code of Practice 1 – Disciplinary practice and procedure in employment, has been complied with. Moreover the written statement may be used in evidence against the employer at any industrial tribunal hearing.

Redundancy

Before the passing of the Redundancy Payments Act 1965, which came into force on 6th December, 1965, there were no statutory provisions governing redundancy. The Act was introduced to assist employees who are dismissed because of redundancy or are laid off or on short time for a lengthy period.

The relevant provisions are now contained in Sections 81 to 120 of the Employment Protection (Consolidation) Act 1978. Again it must be noted that these provisions are the minimum at law. It is now usual practice for employers to pay redundant employees greater sums than the minimum sums mentioned under the Act. This they do either by some prior agreement with the employees' trade union or by making the offer when the redundancy situation arises. When an employer follows this practice he discharges at the same time his statutory obligations under the Act.

The Act applies, in general, to all employees who have contracts of employment, express or implied, in writing or oral, and to contracts of apprenticeship. There are, however, exceptions, the main ones being: employees with less than two years continuous employment with the employer; those employees who in general work less than sixteen hours a week; male employees over 65 and female employees over 60; and certain other specified workers such as dock workers or a person employed by their husband or wife.

Before any claim can be made for a redundancy payment two essential features must be satisfied. These are: the employee must have been dismissed because he was redundant, and that employee must have had at least two years continuous employment with that employer since the employee's eighteenth birthday.

An employee is dismissed for redundancy when the employer has stopped or intends to stop the work for which the employee was employed, or has stopped or intends to stop work at the place where the employee is employed, or that the particular need for the type of work the employee does has ended, diminished or expected to end or diminish.

From this it can be seen that an employee is redundant when the whole business closes down or is to close down, or the business is to be moved elsewhere, or the need for the particular skill of that employee no longer exists. An employee may therefore be made redundant with all the other employees, or he may be the sole employee out of a considerable number of employees who is made redundant. Mere length of service of an employee does not bring the redundancy provisions into operation. If he has been dismissed for some reason other than redundancy, for example, misconduct then he is not redundant however long his period of employment.

Added to this is the requirement to have at least two years continuous employment with that employer.

If an employee is given notice because of redundancy but is offered and accepts an offer of further employment with his employer on the same terms he is not entitled to a redundancy payment and his employment is deemed to be continuous. In order for this to apply the offer of further employment must have been made to the employee before his period of notice expired and he must start work not later than four weeks after the ending of his previous period of employment.

An employee is also not entitled to a redundancy payment if he accepts an offer of employment from his employer which is on different terms to his previous employment, or is at a different place, before his notice expires provided he starts work not later than four weeks after the ending of his previous period of employment. In this case, however, he is allowed a trial period of four weeks' employment in his new job. If during that time he wishes to end his employment he may do so and is then entitled to a redundancy payment.

The Act allows an employee who has been given notice for redundancy to end his employment earlier than the date for the employment to end. The reason for this is to allow an employee who might have been given eight weeks' notice to take up other employment where it is essential for him to start his new job before his period of notice has expired. In this case the employee gives a notice in writing to his employer to end his employment. The employer, who clearly may be put in some difficulty by his employee leaving early, may serve a counter-notice requiring the employee to withdraw his notice ending his employment. If the employee then does not withdraw his notice to end his employment the employee is not entitled to a redundancy payment. The employee deprived of a redundancy payment for his failure to continue working for his employer may bring the matter before an industrial tribunal. The tribunal may award the employee the whole or part of the redundancy payment if it appears to the tribunal to be just and equitable to do so. The basis of the tribunal's decision is whether it was reasonable for the employee to refuse to work his period of notice.

A further provision in the Act deals with the right to a redundancy payment when the employee has been laid-off or on short-time working. An employee is laid off when he has no pay for a week because the employer failed to provide work for him. Short time arises when an employee, because of shortage of work, gets less than half a week's pay for that particular week. The reason for this provision is that an employer might deliberately lay-off or put his employees on short-time in order to encourage them to leave his employment. In this circumstance there would be no redundancy and no redundancy payments.

The Act therefore states that an employee who has been laid off or on short-time for four or more consecutive weeks, or who has been laid-off or on short-time for six or more weeks, not more than three of which are consecutive, within a period of thirteen weeks, may serve a notice on the employer of his intention to claim a redundancy payment. The notice must be served on the employer not later than four weeks after the lay-off or short-time ended. An employee who has served a notice is not entitled to a redundancy payment if it was reasonable to expect that the employer would within four weeks provide employment which would continue for at least thirteen weeks without the employee being laid-off or on short-time.

An employer may serve a counter-notice, within seven days of the employee's notice of claim, informing the employee that he will contest the claim. The matter is then referred to an industrial tribunal for settlement. It should be noted that there can be no redundancy payment made until the employee has ended his employment.

The payment made to a redundant employee is fixed by the Fourth Schedule to the Act. Each year of service for an employee between 18 and 21 years of age counts for half a week's pay; one week's pay for each year of service between 22 and 40; and one and a half week's pay for each year of service between 41 and 64 (59 in the case of women). The years of service are reckoned backwards from the age of the employee when he is made redundant. The payment is limited to twenty years before the claim and subject to a maximum, at the present, of £164 per week. The maximum award is £4920.

An employee who has not been paid a redundancy payment to which he believes he is entitled, or he receives a payment which is less than that he believes is due to him, may appeal to an industrial tribunal. The appeal must be within six months of the employment ending.

When an employer has made a redundancy payment under the Act he may claim part of this payment from the Redundancy Fund. The payment made depends on the age of the redundant employee. This redundancy fund is made up of contributions made by employers and employees.

Unfair Dismissal

What is undoubtedly the most important development in recent employment law is the body of law dealing with the unfair dismissal of an employee.

The principle that an employee ought not to be dismissed unfairly and if he was that he ought to be paid compensation by his employer was introduced by the Industrial Relations Act 1971. When that Act was repealed the provisions concerning unfair dismissal were preserved in the Trade Union and Labour Relations Act 1974. The relevant law is now contained in Sections 54 to 80 of the Employment Protection (Consolidation) Act 1978.

The provisions in the Act concerning unfair dismissal apply, with certain exceptions, to all employees. These exceptions include:

1. Employees who have not been in continuous employment for 104 weeks with their employers at the effective date of termination of their employment. The reason for this exception is to allow an employer a sufficient period of time to assess the suitability of a person he has appointed to his employment.
2. Employees who if they are male are over the age of 65 or if female are over the age of 60.
   Both these ages are the normal retirement ages, consequently dismissal of an employee above the relevant age is not treated as creating any hardship.
3. Employees who are registered dock workers.
   This exception arises from the contracts of employment of these workers being governed by separate and specific legislation.
4. Employees who under their contracts of employment ordinarily work outside Great Britain.
   English law normally applies only in Great Britain, and to seek to enforce English employment law to someone working outside the country would be extremely difficult if not impossible.
5. Employees whose contract of employment is for a fixed term of one year or more where the dismissal consists only of the ending of that fixed term. This is subject to the employee having agreed in writing to exclude any rights he has with regard to unfair dismissal.
   This is an important exception to the construction industry where it is common practice for site agents, clerks of works and others to be employed for the duration of one large construction job only. It has always been understood that when that construction job was finished all employees would have their employment ended. This exception preserves that standard practice.

6. Employees who are subject to an order made by the Secretary of State under Section 65 of the Act confirming a dismissal procedure agreement. This exception allows an agreement to be made regarding dismissal procedures which are to apply instead of the ordinary law.

At the present time only one order has been made.

7. Employment which is normally for less than 16 hours a week. This exception follows the intention of the Act that in general these employment provisions shall not apply to part-time employees.

Section 54 of the Act is a short simple provision which is however a corner-stone of employment law. The provision states that in every employment, other than those exceptions already noted, every employee shall have the right not to be dismissed unfairly by his employer.

The meaning of the expression 'dismissal' is set out in Section 55. This states that an employee is to treated as dismissed by his employer if, but only if:

(a) the contract under which he is employed by the employer is terminated by the employer, whether it is so terminated by notice or without notice, or

(b) where under the contract he is employed for a fixed term, that term expires without it being renewed under the same contract, or

(c) the employee terminates that contract, with or without notice, in circumstances such that he is entitled to terminate it without notice by reason of the employer's conduct.

In addition to the above the section also notes that where an employer has given notice to an employee to end his employment and, during the period of that notice, the employee gives notice to the employer to end the employment earlier than when the employer's notice was due to end, then the employee is still deemed to have been dismissed by the employer.

Dismissal under the first of the categories is when the employer gives the employee the prescribed period of notice or he is dismissed without being given notice. Under the second category dismissal occurs when a fixed term contract is not renewed. In this case however it must be kept in mind that an employee whose fixed term of contract was one year or more may have agreed in writing not to make use of the unfair dismissal procedure.

Dismissal under the third category is known as constructive dismissal. It arises when an employer's conduct to an employee is such that it forces the employee to leave his employment. This situation has arisen where the law recognises that it is no longer reasonable to expect the employee to continue to work for his employer.

An employee's employment is ended when the period of notice expires or, if there is dismissal without notice on that date, and in the case of a fixed term contract which is not renewed when the date of that contract expires. In the case of dismissal and payment in lieu of notice, that is the date of dismissal and not at the end of the period of notice for which payment was made.

The dismissal of an employee is in itself insufficient to make the employer liable to that employee. What is necessary is for the dismissal to be shown to be unfair.

Section 57 deals with this determination of a dismissal being fair or unfair. The section places on the employer the duty of showing what was the reason for the dismissal, and if there was more than one reason what was the principal reason. If the employer is to prove that the dismissal was fair he must show that the reason for dismissal was one of those specified or of some other substantial reason of a kind to justify the dismissal of an employee holding the position the employee held.

The specified reasons are:

1. Related to the capability or qualifications of the employee for performing work of the kind which he was employed by the employer to do, or
2. Related to the conduct of the employee, or
3. Was that the employee was redundant, or
4. Was that the employee could not continue to work in the position which he held without contravention, whether by himself or his employer, of a duty or restriction imposed by or under an Act of Parliament.

The word 'capability' is defined in the Section as meaning capability assessed by reference to skill, aptitude, health or other physical or mental quality. 'Qualifications' means any degree, diploma or other academic, technical or professional qualification relevant to the position which the employee held.

The first of the specified reasons, that of capability or qualifications, can be seen to apply where an employee is appointed to a position which subsequently is found to be above his capability to discharge properly. There may also be the instance of a person claiming to have a certain qualification, which in fact he does not possess, in order to obtain employment. That employee may be dismissed fairly once his failure to possess the relevant qualification is discovered, even though he may have been discharging his employment duties satisfactorily.

The second of the specified reasons, that of the conduct of the employee, is one which in practice gives rise to considerable difficulty in its application. As an aid to deciding whether an employee's conduct justifies dismissal and to promote good industrial relations the Advisory, Conciliation and Advisory Service have issued the Code of Practice 1 Disciplinary Practice and Procedure in Employment. A failure to observe a provision in the Code, it should be noted, does not in itself make an employer liable to any proceedings. If however the employer is involved in any proceedings before an industrial tribunal then his failure to observe any provision in the Code may be used in evidence.

The Code gives practical guidance on a number of matters affecting industrial relations. In particular it sets out what ought to be done by a good employer with regard to warning and possibly dismissing an employee because of his unsatisfactory conduct. The Code accepts that an employee's conduct may be so serious as to justify the employer dismissing the employee without any warning. In the majority of cases however the Code's system of warnings should be used. This system suggests a verbal warning which may be formal or informal, for a minor offence. If the offence is more serious then a written warning should be given together with a statement of the likely consequences of a further offence. Further misconduct may lead to a final written warning which would warn that any recurrence would lead to suspension or dismissal or some other penalty.

The third specified reason, that of redundancy, constitutes a fair dismissal provided that the redundancy is genuine. Any attempt to get rid of any employee by wrongly making him out to be redundant is unfair dismissal.

The fourth specified reason, that of the liability of the employee to continue working in his job without some provision in an Act of Parliament being infringed, is best seen by considering the case of a lorry driver who is disqualified from driving by the courts for some traffic offence. Here it would not be possible for him to continue in his normal employment since if he were to do so it would make both the employee and employer liable at law. If the employer is unable to find the disqualified lorry driver alternative employment, and the employer has only to make reasonable efforts in this respect, then the employer is able to dismiss the employee without that dismissal being unfair.

When considering the matter of unfair dismissal it is necessary to note the provisions in Section 58. These state that an employee's dismissal is to be regarded as unfair dismissal if the reason for his dismissal was that the employee was or intended to become a member of an independent trade union; has taken or proposed to take part in the activities of an independent trade union; or has refused or proposed to refuse to become or remain a member of a trade union which is not an independent trade union.

Conciliation

It ought not to be thought from what has been considered so far that employment legislation is solely concerned with establishing rights of employers and employees. There is a recognition of the need to avoid disputes arising and to assist in the settlement of disputes without resort being made to legal proceedings.

The Employment Protection Act 1975 introduced the Advisory, Conciliation and Arbitration Service. This body is charged with the general duty of promoting the improvement of industrial relations. Trade disputes may be the subject of action by the Service in an attempt to resolve the matter. Where an employee makes complaint that he has been dismissed unfairly an officer of the Service known as a conciliation officer will seek to settle the matter without the industrial tribunal having to hear the complaint.

Industrial Tribunal Proceedings

Under the provisions in Section 67 of the Act an employee who claims that he has been dismissed unfairly may make a complaint to an industrial tribunal against his employer. The industrial tribunal is not allowed to consider the complaint unless it is made to the tribunal before the end of three months from the employee's employment ending. This requirement is subject to the provision that the tribunal may consider a complaint made after the three months period where the tribunal is satisfied that it was not reasonably practicable for the complaint to have been made before the three month period ended.

The question as to whether it was reasonably practicable for the complaint to have been made before the three month period had ended is one which has caused some difficulty in the past. Its intention is to assist the dismissed employee who was unaware of his right to make a complaint to the tribunal that he had been unfairly dismissed at that time but who later discovers his legal right to make a complaint. It is not intended to assist an employee who delays unreasonably in exercising his legal right. The question as to whether a later claim may be made may be decided by applying the judgment of the Court of Appeal in the case of *Dedman* v *British Building and Engineering Appliances Ltd.* 1974. In this case the Master of the Rolls, Lord Denning, said: '. . . I would suggest that in every case the tribunal should inquire into the circumstances and ask themselves whether the man or his advisors were at fault in allowing the period to pass by without presenting the complaint. If he was not at fault, nor his advisors – so that he had just cause or excuse for not presenting his complaint within the period – then it was not practicable for him to present it within that time'.

The proceedings in an industrial tribunal are governed by the Industrial Tribunals (Rules of Procedure) 1985. In general these regulations produce a more informal, simpler and speedier procedure than a typical court hearing.

The person making the complaint has to complete an application form setting out his complaint. A copy of this is sent to the employer who is asked to state if he intends to contest the case and if he does he must give particulars of the grounds of his opposition.

The tribunal procedure is that each side addresses the tribunal, then calls witnesses who give evidence and may be cross-examined by the other side, following which each side may address the tribunal. There is no need to be represented by a lawyer and it is usual practice for an employee to be represented by a trade union official. A person may if he wishes put his own case. Tribunal hearings are in public unless there is some special reason for a private hearing.

The decision of the tribunal, which may be a majority decision of the three members of the tribunal, may be given at the end of the hearing or at a later date but in any case it must be in writing signed by the chairman of the tribunal. An appeal against the tribunal's decision may be made on a point of law only to the Employment Appeal Tribunal. The Employment Appeal Tribunal has three members, one is a high court judge and the other two come from the employers' and the trade unions' sides of industry. An appeal may in certain circumstances be made from the Employment Appeal Tribunal's decision to the Court of Appeal and from that court to the House of Lords.

The award of an industrial tribunal when it finds a complaint of unfair dismissal well founded is, under Section 68, to be compensation paid by the employer to the employee. The compensation awarded is a basic award which at the present time must not exceed £4,920 and a compensatory award, which at the present time must not exceed £8,500. The amount of compensation awarded by the tribunal will be reduced by them when the employee had by his own conduct contributed to his own dismissal. The basic award is based on the employee's age and his period of continuous employment. The compensatory award takes into account such matters as the employee's loss of pension rights and other benefits.

The Tribunal may also make a special award, which must not exceed at the present time £23,850 when an employee has been dismissed because of his trade union activities.

A tribunal may instead of making an award of compensation use the power in Section 69 and make an order for the reinstatement or re-engagement of the dismissed employee. This order, which must take into account the wishes of the employee, need not be obeyed by the employer. In that case, the tribunal will make an award of compensation in the ways considered.

Trade Unions

Trade unions are organisations created to protect the interests of employees and to secure for them the best possible conditions and rates of pay. The early history of trade unions is one of continual conflict, not only with employers but also with the state. Several statutes were brought into force with the intention of protecting trade unions, which at one time were extremely weak, and also of controlling the running of the trade unions so that their affairs were properly conducted.

The legislation concerning trade unions is found in the Trade Union and Labour Relations Act 1974 and the Employment Protection Act 1975 with amendments by the provisions in the Employment Acts, 1980 and 1982, the Trade Union Act, 1984 and the Employment Act, 1988. In this and other legislation there are references to independent trade unions and it is to these bodies alone that certain powers are given.

An independent trade union is defined in section 30 of the 1974 Act as, in general, a trade union which is not under the domination or control of an employer or an employers' association and is not liable to interference by an employer or an employers' association tending towards such control. This definition excludes from the powers given to independent trade unions such staff bodies as are sometimes found in banks and insurance companies where the employers give assistance to their creation and running, and in so doing raise doubts as to the independence of such bodies.

Under the 1975 Act the Secretary of State has appointed a person referred to as the Certification Officer. He is given a number of duties, included in which is that of dealing with an application by a trade union for a certificate that it is independent. In addition to the power to grant a certificate of independence the Certification Officer may also withdrew a certificate he has granted. The granting of a certificate is subject to the Certification Officer being satisfied that the application has been made by a trade union which is independent. When he refuses certification he must give his reasons for that refusal. There is an appeal against his decision to refuse to grant or to withdraw a certificate to the Employment Appeal Tribunal.

Trade unions are subject to certain controls under the 1974 Act with regard to the making and submission to the Certification Officer of an annual return as to their affairs and to keeping proper accounting records with respect to their financial matters.

Trade unions have for a considerable time enjoyed certain legal privileges. These are now set out in the Trade Union and Labour

Relations Act 1974 as amended. There has also been a considerable amount of case law concerning these legal privileges. The total body of this law is too large and complex to be considered in detail here but some general provisions may be noted.

Section 13 of the 1974 Act states that an act done in contemplation or furtherance of a trade dispute shall not be actionable in tort solely because it induces a person to break a contract or interferes or induces any other person to interfere with its performance; or that it consists in that person threatening that a contract will be broken or its performance interfered with or that that person will induce another person to interfere with the performance of a contract. This protection also extends to a person threatening to do these things; without this protection an employer could sue a striking employee for the loss suffered by the employer as a result of that strike.

Section 15 of the 1974 Act also provides a form of protection for peaceful picketing. This allows one or more persons in contemplation or furtherance of a trade dispute to go to a place where another person works or carries on business or where he happens to be, other than his residence, for the purpose of peacefully obtaining or communicating information or peacefully persuading any person to work or not to work.

Events have shown in recent times that not all picketing has been peaceful. With some picketing serious criminal actions have occurred. The position now is that, if a trade union organizes picketing which proves to be not peaceful, legal action may be taken against the union. Substantial fines have been imposed on some trade unions.

Negotiating Machinery

Each industry has its own system of negotiating wage rates and conditions which shall apply in that industry. Originally such matters were left to be negotiated between individual employers and employees but in more recent times it has been recognized that it is to everybody's advantage to settle these matters on a national basis, where this is possible. The effect of such settlement is to achieve national conditions of work and wage rates. The usual arrangement within industries is for representatives of employers and employees to form a joint council which can then decide what conditions and wage rates shall apply. A common feature of this arrangement is that decisions made by the joint council shall be ratified by each representative body.

The National Joint Council for the Building Industry is a body similar to that described above; it is made up of employers' and employees' representatives, and has power to deal with wages and conditions generally within the industry and, when some difficulty arises, to interpret its decisions. To assist the Council there are Regional Joint Committees in different localities. These committees may, if they so desire, set up Area Joint Committees which help them as they in turn help the National Joint Council. Local Joint Committees are also formed; their purpose is to administer the National Working Rules, and Regional and Local Working Rules, and to settle any disputes which may arise within their respective localities. The power of the Local Joint Committee is subject to the jurisdiction of the Regional Joint Committee and of the National Joint Council.

The working rules of the National Joint Council apply throughout the country. It will be readily appreciated, however, that local circumstances may be such that some variation is necessary. Such variation of a national working rule is brought about by a proposal from the Regional Joint Committee concerned requesting the National Joint Council to vary the rule so far as it concerns that area.

Each side of the National Joint Council may seek alteration to a national working rule; the proposed alteration is brought before the National Joint Council by the interested party and the Council may then refer the matter to one of its committees for consideration. Following the report of the committee the Council then makes its decision on the proposed alteration. Ratification of this decision is then made by the employers' organization and the employees' organization.

Within the structure of the National Joint Council and its constituent Regional Joint Committees is an arrangement for conciliation panels to deal with disputes or differences between parties which are affiliated to the National Joint Council.

Legal Effect of Collective Agreements

When a trade union negotiates with employers a new scale of wage rates for workers, it is invariably put into force and applied as the parties agreed it should be. What is the position if the employers have second thoughts and refuse to implement the agreement, or an individual in an employers' organization refuses to pay the new rates? It seems to be generally agreed that collective agreements are not legally enforceable: there is no contractual relationship, the agreement is binding in honour only. What does appear to be agreed is that terms of agreements may become part of the contract of employment by implication or usage.

Disputes

Disputes in industrial matters were originally left to be settled by the parties concerned. Later it became evident that the State should intervene to bring about speedier settlements and to maintain the economy of the country. Various legislative measures have been used to bring about settlements: in the First and Second World Wars compulsory arbitration was introduced and other supporting measures were passed by Parliament. After 1945 most of the measures continued but it was subsequently found that they were inappropriate in peace-time and so had to be revoked.

One statute introduced was the Industrial Courts Act 1919. This provided a form of arbitration for trade disputes and for claims that established terms or conditions in a trade or industry were not being followed. There was an independent chairman and representatives of employers and employees making up the arbitration body.

Although part of the Industrial Courts Act 1919 is still in force almost the whole of the machinery for promoting good industrial relations is found in the Employment Protection Act 1975, which was not consolidated into the Employment Protection (Consolidation) Act 1978.

There is now an Advisory, Conciliation and Arbitration Service which, when a trade dispute exists or is apprehended, may offer its assistance to the parties to the dispute with a view to bringing about a settlement. This is done by the use of conciliation officers of the service.

A further power under the Act when a trade dispute exists or is apprehended is, subject to the consent of all parties, to refer the matter to the Central Arbitration Committee. The Central Arbitration Committee is part of the Advisory, Conciliation and Arbitration Service. The Committee is made up of a Chairman experienced in industrial relations and other representatives with experience as representatives of employers and employees.

The Service may if it thinks fit inquire into any question relating to industrial relations generally or in any particular industry or undertaking. The Service's finding of any such inquiry may be published.

The Service may also give advice and issue codes of practice, both of which might well prevent a trade dispute arising. The advice, which is given without charge, may be given on a wide range of employment topics to employers, employers' associations, workers and trade unions. The codes of practice, several of which have been issued, are designed to promote the improvement of industrial relations.

In recent times the Service has by the use of its various powers brought trade disputes to an end earlier than would otherwise have been the case and have probably minimized the number of trade disputes which have arisen.

10

Industrial Legislation

Industrial legislation is a branch of law which has seen the most dramatic developments in recent years. Formerly there was one piece of legislation only, that was the Factories Act 1961. This Act had its origins in the early part of the twentieth century and in any case was restrictive in that it only applied to workers in factories. Its powers, even where they applied, were considered by many to be inadequate.

In 1963 the Offices, Shops and Railway Premises Act was introduced. This extended to certain workers some of the legal protection previously enjoyed solely by workers in factories. As welcome as this measure was it was felt to be unsatisfactory since it was based in the main on the legal provisions found in the Factories Act, which had been the subject of strong criticism for some time. There was, therefore, a feeling of dissatisfaction as to this branch of law.

This dissatisfaction grew, and in any case there was in support an increasing realization of the economic loss caused to the nation by accidents in industry. In 1970, therefore, a committee was appointed under the chairmanship of Lord Robens to review the health and safety of those at work, the relevant law and the need for additional measures to safeguard the public from hazards. Two years later the Robens Committee made their report. They had found many deficiencies. They found in particular that there were six million people at work who were not covered by the Factories Act or the Offices, Shops and Railway Premises Act. They reported that there was insufficient attention paid to the involvement of staff in matters of health and safety. They also expressed their dissatisfaction as to the administration of the existing law.

The Committee's report and recommendations were soon given legal effect by the passing of the Health and Safety at Work Act 1974. The Act itself does not do as a number of Acts do, that is repeal existing law. The intention is that over a period of time the existing law will be replaced but until that happens it remains in force and its administration is strengthened by these new provisions. The Act of course has a different approach in that it deals with all those at work. In this way the six million at work not previously protected are now given protection. The Act has been brought into force in stages over some years but its full effect will not be seen for some time. What it has undoubtedly done so far is to make many more people aware of the need for health and safety at work.

Health and Safety at Work Act 1974

The Act is comprehensive but it can be said that it sets out to achieve its purpose of improving the health and safety of those at work by three means. These are: 1. general duties, 2. health and safety regulations, and 3. codes of practice. The general duties came into force when that part of the Act became operative. The other two are being brought into force over a period of time. Some regulations and codes of practice have been issued but much remains to be done. Before dealing with these matters in any detail it may be helpful to consider the administrative structure set up under the Act to enforce its provisions.

Administration

The Robens Committee Report was critical of the administration of the existing laws affecting workers. Their recommendations on this matter received the support of Parliament.

The administrative structure is made up of two bodies, the Commission and the Executive. The Commission is the policy making body and the Executive is the body putting into effect the Commission's policy and enforcing the provisions of the Act.

Section 10 of the Act states that there shall be a Health and Safety Commission which shall have a chairman appointed by the

Secretary of State and not less than six or more than nine other members also appointed by the Secretary of State. Before appointing members, other than the chairman, the Secretary of State is to consult with employers' organizations and employees' organizations.

In Sections 11, 12, 13 and 14 the duties, functions and powers of the Commission are set out. In general these include such matters as: to carry out research, to make proposals for regulations, publicity of training and information, carry out any directions given to the Commission by the Secretary of State, to see to the carrying out of the general purposes of the Act, and to direct that the Executive or some other person investigate and make a special report on a matter such as an extensive industrial accident.

Section 10 of the Act also requires the establishment of the Health and Safety Executive. The Executive is made up of a director and two other members, all of whom are appointed by the Secretary of State. The general functions of the Executive are contained in Section 11. These are that it is to exercise those functions of the Commission the Commission directs it to exercise, and to give effect to directions given by the Commission. These matters are in addition to the general requirement to see that the provisions of the Act are enforced.

General Duties

Section 2 of the Act states that it shall be the duty of every employer to ensure, so far as is reasonably practicable, the health and safety and welfare at work of all his employees.

The Section then continues by stating specific matters such as: the provision and maintenance of plant and systems of work; the use, handling, storage and transport of articles and substances; the provision of information, instruction, training and supervision of employees; the maintenance in a safe condition of the place of work and the means of access and egress; and the provision and maintenance of a safe and healthy working environment with adequate facilities and arrangements for the welfare of the employees.

What is common to all that has just been set out is that on matters of safety the employer is under a duty to do what is reasonably practicable. The employer is not under a duty to see that an accident never happens to one of his employees. Although the term 'reasonably practicable' is not defined in the Act there is case law on this term where it has been used in earlier legislation. From this it seems to be that it is the amount of risk involved against the time, trouble and expense of safeguards. That is if the employer can show that he has taken the time, trouble and expense to guard against a risk so that there is little if any likelihood of an accident happening then he has done what is required of him.

Section 3 is of particular importance to the construction industry. The first point to note is the duty of every employer to conduct his undertaking in such a way as to ensure, so far as is reasonably practicable, that persons not in his employment who may be affected are not thereby exposed to risks to their health and safety.

This puts, for example, an obligation on a main contractor to ensure that his work does not create risks to the health or safety of sub-contractors, whether self-employed or not, who are on the construction site and who are not his employees. This obligation can be seen from the decision in the case of *R* v *Swan Hunter Shipbuilders Ltd.*, 1982. Here a ship was being built with a main contractor and various sub-contractors. The main contractors were aware of the great fire risk if oxygen escaped from welding equipment into the confined spaces of a ship. The main contractors therefore produced and distributed to their staff a booklet warning of this danger. Sub-contractors, who were working in close proximity with the main contractors' staff, were not given copies of the booklet or warned of the danger. An escape of oxygen occurred one evening, and the following morning when a sub-contractors' man started to weld, a fierce fire broke out which caused loss of life. The main contractors were held liable and fined heavily for failing to warn the sub-contractors of the danger. There is also an obligation on a main contractor and others under this duty to ensure that the public is not at risk as a result of their work.

A further duty under Section 3 is that placed on the self-employed. This is a duty to conduct his undertaking in such a way as to ensure, so far as is reasonably practicable, that he and other persons (not being his employees) who may be affected thereby are not thereby exposed to risks to their health or safety.

A difficulty under previous legislation had been that self-employed persons could not be dealt with since they were not employers. Now that self-employed persons are increasing in number it has been necessary to bring them within the control of the law. This provision means, for example, that a self-employed joiner on a construction project owes this duty to all the other workers on that project. His failure to observe this duty will make him liable to prosecution.

Section 6 places a duty on a person who designs, manufactures, imports or supplies an article for work to ensure, so far as is reasonably practicable, that the article is so designed and constructed as to be safe and without risks to health when properly used, to carry out any testing and examination to satisfy this duty, and to take the necessary steps to secure the availability of adequate information as to its use and any conditions which are to be observed to ensure that it will be safe and without risks to health.

This provision would apply, for example, to the production of a tool. Here, if there were any risks with its use and conditions were thereby necessary, those conditions would have to be made available in order to discharge this duty.

Section 9 states that no employer who is required by law to do things or to provide things for his employees is to levy or permit to be levied on any employee any charge in respect of that matter.

This means that a contractor who provides a piece of personal equipment to an employee so as to satisfy some legal provision must not make any charge to that employee. It is important to note that this refers only to things done or provided for an employee in order to satisfy a specific requirement imposed by law. It does not prevent an employer providing, say, protective clothing where such is not required at law for his employees and making a charge for that clothing. The employees' agreement is needed to this arrangement but it is frequently done. The inducement to employees is that the employer often subsidises the cost of the article.

Section 8 places a duty on every person not to intentionally or recklessly interfere with or misuse anything provided in the interests of health, safety or welfare in connection with the relevant law. There have been successful prosecutions under this duty where some person by an act of foolishness has interfered with a safety provision.

Section 7 provides a new provision in this branch of law in that it imposes a duty on an employee to take reasonable care of the health and safety of himself and others who might be affected by the work of the employee. The Section also imposes a duty on an employee to co-operate with his employer so that any duty or requirement of the relevant law imposed on the employer is observed.

So an employee who goes on a scaffold which he knows is not constructed as required by the law, and in doing so imperils his own safety, is liable to prosecution.

Safety Policies Committees and Representatives

Although what is to be considered now comes within the heading of general duties just considered it is of such importance as to require separate consideration. It will be recalled that the Robens Committee Report called attention to the need to involve workers in safety matters to a far greater extent than had previously happened; these provisions do that.

Section 2 of the Act places a duty on every employer to prepare and, as often as may be appropriate, revise a written statement of his general policy with respect to the health and safety at work of his employees and the organization and arrangements for the time being in force for carrying out that policy, and to bring the statement and any revision of it to the notice of all his employees.

The Section also allows an exception to be made to this duty to provide a written policy statement. The Secretary of State has used this power and made the Employers' Health and Safety Policy Statements (Exception) Regulations 1975, which excepts any employer who has less than five employees.

Written statements of general policy of necessity must vary according to the size and complexity of the employer's business. What is required in all cases, however, is the general policy of the employer and the organization and arrangements for carrying it out. It may be necessary with some businesses for the employers to set out matters in great detail, including such matters as rules and procedures. This document is then to be brought to the attention of every employee, usually by giving a copy to each employee, and any revision is to be similarly brought to their attention.

Section 2 also gives power to the Secretary of State to make regulations for the appointment by recognized trade unions of safety representatives from amongst the employees. Those representatives are to represent the employees in consultation with the employer.

The appointment of safety representatives by a recognized trade union must, so far as this is reasonably practicable, be from persons who have worked for the employer for the preceding two years or have had at least two years' experience in similar employment.

The Section also puts a duty on the employer to consult such representatives with a view to the making and maintenance of arrangements to enable them to cooperate effectively in promoting and developing measures to ensure the health and safety at work of his employees.

The Safety Representatives and Safety Committees Regulations 1977 have been made by the Secretary of State in accordance with the above powers.

The regulations set out in detail the functions of safety representatives, which include such matters as investigating potential hazards and causes of accidents, investigating complaints by any employee he represents as to health and safety at work, to make inspections, to attend meetings of safety committees, and to consult at the workplace with the inspectors of the Health and Safety Executive and any other enforcing authority. In order to be able to carry out these functions the Safety Representative is to be given time off by his employer, and to be given time off to undergo relevant training. This time off is to be with pay from the employer.

The regulations state that a Safety Committee shall be established if at least two such representatives request the employer in writing to establish such a committee. The employer is after such a request to consult with other representatives of recognized trade unions whose members work there, and then form the committee. Notice of the formation of the committee is to be posted in a place where the employees may easily read it. The committee is to be formed within three months of the request for it to be formed.

A Safety Representative who claims that his employer has failed to give him time off to carry out his functions, or that his employer has failed to pay him, may make a complaint to an industrial tribunal. The complaint must be made within three months of the date of the failure of the employer or such further period as the tribunal considers reasonable where the tribunal is satisfied that it was not reasonably practicable for the complaint to be made within the three months. The tribunal on hearing the complaint, and being satisfied as to the complaint being well-founded, will make an award of compensation as is just and equitable to be paid by the employer to the employee.

Health and Safety Regulations

For many years it has been the practice to deal with the detailed matters concerning health, safety and welfare at work by means of specific regulations. The Construction (Working Places) Regulations 1966 made under the Factories Act 1961 are an example of this practice.

Many of the existing regulations have been in force for some years and are becoming out of date. In some cases the standards they require are too low and better standards ought to be and can be attained. They are therefore in need of revision. In other circumstances no regulations have been made although there might be a need for them.

Section 15 of the Act gives power to the Secretary of State to make health and safety regulations for the general purposes of the Act. These regulations may be made so that they repeal or modify existing statutory provisions, may exclude or modify in relation to a specified class of case, and may make a specified authority responsible for the enforcement of existing legal provisions. These regulations may make exemption from their requirements and in other ways deal with different situations.

Progress in the making of these regulations has not been fast but the Secretary of State has made the Health and Safety (Enforcing Authority) Regulations 1977, which allocate the responsibility for the enforcement of functions of the Act in certain circumstances to local authorities.

Codes of Practice

The Robens Report recommended and the Act accepted the need to have good standards of guidance provided so that not only would a contravention of some provision in the Act be avoided but there would be created a good standard of health and safety for the employees.

The aim of codes of practice under the Act is the same as that of the Highway Code. By the provision of such a code the most recent information on a particular topic, stated in simple short terms, is provided as practical guidance.

Section 16 gives power to the Health and Safety Commission for the purpose of providing practical guidance to approve and issue such codes of practice as appear suitable, or to approve codes of practice issued by some other body which appear to the Commission to be suitable. So the Commission may prepare and issue its own codes of practice or it may approve a code of practice prepared by some other body.

The Commission is required to consult with government departments and other relevant bodies and then to obtain the consent of the Secretary of State. Codes of practice once issued may be revised. Approval of a code may be withdrawn. A code of practice when issued is to be adequately publicized by the Commission.

Section 17 states that in any criminal proceedings brought under the Act the fact that a person failed to observe a code of practice which is relevant to the matter may be given in evidence. The fact that a code of practice was not observed is not in itself to render a person liable to prosecution.

These provisions follow those that apply with regard to the Highway Code. For example, a person who drives very close to the vehicle in front of him is not observing the Highway Code but no criminal prosecution arises from his conduct. If however his driving causes a collision or creates a hazard for others, then a criminal offence has been committed and in any prosecution the failure to observe the Highway Code will be evidence which may be given to the Court. Codes of practice in health and safety will apply in the same way.

Prohibition and Improvement Notices

Two defects under the previous legislation were that a factory inspector might discover a contravention which in itself might not justify a prosecution or where more would be achieved by remedying the contravention than by prosecution, or a contravention was so serious as to require immediate action to remove a danger; and in these circumstances he could not take any action which would be of immediate benefit. He had to bring a prosecution for the contravention and try in the meantime to persuade the employer to take any necessary steps to remedy the situation.

The Health and Safety at Work Act 1974 has provided two new powers to deal with the situations just considered. These powers are to serve an improvement notice or to serve a prohibition notice.

Section 21 of the Act empowers an inspector when he is of the opinion that there is a contravention of the relevant law or that there has been a contravention which is likely to continue or be repeated, to serve an improvement notice. This notice must state the contravention, give the reasons why the inspector is of that opinion and require the matter occasioning the contravention to be remedied within a time not earlier than 21 days after the notice has been served.

The power to serve a prohibition notice is contained in Section 22. In this case the power may be used not only when the relevant law has been contravened but also where a contravention may occur. No notice may be served unless the inspector is of the opinion that the matter concerned will involve a risk of serious personal injury.

The prohibition notice is to state that the inspector is of the opinion that there is or will be a risk of serious personal injury, the matters which in his opinion give rise to that risk, the contravention of the relevant law, and direct that the activities to which the notice relates shall not be carried on until the matters which in his opinion gave rise to the contravention have been remedied.

The direction given in the notice is to take effect immediately if the inspector states that he is of the opinion that the risk of serious personal injury is imminent. Where there is not that risk the prohibition notice is to take effect at the end of a period stated in the notice.

The service of a prohibition notice, which is to come into effect immediately, is a matter of some consequence since it may require some work activity to be stopped which will cause the lay off of men or even hold up a large project. An example of the use and effect of a prohibition notice in the construction industry was found in 1978 with a construction firm carrying out deep excavation work at an extension to a power station. Two lifts were in use for this work. One of the lifts crashed when taking some of the workers down to their work. Four of the men were killed and others seriously injured. When the Health and Safety Executive inspectors made an inspection of the crashed lift they found faults which made them inspect the other lift which was similar and had been maintained in the same way. As a result of the evidence produced on the examination of the undamaged lift the Health and Safety Executive inspector issued a prohibition notice that the second lift was not to be used until it had been thoroughly examined and overhauled. The effect of the prohibition notice was to stop completely this part of the construction work.

In either an improvement or prohibition notice directions may be made as to the measures needed to remedy any contravention and those directions may make reference to an approved code of practice and may give the person on whom the notice is served a choice between different ways of remedying the contravention.

An appeal may be made under Section 24 against an improvement or prohibition notice to an industrial tribunal. When an appeal is made against an improvement notice that appeal has the effect of suspending the operation of the notice until the appeal is decided or withdrawn. In the case of an appeal against a prohibition notice the notice will be suspended only if the person making the appeal satisfies the tribunal that it should be suspended.

In dealing with appeals of these types, where unusual industrial processes may be concerned, the usual composition of the tribunal may not be suitable. Where this is so the section allows one or more assessors to be appointed to assist the tribunal.

Enforcement

Section 18 places on the Health and Safety Executive the duty to make adequate arrangements for the enforcement of the relevant law. In addition to this the Secretary of State may, and in fact has, made regulations imposing duties of enforcement on local authorities.

Inspectors have been appointed both by the Executive and by local authorities to enforce the provisions of the Act. These inspectors are given various powers, such as the right to enter premises, in order to carry out their duties.

In enforcing the provisions of the relevant law inspectors may institute criminal proceedings and they have the right in a magistrates' court to prosecute even though they are not lawyers.

When a person is convicted of a contravention of the relevant law a court will usually impose a fine. Under powers in Section 42, however, the court may, in addition to or instead of imposing a fine, order him to take steps to remedy the contravention. A time limit may be laid down in the order and this may be extended by the court.

The Factories Act, 1961

The Factories Act 1961, is the last in a series of statutes dealing with factories, conditions in factories and workers employed in factories. The importance of this Act and the regulations made under the Act will diminish as the provisions under the Health and Safety Act 1974 become more widely applied.

Definition

Section 175 of the Act sets out a long and detailed definition as to what is to be considered a factory coming within the provisions of the Act; it also includes certain specified premises which would otherwise not be included in the definition. A very general description of a factory is that it is premises in which persons are employed in manual labour in work which is carried on by way of trade or for purposes of gain. There are three essential elements in this definition: employment, manual labour, and trade or purposes of gain. If any one of these elements is missing the premises concerned are not a factory; on the other hand factories may come within the definition even when they consist of nothing more than open air premises.

Building Operations

Building operations receive special mention in the Act since they are by their nature different to the normal factory and its work; certain parts of the Act do not apply to 'building operations'. 'Building operations' as defined in section 176 of the Act means in general the construction, alteration, demolition, repair or maintenance of a building. Section 127 states which parts of the Act are to apply to building operations and includes a requirement that not later than seven days after building operations begin a written notice has to be served on the factory inspector for the district giving details of the operations and the place where the work is to be carried out. This requirement however does not apply if there is reasonable ground for believing that the work will be finished within six weeks. It should be noted that building operations do not include permanent premises such as builder's yards or joiner's shops: here the Act will apply in its entirety.

Administration

The administration of the provisions of the Act is divided between the factory inspectors and local authorities, with the main burden of the administration of the Act falling on the former. An inspector is a civil servant specially selected and trained for his work. Section 146 empowers an inspector and officers of a local authority to enter and carry out inspections of factories at all reasonable times, which include day and night. The obstruction of any person performing his duty under the Act renders the person causing the obstruction liable to a penalty; failure to comply with a requirement of the Act constitutes an offence. All offences under the Act are tried in magistrates' courts.

Section 138 requires an abstract of the Act and other specified information to be posted at the principal entrance to the factory. The purpose of this is to enable the workers in the factory to have readily available to them information concerning the Act.

Section 140 places a duty on the occupier of the factory to keep a register, which must be in the prescribed form. This register is known as the general register and must contain certain information regarding accidents and other matters.

Health

Section 1 requires factories to be kept clean and refuse to be removed daily. Walls and ceilings in the factory are to be washed down with hot water and soap every fourteen months if they have a smooth impervious surface, if painted or varnished to be repainted or revarnished every seven years; in other cases they are to be whitewashed or colourwashed every fourteen months.

Section 2 requires that factories shall not be so overcrowded as to cause risk or injury to health to employed persons; there is a general requirement that there shall be not less than 400 cubic feet of air space available for each worker.

Section 3 states that in each workroom there is to be maintained a reasonable temperature. Where little physical effort is involved and most of the work is done sitting there shall be a temperature after one hour of work of at least 60°F. (15.6°C.); thermometers must be provided.

Section 4 requires that each workroom shall be adequately ventilated.

Section 5 requires suitable and sufficient lighting to be provided; the Secretary of State is given power to make regulations on this matter.

Section 7 deals with the provision of sanitary accommodation. There are to be separate conveniences for each sex. Regulations have been made setting out what numbers of conveniences shall be provided according to the numbers of workers employed in the factory.

Welfare

Section 57 makes a requirement that there shall be an adequate supply of wholesome drinking water provided at suitable points in the factory.

Section 58 states that suitable facilities for washing shall be provided, including clean running hot and cold or warm water, soap, clean towels or other means of drying; these facilities are to be conveniently accessible. The Secretary of State has power to make regulations as to the number of wash-hand basins to be provided.

Section 59 requires the provision of suitable accommodation for clothing which is not used in working hours. Drying facilities, where reasonably practicable, are to be provided. The Secretary of State has power to make regulations concerning this matter.

Section 61 lays down a prescribed standard for the provision of first-aid equipment. Where fifty or more persons are employed a first-aid box is to be in the care of a person trained in first-aid treatment.

Safety

There are numerous provisions in the Act regarding safety. In general it may be said that dangerous machinery has to be securely fenced and that the fencing provided shall be maintained so as to give proper protection.

Young persons or women shall not clean machinery if some moving part exposes them to risk of injury. Further, young persons are not to work at machines which are prescribed by the Secretary of State as being dangerous, unless the young persons have been given sufficient training in the use of the machine or are working under adequate supervision of a person with experience of that machine.

Hoists and lifts are to be of proper construction, strength and mechanical condition, and must be properly maintained. Every hoist or lift is to be examined every six months by a competent person and a report by that person attached to the general register.

Chains, ropes and lifting tackle are to be constructed of sound material and shall be sufficient in all respects for the use to which they are to be put. No chain, rope or lifting tackle shall be used for weights greater than its working load. Every chain, rope or lifting tackle is to be examined every six months by a competent person. Before being first used every chain, rope other than a fibre rope, or lifting tackle is to be tested and a certificate of test and examination of safe working load given and kept available for inspection.

Cranes and other lifting machines are to be of proper construction and adequate strength and to be properly maintained; there is to be examination by a competent person every fourteen months and particulars of such examination are to be entered in a register. Safe working loads are to be clearly marked on every lifting machine. Jib cranes are to have automatic indicators of safe working load.

Factories are to be provided with proper means of escape in case of fire. A certificate as to the provision of means of escape is given by the fire authority. Use of a factory in contravention of this requirement as to means of escape in case of fire is an offence. Means of escape are to be properly maintained and kept at all times free from obstruction.

The Construction (Health and Welfare) Regulations, 1966

These are regulations made under power contained in the Factories Act, 1961 and administered by the factory inspector. Their aim is to require employers to provide facilities for their employees' health and welfare. Failure to comply with the regulations is an offence for which a criminal prosecution may be brought.

The regulations, which apply to building operations and to works of engineering construction, empower the Chief Inspector of Factories to grant a certificate of exemption so that all or some of the regulations do not apply to certain works.

The requirements as to the provision of first-aid equipment vary according to the number of persons employed on a site. First-aid boxes in accessible positions are to be provided where more than five persons are employed; if the number of employees is more than 250 there must be a first-aid room in the charge of a person trained to give first-aid treatment.

The welfare requirements include the provision, in case of bad weather, of adequate and suitable accommodation for accommodating clothing not in use and facilities for taking meals. Sanitary conveniences and facilities for washing must be provided. An adequate supply of wholesome drinking water is also required.

The Construction (Working Places) Regulations, 1966

These regulations, made under power contained in the Factories Act 1961, repealed many of the regulations of the Building (Safety, Health and Welfare) Regulations, 1948. The administration and enforcement of these regulations are the same as for the Construction (Health and Welfare) Regulations mentioned previously and they apply to the carrying out of building operations and works of engineering construction.

The regulations are mainly concerned with safety of working places. As will be readily appreciated safety and the use of scaffolds forms an important part of the regulations. Scaffolds are to be of adequate strengths, properly erected under the supervision of a competent person, and are to be properly maintained. Minimum sizes are specified for working platforms, suspended scaffolds and planks. Guard rails and toe boards are to be provided to scaffolds where a person using the scaffold is liable to fall more than six feet six inches. Gangways are to be kept in such a condition as to give proper footholds and no unnecessary obstruction is permitted.

The Construction (General Provisions) Regulations, 1961

These regulations were made under power in the Factories Act, 1937, and 1948, and continue in force by reason of the Factories Act 1961. They revoked some of the regulations of the Building (Safety, Health and Welfare) Regulations, and provided new measures for building operations and works of engineering construction. Administration and enforcement of these Regulations are as mentioned previously.

An important feature in the Regulations is the requirement that every contractor and employer of workmen shall, where he has undertaken works to which the Regulations apply and where he normally employs twenty or more, appoint in writing one or more persons who are suitably experienced to act as safety supervisors. The safety supervisor must promote safe conduct in work and exercise general supervision of the observance of the Factory Act; his name must be entered on an abstract of the Regulations which must be prominently displayed. The regulations do not require that the appointed safety supervisor shall do no other work but there is a requirement that any other duties shall not prevent him efficiently discharging his duties as a safety supervisor. A practice has arisen of firms joining together to appoint a safety supervisor to visit a number of firms. In this way the law is enforced. In other cases employers' organizations have made an appointment and the participating employers pay for his services.

The other regulations require measures to secure safety in excavations and similar works; suitable and adequate timbering to be provided for such excavations; and timbering work to be carried out under the supervision of an experienced competent person. When such timbering works have been completed no person is to be employed until there has been a proper inspection. Any excavation which is liable to cause injury by reason of the collapse or fall of any structure must not be commenced or continued until adequate steps are taken to ensure safety.

Offices, Shops and Railway Premises Act, 1963

Before this statute was passed by Parliament there was little, if any, legislation dealing with the health, welfare and safety of employees in offices, shops and similar premises. The need for protection for workers in these premises had been recognized for some time but it was not until the Gowers Committee reported in 1949, that any statutory control of the health, welfare and safety of these workers seemed possible. The Offices, Shops and Railway Premises Act, 1963, is the result, however long delayed, of such investigation the Gowers Committee made and of its recommendations.

The Act applies to over a million premises and affects over eight million workers.

The definitions of the various premises to which the Act applies are found in Section 1 of the Act. Several premises are mentioned specifically so as to bring them within the Act.

The Act does not apply to premises where the normal working week does not exceed 21 hours, or to premises where the only persons employed there are certain close relatives of the employer, or where the only person working there is self-employed.

The Secretary of State has power to grant to any class of premises he chooses exemption from some of the provisions of the Act. Similarly local authorities can grant stated exemptions in the case of individual premises.

Administration

Administration of the Act is divided between the factory inspectors, fire service authorities and local authorities. The factory inspector is responsible for administering the Act in Crown premises, local authority buildings and in shops and offices at building sites. Fire service authorities administer the provisions in the Act relating to fire with the exception of those premises dealt with by the factory inspector. Local authorities are responsible for the administration of the other parts of the Act in the premises not otherwise dealt with; this includes the greater number of offices and shops.

Inspectors under the Act have power to enter premises to which the Act applies at any reasonable time; they are empowered to inspect, make examinations and ask for certificates to be produced. It is an offence under the Act to obstruct any inspector who is carrying out his duties under the Act; offences against the provisions of the Act are punishable by fine. Employers are required to publish abstracts of the Act in a prescribed form in the premises so that employees are aware of the terms of the Act.

To assist in the administration of the Act there is a requirement that premises coming within the Act have to be registered with the appropriate authority.

Health, Welfare and Safety

There is a requirement in Section 4 that premises, furniture and fittings shall be kept in a clean condition: refuse must not be allowed to accumulate and floors must be cleaned at least once a week.

Section 5 contains important provisions relating to the overcrowding of rooms: a room has not to be so overcrowded as to be likely to cause risk of injury to health; further, the room must have 40 square feet of floor space for each person who works in the room. Where the ceiling is lower than 10 feet there must be not less than 400 cubic feet of air space for each person employed in the room.

Section 6 requires that there shall be a reasonable temperature in every room where persons are employed other than for short periods only. This applies where there is little physical effort on the part of the employee. The reasonable temperature is not less than 16°C after the first hour of work; a thermometer must be provided on each floor where this Section is operative.

Section 7 states that proper provision shall be made for ventilation of the rooms of a building to which the Act applies.

Section 8 requires the provision of proper lighting which may be by natural or artificial means.

Section 9 imposes a duty to provide proper sanitary accommodation in accordance with regulations made by the Secretary of State. The regulations set out the sanitary conveniences which must be provided for specified numbers of employees in order to comply with the Act; it is possible to comply with the Section by making an arrangement so that employees may use the conveniences provided by another employer. Conveniences which are used under such an arrangement must, however, be conveniently accessible to the employees.

Section 10 requires washing facilities to be provided which must have clean running hot and cold or warm water, soap and clean towels. Regulations have been made as to the numbers of wash-hand basins to be provided. As we saw was the case with Section 9 arrangements can be made with another employer for the use of washing facilities provided by him to be available for other employees.

Section 11 makes a requirement that there shall be an adequate supply of drinking water.

Section 12 requires that there shall be accommodation for employees' clothing not worn during working hours.

Sections 17, 18, and 19 deal with safety in the use of dangerous machinery: no person under 18 is to clean any machinery if there is risk of injury to him from a moving part of that machine; dangerous parts of machines are to be adequately fenced; before any person is allowed to work at a dangerous machine that person must be instructed as to its dangers, and be properly trained how to use the machine.

Section 24 details the provisions to be made with regard to first-aid; where more than 150 persons are employed there must be a trained person in charge of the first-aid equipment.

Fire Precautions

All premises are to be provided with proper means of escape in case of fire. The work being conducted on the premises must be so arranged that there is always free access to the means of escape. In the case of certain premises a certificate must be obtained from the fire authority that the means of escape have been inspected and found to be satisfactory. Where the fire authority is not satisfied as to the provision of means of escape, a certificate will be refused unless certain works are carried out within a specified time. The employment of persons after this time with the work uncompleted is an offence.

Industrial Training Act, 1982

This Act sets out to do three things: to improve the standard of industrial training; to provide a sufficient supply of properly trained workers in industry; and to share throughout an industry the cost of training workers. The need for the Act became apparent when it was discovered the supply of trained workers was inadequate and that some workers were not trained to the required standards. Another fact found was that a few firms trained workers themselves or arranged for their training at colleges while other firms failed to train workers at all. Firms which failed to train or assist in the training of workers were found to recruit workers when skilled after training by other firms. This has been corrected by the introduction under the Act of a system of levies to be paid by all firms.

The Secretary of State is responsible for various matters under the Act. He may make an order specifying the activities and establishment of a training board. Before he does this he must consult with the Manpower Services Commission or accept proposals submitted by the Commission. The Commission is to consult with representatives of employers and employees and certain specified organizations before making proposals.

The Act empowers the Secretary of State to set up industrial training boards each of which will be responsible for the standard of training in a particular industry. Before a board is created for an industry the Secretary of State must consult with employers' and workers' organizations for that industry. The board must have a chairman who has had industrial or commercial experience, and equal representation from organizations of employers and employees in that industry, and representatives from education; the Secretary of State and other government departments are also represented. The boards are required to secure proper training in the industry and to publish recommendations on the content, nature and length of training; they are also authorized to conduct research into training for employment in the industry. An important feature is that the boards may pay allowances to persons being trained and make grants or loans to those providing courses. A board's proposals on its functions must be approved by the Secretary of State and it may appoint committees or join with other boards to appoint joint committees delegating functions to that committee.

The finance needed for a board's purposes – which include the running of training schemes or arranging of courses to be run by others – is provided by government grant and by a levy paid by all employers at the same rate fixed by the board.

The board will pay a grant from its funds to an employer who is providing training for his employees, providing the training satisfies the board's recommended standard of training. An employer who does not train his employees must pay the levy but will not be able to claim a grant from the board.

The maintenance of a board's recommended standard of training is important; for this reason firms will only be paid grants if their training is satisfactory. A board or its committee may appoint inspectors to visit firms and report on the training being carried out.

The position of education authorities is not altered by this Act. The board makes recommendations as to training of workers, which may be at any level, and this training is given by an employer or at an educational establishment. An employer who sends his workers to a course at an educational establishment will, provided the course is considered appropriate by the board, be entitled to a grant.

11

Insurance and Commercial Law

In 1942 the Beveridge Report suggested there was a need to have a national system of benefits payable to members of the community who fell sick, became unemployed or suffered injury at work. Before this report there was little legislation on these matters and what there was was not very effective. The best example was the Workmen's Compensation Act which dealt with injuries sustained at work by means of an employer's scheme. The Act was extremely complex and the procedure cumbersome. The system for retirement pensions was also inadequate. In 1946 the present system of state protection against sickness, unemployment, industrial injury and provision for proper retirement pensions was introduced. There were two main Acts, the National Insurance Act and the National Insurance (Industrial Injuries) Act. These Acts were added to over the years as the original intentions of the Acts were widened and strengthened. A new measure was the introduction of a new scheme of retirement pension, which was based on the earnings of the employee and was additional to the original scheme which still continues. This last measure of an additional pension has brought about a revision of the original law. From 1 July 1988 it has been possible for employees to contract out of this by joining a private pension scheme. The law on these matters is now contained in the Social Security Acts 1973–86.

Social Security Acts 1973–86

There is under this law a scheme which makes provision whereby a worker who suffers a loss of earnings from inability to work owing to an accident at work or the effects of an industrial disease is compensated. The scheme in general covers all workers. All that is needed to obtain benefit under the scheme is to show that the claim arises from some accident at work. It is not necessary to show that there had been fault on the part of someone. The essential is to show that the accident or industrial disease arose out of and in the course of employment. Payments under these provisions do not affect a person's right to sue for damages at common law.

Disputes do arise under this scheme, principally on the ground that the accident may not have occurred in the course of employment. Any such dispute as to whether a benefit ought to be paid is settled by tribunals set up under the Act; a person aggrieved by a decision of a tribunal may appeal to a Commissioner. A Commissioner is a barrister of not less than ten years' standing to whom appeals on points of law are made and his decision may only be questioned in a court on the ground that he has exceeded his jurisdiction.

The benefits payable for industrial injury have changed recently. Death benefit has been abolished, sickness benefit is now paid for absence from work because of industrial injury for 15 weeks, after which disablement benefit is paid. To qualify for a disablement pension the disability must be not less than 14%.

The protection in the form of benefits for sickness, unemployment, retirement and other matters provided by the scheme is probably the most important part to the average employee. These benefits are only paid if a required number of contributions have been paid by the employee making the claim. For example, a person who has failed to make the required number of contributions in the course of his working life will not qualify for the full rate of retirement pension. In certain circumstances a person may disqualify himself for benefit by reason of his conduct; an employee may be refused benefit if he leaves his job without reasonable cause. Any dispute as to whether any benefit is payable or not is determined by a tribunal with a right of appeal to a Commissioner.

The most recent benefit under the scheme of social security benefits is that of an additional pension to the basic pension. This additional pension is related to the earnings of the worker. Payment is made up to the age of 65 for men and 60 for women. The pension paid depends on the number of years of contributions, up to twenty, and the average earnings over those years. As was mentioned earlier it is now possible to contract out of this scheme. Where an employee is a member of his employer's own pension scheme, and that scheme has been approved as been up to the standard of the state scheme, then such an employee is exempt from having to contribute to the state scheme. He will still contribute for and in due course will receive the basic state pension. For the other pension he will receive payment from his employer's scheme according to its conditions.

All these benefits have to be paid for and this is done by means of contributions from both the employee and the employer. The Acts put insured persons into three classes, which are:

Class 1. Employed persons. These are persons working for a wage or salary.

Class 2. Self-employed persons. These are persons working on their own account.

Class 3. Non-employed persons. These are those who are insured but do not belong to Class 1 or 2.

Class 1 contributions are up to 9% for employees and up to 10.45% for employers where the employee is a member of the state pension scheme. If the employee is contracted out of the state pension scheme both rates are reduced. Class 2 contributions are at a flat rate of £4.05 per week. Class 3 contributions are at a flat rate of £3.95 per week. There is also an additional contribution paid by the self-employed known as class 4, this is 6.3% of profits between £4,750 and £15,860 a year. As some employees are on very low rates of pay the payment of contributions by them could create hardship. There are therefore lower earning limits below which no contributions are payable.

Carriage of Goods

The building industry, like most other industries, needs motor vehicles to carry goods for its work. The state controls to a certain extent the use of goods vehicles on the road by a system of licences. Although there is a mass of law on this matter, not all of which is essential for our purposes, some brief mention may be helpful.

The Transport Act, 1968, governs these matters. There are two classes of operator's licences under the Act. The restricted operator's licence is a licence for goods vehicles which are used for the carriage of goods for or in connection with any trade or business carried on by the holder of the licence, not being the trade or business of carrying goods for hire or reward. This class of licence covers the ordinary trader or businessman who uses his goods vehicles to carry his own goods. The other class of licence is the standard operator's licence. This is a licence for the use of a goods vehicle for hire or reward or for or in connection with any trade or business carried on by the holder of the licence. As can be seen this class of licence is much more extensive than the restricted licence, it allows the holder to carry goods for another person and to make a charge for doing so. In addition to that the holder may also carry goods in connection with his own trade or business. There is power to revoke or vary a licence that has been granted. Wrongful use of a licence is an offence punishable by fine.

Employer's Liability

Two difficulties concerning employer's liability have arisen in recent times. The first difficulty was in determining the liability of an employer for injury to his employees which resulted from defective equipment provided by him in connection with his business. The second difficulty arose when an employer conducted his business without insurance cover for injury to his employees; this meant that an award by a court to an injured employee could not be satisfied.

The first difficulty was noted in the case of *Davie v New Merton Board Mills Ltd.*, 1959. The facts in this case were that an employee using a piece of equipment was injured when a piece of metal broke off a steel drift. The equipment had been bought by the company from a reputable supplier and the defect was not such as could be observed from any reasonable inspection. The employer was held not to be liable to the employee since he had purchased the equipment from a reputable supplier and the defect was not one which could be found by making a reasonable inspection. The effect of this decision was to mean that in similar circumstances an injured employee would have to sue the manufacturer or supplier who might be situated abroad and difficult to trace, or he may be bankrupt. The legal position brought about by this decision was the subject of much criticism and it was accepted that there was a need to change the law.

To remedy this difficulty the Employer's Liability (Defective Equipment) Act, 1969, was passed. The Act states that where an employee suffers personal injury in his employment because of a defect in equipment provided by the employer for his business and the defect is wholly or partly the fault of someone other than the employer or employee, then the injury is deemed to be also negligence of the employer. This means that the employer is held to be liable for negligence when defective equipment secured by him from a manufacturer or supplier is the cause of personal injury to an employee. The employer is allowed by the Act to seek contribution from the manufacturer or supplier if the manufacturer or supplier can be held to be negligent. The employer may also, if this is appropriate, seek to have the employee's own negligence, if any, taken into account in determining the damages to be awarded.

The difficulty with regard to employers who did not have adequate insurance for personal injury to their employees was dealt with by the passing of the Employer's Liability (Compulsory Insurance) Act, 1969. This Act, together with the regulations made under it, requires that, subject to certain exceptions, every employer carrying on business shall insure and maintain with an authorized insurer an approved policy against liability for bodily injury or disease sustained by his employees arising from their employment. The exceptions are family relatives and certain bodies such as nationalized industries and local government authorities. An approved policy is one which gives cover for not less than £2 million and does not contain certain conditions which, if they were included, would possibly allow the insurers to repudiate a claim. A certificate of insurance must be issued and copies of the certificate displayed at each place of business where persons are employed who are covered by the policy. The certificate or a copy must be available for inspection by an inspector of the Secretary of State for Employment. Failure to comply with the requirements of the Act are offences for which on conviction fines may be imposed.

This statutory requirement to have insurance cover for liability for personal injury to employees has in a number of cases had little effect on employers. The reason for this is that they had already insurance cover which satisfied the Act. Such employers have, of course, to observe the duty of posting certificates and the other requirements in the Act and regulations.

Finally it should be noted that there is another form of compulsory insurance. This is in connection with the use of motor vehicles. The minimum insurance cover permitted by law is for third party risks, which since 1972 has included cover for passenger insurance. A more usual form of insurance is comprehensive which includes not only the legal minimum for third party risks but cover also for such other matters as damage to the vehicle.

Negotiable Instruments

Money transactions between parties have, except in the case of small amounts, to be made by the use of documents which are known as negotiable instruments. These also allow a person who has received a negotiable instrument to use it in turn without cashing it to pay any debt that he himself owes. This transferability, which may be done simply by delivering it to another, makes negotiable instruments a useful and desirable way of dealing with sizeable sums of money. There are a number of negotiable instruments which are specified in the Act of Parliament dealing with these matters, the Bills of Exchange Act, 1882, but the two of most importance to builders are bills of exchange and cheques.

Bills of Exchange

A bill of exchange is defined by Section 3 of the Bills of Exchange Act, 1882 as 'an unconditional order in writing addressed by one person to another, signed by the person giving it, requiring the person to whom it is addressed to pay on demand, or at a fixed determinable future time, a sum certain in money to, or to the order of, a specified person or to bearer'.

If we consider this definition in a little detail we can see that in order to create a bill it is necessary to give an order that a payment shall be made. It is insufficient just to authorize the payment of a sum of money. As will also be seen the bill must be in writing; it is not possible to create a bill by word of mouth. The bill has to be addressed by one person to another and signed by the person giving it. This means that the bill must bear the name of the person who created it, he is the drawer of the bill; it must bear the name of the person to whom the order to pay the money is given, he is the drawee; and it must bear the name of the person who is to receive the payment, he is the payee. The signature of the person drawing the bill may be printed or produced in some other way if it is certain that the intention was to produce the signature of the drawer.

The definition allows a bill to be produced as payable on demand, that is the person to whom it is addressed has to pay the sum specified when the bill is presented for payment. It may also be created so that it does not become payable until a fixed time or a time which can be determined has occurred. So a bill may be created so that it is payable on, say, the 30th June or it may be made so that it becomes payable when, say, 90 days have elapsed after the date marked on the bill.

The bill has to be for a sum which is certain in money. By other provisions in the Act, however, the bill may be payable with interest or by instalments. The definition that the bill is to or to the order of a specified person requires that that person shall be named or otherwise readily identifiable. The Act does however allow a bill to be made payable to two or more payees. Where the bill is marked, as the definition indicates, to bearer then it is payable to the person who is the bearer at the time the bill becomes payable. The Act also provides that if a bill is made payable to a fictitious or non-existing person then it is to be treated as payable to bearer.

The question may be asked as to why bills of exchange are used. The advantages are the following:

1. the person who has the bill whether it was made payable to him or he has acquired it has a document which provides clear evidence of the promise of a person to pay a certain sum of money. Furthermore unlike a normal legal action the person who created a bill cannot make a counter claim in order to avoid paying.
2. a person who holds a bill which will not be payable until some future date may obtain earlier payment for a lower sum of money by selling it to a bank or a discounting house. The bank or discounting house then holds the bill until it matures and presents it for payment.
3. a person who holds a bill may pay a debt he himself owes by transferring it to his creditor. By this practice of negotiating a bill the bill may pass through several holders before it is finally presented for payment.

A bill of exchange may be marked that it is payable solely to the party named. In this circumstance the bill is not negotiable. If however it is not so marked and is negotiable then it may be negotiated according to the kind of bill it is. If it is a bearer bill then it is negotiated by delivery. That is it is simply handed over by its existing holder to its new holder as is agreed between them. In the case of a bill made payable to the order of a named person then that person must endorse the bill by writing his signature on it. In the case of a bill where there are two or more persons named then all must endorse the bill unless one person endorses the bill with the authority of the others. To be an effective negotiation the endorsement must be for the whole amount of the sum named.

A bill of exchange is discharged when the specified amount is paid either by or on behalf of the acceptor. The acceptor is the drawee who has signed the bill indicating that he accepts the liability to pay the bill. It may be discharged also when the holder of the bill gives up all his rights in the bill; by the holder intentionally cancelling the bill; by the acceptor taking the bill back in payment of a sum due to him; and if the bill becomes statute barred under the Limitation Act 1980, this is six years from a cause of action arising.

Cheques

A cheque is defined in the Bills of Exchange Act, 1882, as 'a bill of exchange drawn on a banker, payable on demand'.

As can be seen from this definition, to which must be added the definition of a bill of exchange considered earlier, a cheque is a form of a bill of exchange which is an unconditional order in writing, directing a banker to pay a specified sum of money to or to the order of a specified person or to a bearer, and the cheque is signed by the person issuing the cheque.

Cheques are now in widespread use as a means of paying accounts of any amount. There is therefore a risk that a cheque may be used as a means of dishonesty so that a person who accepts payment of an account by means of a cheque may then find that it is dishonoured. In order to prevent a cheque getting into the wrong hands and being paid to a person who is not entitled to payment the common practice is to cross cheques.

An uncrossed cheque is one which is made out to a named

person and permits him, once he has signed the back of the cheque, to demand payment in cash over the counter at the bank. It is therefore very easy for a dishonest person who obtains an uncrossed cheque made out to someone else to forge that person's signature and obtain payment. For this reason banks discourage the issuing of uncrossed cheques.

The Act allows cheques to be crossed in a number of ways. A crossing may consist only of two parallel transverse lines across the face of the cheque. The words 'and company' or 'and Co.' may be written inside the lines. The words 'not negotiable' may also be written inside the lines. This makes the cheque no longer a negotiable instrument. That is, being signed on the back of the cheque by the person it is made payable to so that it can be transferred to someone else. Cheques crossed 'not negotiable' are however transferred but when this is done the person who takes the cheque is at risk since he cannot acquire a better title of ownership than the person had who transferred it to him.

Cheques may also be crossed 'Account payee'. This has the effect of requiring the bank which collects the proceeds of the cheque to pay the sum into the account specified.

The effect of crossing cheques is to prevent payment of cash to the person who presents the cheque. It requires the bank to collect the money and deposit it in the account of the person entitled to that amount. As it is a procedure which takes several days the practice of banks is to restrict the person who presented the cheque drawing on the proceeds until the bank has in fact obtained the proceeds.

A bank which fails to observe the requirements specified in the crossed cheque, for example, paying cash over the counter, becomes liable to the true owner of the cheque provided that person has suffered a loss as a result of that action. Where a person who has issued a cheque has cause to believe that it has gone astray and may fall into wrong hands he may instruct his bank not to pay if the cheque is presented for payment. This 'stop' operates until it is withdrawn. The fact that a 'stop' notice has been given to the bank does not affect the right of the holder of the cheque who has a good title to it to require payment. In such a case either the 'stop' is withdrawn or the holder is paid direct.

In most circumstances a cheque is presented for payment reasonably promptly. As there may be occasions, for whatever reason, when this is not so the Act deals with the situation. It provides that if a cheque has not been presented within a reasonable time, and the person who drew the cheque has thereby suffered actual damage for the delay, then his liability under the cheque is reduced by that amount. What is a reasonable time is determined by the circumstances of the matter, trade practice and banking practice. It is usual to require that if a cheque is presented for payment more than six months after its date it is to be returned to the drawer for his confirmation.

A bank's authority to honour cheques of a customer is ended in a number of ways. These include, when the customer instructs the bank not to pay on any cheques; when the bank learns of his death; the bankruptcy of the customer; and the customer transferring the credit balance of his account. Where the account has insufficient funds to meet the cheque the bank has the option of honouring the cheque or not as it wishes.

12

Law of Highways

The law of highways, found both in statutes and at common law, is of particular importance to builders. They need, in carrying out building work, to excavate in roads, to have roads closed, to make new roads, to have roads adopted as maintainable by the public, and they must use the road in a lawful manner.

Statutory and Common Law Position of Highways

A highway at common law means a way which is open to members of the public for them to pass and re-pass; the right the public possess is no greater than this. Any private way is under the control of the owner or owners of the way and use of that private way by others is by permission of the owner or owners.

A highway may be created by prescription, by dedication, or by the use of some power in a statute.

Prescription arises where a way has been used by the public for twenty years or more without interruption. There is a presumption that the way is to be a highway unless there is evidence to show that there was no intention to dedicate the highway to public use. The fact that a highway can be created in this way is of importance to owners of open space which the public may use. To prevent a way on such open space becoming a highway the law requires the owner to take some action to show that he has not dedicated the land as a highway. The usual form of action is the erection of a notice stating the land is not dedicated as a highway, or the erection of an obstruction on the way for a day each year. The owner of the land may also deposit a map with the local authority showing the ways which he has dedicated as public rights of way on his land.

Dedication arises where the owner of a way dedicates that way to public use. The dedication may be by means of an agreement or be implied from the owner's actions. If an owner unintentionally acts in a manner so that it may be implied that he is dedicating a way he may protect his rights by taking action as set out above.

Most highways are, of course, constructed by local authorities or by the Secretary of State for Transport under power contained in statutes. Section 24 of the Highways Act, 1980, gives such power to construct new highways.

The question of the maintenance of a highway is of great interest. Not all highways are maintainable at public expense; those that are defined in Section 36 of the Act.

The section begins by removing the liability for maintenance of highways from the inhabitants at large of an area. This liability was a remnant of ancient law, the application of which invariably created difficulties for a person bringing an action for injury suffered because of the condition of the road. Highways maintainable at public expense under the Section are: a highway built by a highway authority after the Act came into force; a trunk road or special road; a highway being a footpath or bridleway created by order or dedication after the Act came into force; a highway built by a district council under provisions in the Housing Act, 1985; and those highways which, before the passing of the Act, were maintainable by the inhabitants at large or a highway authority. There are also certain other provisions in the Act and elsewhere to make a highway become maintainable at the public expense. To express the import of the Section we can say that it makes most highways maintainable at public expense. Furthermore, as time progresses, the provisions in the Act will make more highways maintainable at public expense.

The maintenance of such highways is carried out by the highway authority and the cost recovered from the rates. What, it may be asked, is the position if a highway authority fails to maintain properly a highway and damage arises from that failure? Who is responsible? The position now is that, by the provisions in section 58 of the Highways Act, 1980, the highway authority is liable for damage caused by non-repair of the highway. This does not however mean that in all circumstances it is liable; a highway authority may, in defence, show that it has taken reasonable care to see that the highway was not in a dangerous condition.

Lawful Use of the Highway

Unlawful interference with or use of a highway may give rise to an action at common law by a person who has suffered loss or injury which is greater than that suffered by other users of the highway. The action may be for damages or injunction or both. Where the interference is affecting the public generally then the Attorney General may bring an action for an injunction to protect the public.

The position of the public highway and unlawful use with consequent injury was considered in *Harper* v *Haden & Sons Ltd.*, 1933. The court suggested that a temporary obstruction of the highway, or to the enjoyment of premises adjoining the highway, will not give rise to a remedy at law provided the temporary obstruction is reasonable in all respects; that is, that it causes an obstruction for no longer than is absolutely necessary and is no greater than the work ought to cause. Where this is not the case action may be brought.

From the above it can be seen that in effect what the court is saying is that reasonable use of the highway with a little 'give and take' is not going to cause undue difficulty for anybody. Where small difficulties do arise these should be accepted without giving rise to a right to bring an action. On the other hand, it is clear that 'give and take' and use of the highway are not to be so construed as to mean a person must suffer some substantial hardship for a prolonged period and be without a remedy at law. The desire of the courts is to prevent legal actions being brought for trivial matters arising from the use of highways.

An example of 'reasonable' use of the highway is seen in the case of *Trevett* v *Lee*, 1955, where a half-inch hose pipe in a time of drought was laid across a road in order to supplement a water supply at the defendant's premises. The plaintiff saw the hose pipe but nevertheless tripped over it and suffered injury. The claim failed. The Court of Appeal decided that this was reasonable use of the highway and there was neither negligence nor nuisance.

In *Harper* v *Haden & Sons Ltd.*, 1933, the facts were that a wooden hoarding was erected to enclose a space intended to be used to deposit builders' rubbish from alterations at some near-by premises. The hoarding, which was next door to the shop of the plaintiff, had a platform and handrail, stood seven feet high and was nine feet in length along the pavement. The plaintiff claimed that the hoarding was an obstruction which had caused him direct injury from loss of custom to his shop and that it constituted a public nuisance. The court decided the hoarding was reasonable in extent and had not been erected for longer than was necessary to enable the alterations to be completed.

Another interesting case was that of *Almeroth* v *Chivers & Sons*, 1948. Here a pedlar had his barrow on the road and as he stepped on to the pavement to make a sale he tripped over a heap of slates which had been left at the kerb. The pedlar sued the builders who had left the slates after carrying out work at some property. The court decided that the defendants were liable for negligence and nuisance. The obstruction in the highway was not reasonably necessary for the work in hand.

Trees which overhang a highway have formed the subject matter of several cases. The principle at common law in this matter is that if an overhanging tree is diseased or decayed so that it is dangerous, and this fact is apparent on reasonable examination, the occupier of the land on which the tree stands is liable. This principle was upheld in *Caminer* v *Northern and London Investment Trust*, 1951, where the House of Lords considered the case of a tree falling on to a passing motor car and causing injury. The tree was found to be diseased but this fact could not be observed by an examination of the tree above ground. The House of Lords decided that, on the facts before them, there was no evidence to show lack of care by the occupier of the land and so he was not at fault by reason of negligence or nuisance.

The fixing of a heavy object to a building which adjoins the highway places the occupier under a duty to see that it is secure. If the object should fall the occupier is liable for any injury caused. In *Tarry* v *Ashton*, 1876, a lamp fixed to the wall of the defendant's premises fell and caused injury to a passer-by on the highway. The defendant did not know of the dangerous state of the lamp, nor could he have suspected danger since he had recently employed an independent contractor to carry out repairs to the lamp. The fact that he had engaged an independent contractor did not absolve him of blame. He, as the occupier of the premises, was liable.

It is at this point probably timely to warn again against any belief that where the occupier of premises is held liable for dangerous work, and an independent contractor has been engaged, that the independent contractor escapes liability. This is not so. It is most probable the independent contractor will be sued by the occupier of the premises for breach of contract in that he failed to carry out his contractual obligation in a proper workmanlike manner.

Closing and Obstruction of Highways

The development of sites in built-up areas is often hampered by the existence of a highway on the site. To build on the site and preserve the highway may well be uneconomical and prevent the best use of the site; the fact that a highway is present, however, does not necessarily mean that such a site has to be developed in an unsatisfactory manner, or the project abandoned.

Section 116 of the Highways Act, 1980, gives a magistrates' court power, on the application of the appropriate authority, to order the highway to be stopped up or diverted. Before the court can make the order it must be satisfied that the highway is unnecessary or that it can be diverted in a manner satisfactory to the public. On the hearing of the application any user of the highway or other interested party may make objection and no order is to be made unless the planning authority and persons having a legal interest in the land over which the diverted highway will run give their consent. The appropriate authority referred to in the Section means a highway authority which is the county council.

In some cases the property developer or builder may wish to close a highway. He too may, by following the proper procedure, secure the closing or diverting of a highway. Section 117 allows a person who wants a highway to be stopped up or diverted, but who is not authorized under Section 116 to make an application, to request the appropriate authority to make application on his behalf and at his expense.

Private Streets

What is for the builder probably the most important part of the law of highways is that concerning the construction of private streets, and their subsequent adoption by the highway authority as highways maintainable at public expense. So far as the builder is concerned his main interest is the 'Advanced Payments Code' in the Highways Act. This code requires that where a building is to be erected which is subject to approval by the local authority and will front on a private street, then no work shall be done on the erection of the building until the owner of the land or a previous owner has paid to the authority or otherwise secured to their satisfaction the payment of a sum of money as may be required in connection with the street work; there are, however, a number of circumstances where this requirement does not apply. When the work has been completed the balance of the deposit is either paid to the authority or refunded to the owner.

Another means to secure the construction of a private street and its subsequent adoption as a highway maintainable at public expense is found in Section 38 of the Act. This allows a developer to enter into an agreement with the authority whereby the developer will construct the road to the specification of the authority; the road is then dedicated to the public and becomes a highway maintained at public expense. This allows the builder to develop an estate knowing that the roads, if constructed to the specification of the authority, will be adopted as highways maintained at public expense. Furthermore, no deposit is required under a Section 38 agreement, but the authority usually require a bond for satisfactory completion by the developer.

Making up of Private Streets

What we have considered above concerns the construction of private streets where new estates are being developed, or buildings erected on a private street. But we also have to consider the problem of making up private streets on which there are existing buildings so that the streets will become highways maintained at public expense.

Although some authorities make use of powers in local Acts of Parliament enabling them to make up private streets, most authorities use the power in the 1892 Code in the Highways Act 1980. The title of this code comes from the fact that there was originally an Act of Parliament of 1892 which dealt with private street works. Those provisions are now incorporated in the Highways Act 1980. The 1892 Code enables the authority to serve notice on the owners of the land affected of the intention to make up the private street and to recover the cost from them. Under the Code this cost may be apportioned according to the benefit the particular premises will enjoy from the highway. This allows more of the cost to be charged to, say, business premises with a fleet of motor vehicles than houses standing in the same street.

The procedure for operating the 1892 Code, is that where an authority is satisfied a private street is not properly made up and ought to be so made, a resolution is passed that the surveyor shall prepare all the necessary plans and specifications. These are then approved by a resolution of the authority, the fact that it is the intention of the authority to execute these works is advertised in the local papers and notice is served on the owner of the premises. The notice on the owners must state the amount to be charged. An appeal may then be made to the local magistrates' court on a number of grounds. Once an appeal, if any, has been settled the authority executes the work and recovers the expense of the work. There is power to allow payment to be made to the authority over a period of thirty years.

Building Lines

In building work reference is often made to 'building lines' without clearly understanding just what the term means. The Highways Act, 1980 makes reference to various kinds of 'lines', which are generally referred to by builders as 'building lines'. The effect of the introduction of building lines in the control of building work is such that a clear understanding of their importance is essential.

The Act refers to a 'building line' in Section 74. Power is given to a highway authority, which it should be noted need not necessarily be the local council, to prescribe a frontage line (building line) for both or either side of a highway which is their responsibility to maintain. The effect of the creation of a building line is to prevent the erection of a new building, except a fence or boundary wall, or a permanent excavation below the level of the highway, nearer to the centre of the highway than the building line. The highway authority may, however, consent to work being carried out beyond the building line, subject to any conditions it may impose. This prohibition on work in the highway does not apply to excavations for such work as gas or water mains. A building line, when prescribed, may be registered as a charge in the local Land Charges Register and in general is binding on all future owners and occupiers of land affected by the building line. A highway authority may revoke a building line if it is satisfied the line or any part of it is no longer necessary. A person whose property is seriously affected by the making of a building line, which in practice would prevent development of his land, may recover compensation from the highway authority. A person who has contravened a building line or permitted work in contravention of a building line is liable to prosecution.

A somewhat similar provision to the above is found in Section 73. This Section gives a highway authority power to prescribe an 'improvement line'. Such a line may be made where a highway is narrow or inconvenient or where it is necessary or desirable to widen the street. The purpose of an improvement line is to preserve land for road improvements by preventing buildings being erected on land which will be needed for such improvement. A building line does something rather different; it does no more than preserve the state of an existing highway by preventing building work beyond a fixed line. Where an improvement line has been made no new building is to be erected or permanent excavation made in the highway nearer to the centre of the highway than the improvement line. The highway authority may, however, consent to work being carried out beyond the improvement line subject to conditions, if any, they may impose. The making of an improvement line, where it injuriously affects the property of a person, may mean that the highway authority has to pay compensation. An improvement line, or any part of the line, may be revoked if it is no longer necessary. The line is registrable in the local Land Charges Register and so is binding on future owners and occupiers of land affected by the line. Contravention of the provisions of the Section is an offence.

Although there are these specific legal provisions under the Highways Act 1980, in recent years they have not been used. The same degree of control has been achieved by waiting until an application was made under the Town and Country Planning Act 1971 for planning permission to develop the land. When permission has been granted it has been such that the building could not be erected nearer to the highway than would have been allowed using the powers in the Highways Act 1980. This practice also avoids the authority having to pay compensation as they would have to do under the Highways Act 1980.

New Streets

The law relating to new streets is contained in the Highways Act, 1980, and in bye-laws made under the Act. The purpose of this legislation is to enable local authorities to exercise control over such matters as the width of streets, falls, kerb heights and similar matters. Local authorities exercise control by means of approval of plans and by the giving of notices. A 'new street' is most usually created when a builder erects houses on land in such a manner that a street is formed. Other circumstances where a new street is created are: old highways which have had houses built by the side so that the highway is now a street in the generally accepted meaning of the word; the continuance of an existing street; or the use of the power in Section 188 of the Act to declare an existing highway to be a new street.

The appropriate authorities for 'new streets' are the councils of counties and, in the Greater London area, the councils of the London boroughs.

Section 186 gives the appropriate authority power to make bye-laws as to the level, width and construction and the sewerage of new streets; where the authority have defaulted in this matter the Secretary of State may make bye-laws. These include the giving of notice, deposit of plans, inspection and testing of work, and power of local authorities to take samples. These bye-laws are subject to the confirmation of the Secretary of State.

The application of the new street bye-laws may well be unreasonable in some cases. To deal with such a situation the appropriate authority may, with the consent of the Secretary of State, relax the requirements of the bye-laws or dispense with compliance with the bye-laws. Notice has to be given of this action and the Secretary of State must take into account any objection made to him.

Section 191 requires the authority to approve plans of proposed work if that work complies with the bye-laws. Where there is some defect or contravention of the bye-laws the authority shall reject the plans and give notice of this fact to the person who deposited the plans or on whose behalf the plans were deposited. Any dispute between the authority and the person depositing the plans as to whether or not they ought to be passed may be settled by a magistrates' court.

The plans of proposed works when approved by a local authority have a life of three years. That is, the proposed work, if not begun within three years of the date of deposit of the plans, may not commence if the authority give notice to the person who deposited the plans, or on whose behalf the plans were deposited, that the plans are of no effect.

If work is carried out which is not in accordance with the new street bye-laws the authority may give notice to the person executing the work, or on whose behalf the work was executed, to remove the work, or if he so wishes to make the necessary alterations to comply with the bye-laws. In addition to this the offender may be taken to court and a fine may be imposed. Where the notice is not complied with within 28 days the authority may carry out the necessary work and recover their expenses. A right of appeal exists to a magistrates' court against the notice of the authority.

Section 193 gives the council of the appropriate authority power to require that in certain cases the width of a new street shall be greater than that proposed. This power may only be exercised where a new street will, in the opinion of the council, form a main thoroughfare or continuance of a main thoroughfare, continuance of a main approach or communication between main approaches in its area. The authority, where it exercises this power, must pay compensation for any loss or injury arising from its requirement. The authority must also pay any cost over and above that which would have been payable if a street had been constructed of normal maximum width. A person aggrieved by a requirement under this Section has a right of appeal to the Crown Court.

Building Operations and Excavations

In addition to the common law mentioned earlier, which is relevant to building operations, the Highways Act of 1980 contains a number of provisions which concern building operations, excavations and highways.

A Section of particular importance to the builder is Section 59 of the Highways Act. This deals with damage caused to a public highway, maintained at public expense, by excessive weight passing along the highway or by extraordinary traffic. The highway authority are empowered to recover expenses incurred by reason of the damage caused by the excessive weight or extraordinary traffic; these expenses are recovered by the highway authority after receiving a certificate from the surveyor of the expenses which will have been or will be incurred in maintaining the highway because of the excessive weight or extraordinary traffic. The expenses may be recovered by court action. Where the person responsible for the excessive weight or extraordinary traffic admits liability before damage is caused, the highway authority may agree on a sum of money for his liability or the matter may be referred to arbitration for determination of the sum. Proceedings to recover the expenses must be commenced within twelve months of the damage being caused. But where damage is caused by work in connection with a building contract or work which extends over a long period the action must be commenced within six months of the date of completion of the contract or work. The reference in the Section to excessive weight or extraordinary traffic means that these are two separate matters. Excessive weight is likely to arise where a cargo, possibly carried by a single vehicle, is such as to cause damage to the highway. Extraordinary traffic is considered to be use of the highway which is over and above that of the ordinary use of the highway. The application of this Section to building operations may best be seen where repeated use of a particular highway by vehicles carrying materials to a job increases the use of a highway and so causes damage. Expenses which are recoverable under the Section are those expenses which are over and above the average expense for repairing comparable highways in the neighbourhood.

Section 131 makes it an offence for any person, without lawful authority, to excavate in the highway or deposit anything on the highway which can cause damage.

Section 133 states that where damage is caused to a footway of a street, which is a highway maintainable at the public expense, by work on adjoining land, the expense incurred in repairing the damage is recoverable from the person at fault or the owner of the land.

Section 143 gives a highway authority power to serve notice on a person who has erected or set up a structure on a highway. An appeal against the notice may be made to the Secretary of State. The highway authority may, if the notice is not complied with, remove the structure and recover their expenses for the work involved.

Section 153 empowers a local authority, by notice, to require that a door, gate or bar on a building which opens on to a street shall not be so made as to open outwards.

Section 165 allows a local authority to serve notice requiring remedial works on the owner or occupier of land adjoining a street that is unfenced or inadequately fenced and dangerous. An appeal may be made to the magistrates' court. The local authority may execute works and recover costs in the case of non-compliance with the notice.

Section 171 is an important section to the builder; it empowers a highway authority to give consent for building materials, rubbish or other things to be deposited in a street which is a highway repaired at public expense. In giving consent the highway authority may impose conditions. These conditions may be to prevent damage or to ensure that statutory undertakers have access to their apparatus in the highway. Temporary excavation may be authorized also. Refusal to grant consent may be the subject of an appeal to the magistrates' court. A person who places building material, rubbish or other things in the street or carries out an excavation, must see that it is properly fenced and, if so required by the highway authority, provide proper lighting. The authority can require the removal of an obstruction or the filling in of an excavation. A further requirement is that the obstruction or excavation must not remain longer than is necessary. Contravention of the Section is an offence punishable by fine.

Section 172 states that a person who is proposing to carry out work to a building in a street shall erect, to the satisfaction of the local authority, a proper close boarded hoarding that will separate the building from the street. A local authority may, however, dispense with this requirement. The erection of this hoarding may entail other works, such as a platform, handrails and lighting, if the local authority so require. Refusal of consent by the local authority gives rise to a right of appeal to a magistrates' court. Contravention of the Section is punishable by fine.

Section 173 requires that a hoarding or similar structure in or by the side of a street shall be securely fixed. It is an offence not to comply with the requirements of the Section.

The problem of builders' skips on highways has been solved by Section 139 of the Highways Act, 1980, which states that they may only be deposited on a highway with the permission of the highway authority, which may impose conditions relating to the proper control of the skip, its size, siting, lighting, guarding, removal, identification and marking. Under Section 140, a highway authority or policeman may require a builder's skip to be removed or repositioned or do so themselves, even though the skip is there by permission, since a traffic accident or some other happening may make the removal or repositioning of a legally sited skip essential. Failure to obey is an offence.

Section 139 states that, subject to certain defences, the owner of land or a building on which are being carried out building operations which risk serious bodily injury to passers by shall be guilty of an offence. Liability still exists even if a local authority has taken action to remove the danger. A builder can be liable if the danger arose because of his act or default.

A practice which was not uncommon in the past and which gave rise to problems is now the subject of control by the provisions in Section 170. The practice was that of mixing mortar or concrete on the highway. The main problem was that harmful substances were washed into drains and sewers. Section 170 makes it an offence punishable by fine to mix or deposit on a highway any mortar or cement or other substance likely to stick to the surface of the highway or likely to solidify if it enters the drains or sewers connected with the highway. Certain authorities including highway authorities, local authorities and statutory undertakers are exempt. No offence is committed if the mixing takes place in a receptacle or on a plate so that the substance does not touch the highway or enter a drain or sewer.

A problem which has troubled highway authorities for some time has been the erection of scaffolds on a highway. Some of these scaffolds have been unnecessarily obstructive or have been dangerous. In one or two cases there have been collapses of scaffolds with loss of life to persons on the highway.

Section 169 of the Act has laid down provisions designed to deal with these problems. The Section states that no person shall, in connection with any building or demolition work or the alteration, repair, maintenance or cleaning of any building, erect or retain on or over a highway any scaffolding or other structure which obstructs the highway unless that person is authorized to do so by a licence in writing issued by the highway authority. The licence may contain such terms as the issuing authority thinks fit. The authority to whom an application for a licence is made must issue a licence unless the authority considers the structure would cause unreasonable obstruction or where a structure could be erected in a different way to that proposed and which would cause less obstruction than the structure proposed. The authority may require the applicant to submit such particulars as is reasonable in order to allow the application to be considered properly. The refusal to grant a licence allows the applicant to appeal to a magistrates' court. If he is dissatisfied with the terms of the licence the authority issues he may similarly appeal. The court may order the authority to issue a licence or to alter the terms of the licence. The section places a duty on the person to whom a licence is issued to see that the structure is adequately lit at night, to erect and maintain traffic signs as required by the authority, and to do such other things as any statutory undertakers reasonably request in connection with their apparatus. Failure to observe the requirements of the section is punishable by fine.

13

The Law Concerning Buildings

Building Control

A topic of ever increasing importance is that of controlling the standard and means whereby buildings are constructed. This is not a new topic, in fact the first form of building control was established in the 19th century. This form of control was introduced to prevent the worst of bad building which was common at that time especially with houses. This was by means of building by-laws. The by-laws were made by individual local authorities and varied from one area to another. Over a period of time building by-laws became more detailed and extensive. Until building by-laws were abolished they were made by local authorities under power contained in the Public Health Act, 1936.

A criticism made of building by-laws was that they varied, sometimes substantially, from one area to another. This caused great difficulties to national housebuilders since they had to comply with different requirements in different areas, and this was not an economic way of house building. In order to overcome this difficulty the system of building by-laws was abolished by the Public Health Act, 1961, and a new form of building control introduced. The new system was that of building regulations made not by individual local authorities but by a government minister. These regulations applied nationally and so achieved a uniform standard throughout the country. Although this system was considered to be a great improvement it, in turn, was criticised. The main criticism was that the regulations were somewhat inflexible and restricted architects and builders from using new materials and new forms of technology. A further criticism was that the administration of building regulations was under the control of local authorities. A change was considered desirable.

The change has been made by the provisions in the Building Act, 1984. This Act has allowed the introduction of new building regulations and a different system of administration. It allows the Secretary of State for the Environment to make building regulations. Before making building regulations the Secretary of State has to consult with the Building Regulations Advisory Committee. This committee has its members appointed from all sections of the building industry by the Secretary of State. The benefit to the formation of building regulations of having members of different professions with their skills and experience is obvious. The Secretary of State used the powers given to him and made the building regulations in 1985. A point to note with these regulations is that they apply also to the London area. Before this London had its own system of building control by Acts of Parliament.

Both the Building Act, 1984, and the building regulations exempt certain buildings from the application of the building regulations. Buildings for educational purposes approved by the Secretary of State and most buildings belonging to statutory undertakers, such as British Gas, are, under the Building Act, 1984, exempt from building regulations. Certain specified buildings, such as small buildings and greenhouses, are also exempt.

As will be appreciated, there will always be circumstances where the application of the building regulations may not be necessary and, in fact, their application may prevent some building work being carried out. For this reason the Building Act, 1984, allows the Secretary of State to direct that a requirement in the regulations shall be dispensed with or relaxed. The building regulations allow a local authority to do this on behalf of the Secretary of State. If the application is refused by the local authority an appeal may be made to the Secretary of State.

The Building Act, 1984, also deals with the criticism of the old regulations for being too restrictive. The Secretary of State is given power to approve documents, prepared by him or some other body, which provide practical guidance for meeting the requirements of the building regulations. This he has done. Anyone who builds in accordance with such approved documents is deemed to have met the standards of the regulations. Failure to comply with such a document does not however mean that there has been a breach of the regulations. The effect of this is to mean that a person can use the approved documents, if he so wishes, as a guide to complying with the regulations. If he chooses not to do so, he can build as he wishes but in this case he has to show that what he has done meets the standards of the regulations.

The Building Act, 1984, also deals with the criticism of the administration of the regulations for being in the exclusive control of local authorities. This it has done by allowing certain other persons to be responsible for this administration. In the case of administration by a local authority the procedure may be by depositing full plans or by giving a building notice. In the case of the deposit of full plans the procedure is the traditional one of full details being given, by way of plans and other information, to the local authority for approval. The local authority are then to pass the plans unless they are defective or show a contravention of the building regulations. The time for the local authority doing this is five weeks, with an extension, which has to be agreed in writing, of up to two months. If the local authority fail to pass the plans or fail to give a decision within the stated time then the dispute may be settled by the magistrates' court. If the plans are approved, the building regulations require that notices shall be given to the local authority at various stages of construction so that inspections may be made. If a person decides not to submit full plans he may give a building notice to the local authority. This simply tells the local authority of the intention to carry out the work without going into detail about the proposed works. The local authority may however ask for additional information but there is no question of passing or rejecting plans. The local authority have to be given notices of the progress of construction so that inspections may be made. Local authorities have to be paid fees for the work they do in connection with the administration of building regulations.

As we have seen, the Building Act, 1984, allows for administration of the building regulations by persons other than local authorities. These persons are referred to as 'approved inspectors'. The procedure here is that the person proposing to have the work done and the approved inspector jointly give notice, referred to as an 'initial notice', to the local authority. This notice is accompanied by certain plans and evidence of the insurance cover the approved inspector has to have. The local authority have ten days to accept or reject the initial notice. In the event of rejection there is a right of appeal to the Secretary of State. If the notice is accepted the local authority's powers of administration are suspended. It is the responsibility of the approved inspector to see that the work is to the standard of the building regulations. On satisfactory completion he gives a final certificate to the owner and the local authority. If there is a contravention which is not remedied within three months the approved inspector must cancel the initial notice. Either another approved inspector or the local authority then take over.

Whatever procedure is used the failure to satisfy the standards of the building regulations is a matter for the local authority. The authority may serve a notice, provided it is not later than twelve months after the completion of the works, requiring the contravention to be remedied or the work pulled down or removed. In addition to this a fine may be imposed. It is also possible to obtain a court injunction for the removal or alteration of the works.

Sewers and Drains

The Public Health Act of 1936 and the Building Act, 1984, contain a number of provisions dealing with sewers and drains. The aim of these provisions, when introduced, was to clarify the law which previously had been indefinite on these matters.

A duty is placed on water authorities to provide public sewers for the proper drainage of their areas: power is given to carry out all the necessary work for the construction of public sewers. In addition to this power water authorities may declare that certain sewers in their districts shall be public sewers. They may also enter into agreements that sewers which are to be constructed shall at some future date become public sewers. This form of agreement is frequently used in the development of private housing estates, so that when the estate is completed the sewers become public sewers, the responsibility for maintenance of which falls on the water authority. The Public Health Act 1936 also contains a sensible provision that where a sewer is to be privately constructed the water authority may require that the sewer shall be so constructed as to form part of the local authority's system of sewers. Any extra cost incurred in meeting this requirement has to be borne by the water authority.

Both Acts in dealing with sewers and drains refer to three definitions and make various provisions according to these definitions. A public sewer is a sewer which is vested in a water authority and which, in general, it is liable to maintain. A certain number of public sewers are, however, maintained at the expense of the owners of the properties the sewer serves. Private sewers are sewers which are not vested in a water authority, and their maintenance is the responsibility of the owners of the properties the private sewer serves. Private sewers came into existence by reason of the power in Section 22 of the 1984 Act. This power enables a local authority, when plans of proposed buildings are being considered, to require that the buildings shall be drained in combination. This power is used when it is more advantageous or economical to drain buildings by means of a combined drainage system. Where a local authority make use of this power they must fix the proportions of expense of construction and maintenance which are to be borne by the different owners of the properties concerned. A drain is a pipe taking the drainage of a building or buildings within the same curtilege. The construction and maintenance of a drain is the responsibility of the owner or owners of the building or buildings concerned; this responsibility includes the part of the drain under the road, in fact all the drain until it connects to the public sewer.

If we consider the practical application of this law to a new housing estate development we shall see the following: the main sewer laid under the centre of the road would be constructed by the builder and an agreement made for its subsequent adoption by the water authority; the drains from the houses connected to the main sewer would be drains which, under the Act, are maintained at the expense of the individual owners of the houses; where the local authority required the combination of drainage from houses then private sewers would be created, the maintenance of which would be the responsibility of the individual owners of the houses.

The 1984 Act gives power to local authorities to require, by notice on the owner or occupier, the maintenance of drains and private sewers. Where the requirements of the local authority are not carried out the local authority themselves may carry out the work and recover their expenses.

Drainage and Sanitation

Section 21 of the 1984 Act requires a local authority to reject plans of a building deposited with the authority for approval unless the plans show that there will be proper provision for the drainage of the building. The refusal of a local authority to approve plans under this Section may be the subject of an appeal to the magistrates' court. A drain is not to be considered a satisfactory drain unless it is connected with a sewer or discharged into a cesspool or other place. A drain cannot be required by the local authority to connect with a sewer unless the sewer is at a level to allow connection, unless the sewer is within 100 feet of the site of the building, and unless any intervening land is land through which that person has a right to construct his drain. The requirement that the sewer is within 100 feet of the site of the building does not prevent a local authority requiring the connection of the drain to the sewer which is more than 100 feet from the site of the building; the local authority must, however, pay any expense which arises because the site of the building is more than 100 feet from the sewer.

Defective drainage to buildings may be remedied by a local authority, exercising its power under the 1984 Act by service of notice on the owner or occupier of the building, requiring the carrying out of specified works within a stated period. The local authority has power to carry out the work if the owner or occupier defaults and to recover the cost incurred.

A most useful power is given to specified officers of a local authority to open up a drainage system, if some fault is suspected, and to carry out an examination, including testing of the drains. The cost of this work falls on the local authority.

Sanitation of buildings is dealt with in Section 26 of the 1984 Act. This states that where plans of a building or extension of a building are submitted for approval, the plans shall be rejected unless they show sufficient and satisfactory sanitary accommodation or the local authority believe that sanitary accommodation is not necessary. Any dispute between the local authority and the person by whom or on whose behalf the plans were submitted, as to whether sanitary accommodation should be provided or as to the number of conveniences to be provided, may be determined by a magistrates' court. It should be noted that this Section refers to any building and not just to houses.

Local authorities are empowered under the 1984 Act to require the repair or renewal of sanitary conveniences which are prejudicial to health or constitute a nuisance. The power is given to local authorities to serve notice making specific requirements which must be fulfilled within a stated time. If the notice is not complied with the local authority may carry out the work and recover its expenses.

Water Supply

A feature concerning houses and the supply of water for domestic purposes is the requirement, in Section 25 of the 1984 Act, that where plans of a house are submitted to a local authority for their approval, they shall reject the plans unless a proposal is put before them for providing a supply of wholesome water sufficient for the domestic purposes of the occupants of the house. The supply has to be connected to the house by means of a piped supply from the supply of the local authority or other statutory water undertaking; if this is not possible at reasonable expense then a piped supply connected to some other supply must be provided; if these measures are not practicable at reasonable expense a supply must be provided within a reasonable distance of the house. Any dispute between the local authority and a person submitting plans concerning this matter may be settled by a magistrates' court.

Dangerous Premises

There are important provisions in the Building Act 1984 concerning dangerous premises. Section 77 gives power to a local authority to act where it appears to them that a building or structure or any part is dangerous or is being used for carrying such loads that danger exists. The danger need not be to the occupants of the building alone, danger to persons in a street is also included.

The action the local authority may take is to bring the matter before a magistrates' court. The court may, in the case of dangerous premises, require the owner of the building to execute works specified in the court order within a stated time. The owner may, if he so wishes, elect to demolish the building, structure or part, instead of carrying out the specified works. Any rubbish resulting from such demolition must be removed. In the case of a building which is dangerous because of overloading, the court order may require that the use of the building be restricted until any necessary works have been completed. Where there is failure to carry out the works or the demolition and removal of rubbish specified in the order within the specified time, the local authority may carry out the work and recover the cost incurred.

Where a local authority use the power described above the whole process inevitably takes some time; the matter has to be considered by the local authority and then application has to be made for the necessary court order; after the court has considered the matter an order is made requiring the execution of works within a specified time. It can readily be seen that all these procedural measures may cause a considerable delay in dealing with a known danger.

Section 78 provides emergency powers to deal with dangerous buildings, structures or parts. These emergency powers may, if the danger is imminent, be exercised by the surveyor of the local authority instead of the local authority. The Section gives power to a local authority to take immediate action where it is, in their opinion, necessary to deal with the danger. Where it is possible, before such action is taken notice is to be given by the local authority to the owner and occupier of the building or structure. The expense incurred by the local authority may be recovered from the owner. These expenses cannot be recovered if action could have been taken under Section 77; nor may expenses be recovered for fencing off or having the building watched if the danger has been removed. An unusual feature of this Section is that in any proceedings to recover expenses, the court may inquire if some other person ought to bear the expense either wholly or in part. If the court is satisfied that some person other than the defendant ought to pay the expenses or some part they may make an order to this effect.

Housing Act 1985

This Act is the latest in a long line of Acts which have set out to deal with bad housing by way of repair, demolition and improvement. These provisions are detailed but the main provisions are set out below.

Standard of Fitness

Section 604 of the Housing Act, 1985, provides the guidance needed by local authorities to decide whether a house is unfit for human habitation. A number of matters are mentioned to which attention shall be paid, these are: repair, stability, dampness, internal arrangement, natural lighting, ventilation, water supply, drainage and sanitary conveniences, the means available for preparing and cooking food, and the means for disposal of waste water. Where one or more of these matters makes the house not reasonably suitable for occupation, that house is to be considered unfit for human habitation.

This standard is considered by many to be a low standard; most people would accept that the provision of hot water and a bath are essential in any house. The standard in Section 604 ignores these and because of the concern at the inadequacy of this standard the Secretary of State for the Environment is considering the making of a new standard of fitness.

Individual Unfit Houses

The individual unfit house frequently gives rise to action by a local authority. Section 189 gives power to a local authority, when satisfied a house though unfit for human habitation is capable of repair at reasonable expense, to serve a notice on the person having control of the house to execute stated works within a reasonable time, which must be not less than twenty-one days. A right of appeal exists to the county court for a person aggrieved by the service of a notice. Where no appeal is made or the appeal dismissed, and the time allowed for the work has expired, the local authority may carry out the work required in the notice. The cost of this work is recovered by the local authority from the person in default.

A house which is unfit for human habitation and cannot be repaired at reasonable expense may be dealt with by a local authority. The procedure is that the local authority serves a notice on the person having control of the house informing him that the future of the house is to be considered at a meeting to be held at a time and place stated in the notice. At the meeting the person on whom the notice was served may make an offer to carry out works to the house. The local authority may accept this offer or agree to the house being used for some purpose other than human habitation. Where no offer is made, or if made the offer is not accepted, the authority may make a closing order or demolition order; a right of appeal to the county court exists against such action. A closing order is usually made where the demolition of a house would affect other properties. A demolition order requires the demolition of the house within a stated period; failure to carry out this demolition within the stated time gives the local authority the right to enter, carry out the demolition, and recover expense.

Clearance Areas

Where an area contains a number of unfit houses the problem is different from those discussed above. A local authority has, under Section 289, power to deal with groups of unfit houses. Before this power may be used the authority must be satisfied that the houses are unfit for human habitation or are, because of their bad arrangement or the narrowness or bad arrangement of the streets, dangerous or injurious to the health of the inhabitants of the area. The procedure is that the local authority, on being satisfied as to the above matters, pass a resolution that they intend to deal with the area by using the power in this Section. Notice of this resolution must be given forthwith to the Secretary of State and advertized in the local newspapers. The Act requires that after passing the resolution the local authority shall not act on it until they are satisfied they can rehouse any displaced occupants of the houses.

After an area has been declared to be a clearance area the local authority have to clear the houses by means of a compulsory purchase order. Once the compulsory purchase order is confirmed the houses and the land pass to the local authority who then carry out the demolition of the houses. The owners of the houses are paid as compensation the site value of the land only. To enable a local authority to carry out redevelopment of a clearance area they are given power to purchase other land so that they have an area of land of suitable size and shape.

A right of appeal against the proposals of a local authority exists to the Secretary of State who may hold a public local enquiry into the proposals. The public local enquiry is conducted on behalf of the Secretary of State by one of his inspectors, who is usually a qualified architect or surveyor. Evidence is given at the enquiry by the local authority to support their proposals, and rebutting evidence is given on behalf of the persons who are making the appeal. The Secretary of State after considering the evidence gives his decision in the matter. This decision may be questioned only on a point of law to the High Court within six weeks.

Housing Improvement Grants

Since the end of the war the urgent need for houses and the desire to remove unfit houses has meant that great attention has been paid to the whole question of housing. The preservation of existing houses and their improvement, where they are lacking in facilities normally accepted as essential for a house, has been recognized as a necessity. Improvement of houses, therefore, provided certain matters are satisfied, is now encouraged by the government by means of a system of grants. The improvement of houses falls into three classes:

1. *Intermediate Grant* This requires the provision of standard amenities. These are the provision of a fixed bath or shower, a sink, a wash-hand basin, a water-closet, and a hot and cold water supply to the sink, wash-hand basin, fixed bath or shower and thermal insulation to the roof space conforming to the Building Regulations.
2. *Improvement Grant* This requires the provision of the standard amenities and certain other facilities so that a higher standard of housing is secured.
3. *Special Grant* This is to improve houses in multiple occupation by means of an intermediate grant.

Intermediate Grant

As has been indicated, this is paid to secure the improvement of a house by the provision of the standard amenities. Local authorities are under a duty to pay this grant provided certain conditions are satisfied. These conditions are that the house must have been built before 2 October 1961, and on completion of the work it must be fit for human habitation and be available for use as a dwelling for at least fifteen years. The grant paid is usually half the cost of the work up to £2,275, made up as follows: a fixed bath or shower £340, a hot and cold water supply at a fixed bath or shower £430, a wash-hand basin £130, a hot and cold water supply at a wash-hand basin £230, a sink £340, a hot and cold water supply at a sink £290, and a water-closet £515. No grant is paid for thermal insulation under this scheme but a grant may be payable under the Homes Insulation Act 1978. In certain circumstances a grant may be made in addition to that for the provision of the standard amenities. This grant is for necessary repairs and has a limit of £3,000. If a house has some but not all of the standard amenities, a grant may be claimed for the provision of those needed to satisfy the standard. The person entitled to claim the grant is the freeholder or leaseholder provided he has an unexpired term of not less than five years at the date of application. In general the grant is paid by the council after the work has been completed, although there is power to pay the grant subject to completion within a prescribed time. When the improvements have been made the landlord of a tenanted house may claim a rent increase of 12½ per cent per annum of his share of the improvement work or the rent may be fixed by the rent officer depending on the tenancy held.

Improvement Grant

This form of grant is paid at the discretion of the local authority. It is paid for the improvement to the stated standard of a house built before 1945, provided the house will have after the work has been completed a life of at least thirty years. In exceptional circumstances the local authority may pay a grant when the house will have an expected life as short as ten years. The usual requirement as to who can make application for a grant apply. The grant is to be not more than one-half of the approved sum subject to a maximum payment of £6,600 for a single dwelling. In the case of the conversion of a house or building of three or more storeys the maximum is £7,700. It is possible, however, with the Secretary of State's approval to pay a higher grant. It should be noted that this form of grant is paid at the discretion of the particular authority; some authorities refuse to operate this type of grant, but this is contrary to government policy. The power to increase the rent previously mentioned also applies to this form of grant.

Special Grant

This is a type of grant introduced for the improvement of houses in multiple occupation by the provision of standard amenities. The grant is made at the discretion of the local authority and is subject to their satisfaction of the proper completion of the works.

General Improvement Areas

The success of the scheme for the improvement of individual houses has led Parliament to consider the introduction of some scheme whereby houses could be improved in groups. The improvement of the houses in this manner is more economical and means that all the houses in that area are of a proper standard. With the improvement of individual houses, on the other hand, there is a mixed area of houses, some being of a proper standard, others not being of an adequate standard; the expected life of houses in such an area is not the same and so difficulties are created.

To meet this need, Parliament gave local authorities power to deal with the improvement of houses in predominantly residential areas. This they can do by declaring areas to be general improvement areas and securing the improvement of the houses in those areas. Since it is now recognized that the improvement of houses in themselves is often insufficient to improve the environment of the area, there is now power for local authorities to carry out improvements in the area other than improvements to the houses. For example there is power, subject to approval by the Secretary of State, to convert a highway into a footpath, in this way creating a traffic-free area. There is also power to acquire land for use as recreational areas, play areas or parking areas. Local authorities who carry out these environmental improvements in general improvement areas may claim a grant from the Secretary of State of up to £400 for each house in the area.

A general improvement area is created when a local authority have a report submitted to them that a predominantly residential area in the district is one where the living conditions in the area ought to be improved by the improvement of the amenities of the area or of the dwellings or both, and being satisfied that an improvement can be effected, the local authority define the area on a map and pass a resolution declaring it to be a general improvement area. The fact that this has been done must be published in local newspapers and brought to the attention of the persons living in the area. The local authority are also under a duty to bring to the attention of the persons living in the area the action they propose to secure the improvement of the area and the assistance available for improvement of the amenities of the area or of the dwellings.

The aim of a local authority in a general improvement area is to improve houses to the highest standard. It is believed that by adequate publicity owners will be willing to improve their property, but where an owner is reluctant to improve his property there is power given to the local authority to acquire the property compulsorily to secure its improvement. Any such compulsory purchase is subject to the confirmation of the Secretary of State.

By the use of these powers it should be possible to change an area of well-built houses lacking in amenities in an area devoid of environmental amenities such as open spaces and recreational areas into an area where every house has full amenities and the surrounding environment possesses recreational and traffic-free areas.

Housing Action Areas

A further development was the introduction of housing action areas. Any such area is where the local authority is satisfied on a report submitted to them that the physical state of the housing accommodation in the area as a whole and the social conditions are such that the area ought to be dealt with as a housing action area within five years.

Any such area may be found in the run-down parts of towns and cities throughout the country. What is required for this declaration of a housing action area is that the living conditions must be unsatisfactory, the social conditions of those living in the area must be bad and there must be an obvious need to have proper and effective management of the area. In total there is an apparent need for remedial action to be taken within the period of five years because of the extremely bad housing conditions.

The procedure to be followed by a local authority in making an area a housing action area is that they must pass a resolution to this effect and publish that fact in local newspapers. Details must also be sent to the Secretary of State for the Department of the

Environment for his consideration and he has power to overrule the local authority's proposal. As the effects of the housing action area will be felt most by those living in the area the local authority have to pay special attention to explaining its effects on the residents of the area.

The housing action area is dealt with by way of improvement of the houses and of the area generally. As the houses in such area are usually of a low standard and in a bad state of repair with consequent greater expense in their repair and improvement, and as an indication of the government's and the local authority's wish to secure better housing conditions in such areas, the improvement grant paid is increased from its usual 50 per cent to as much as 90 per cent.

The Legal Position of Statutory Authorities Supplying Services to Buildings

The essential services for buildings such as gas, electricity, water and drainage are, in general, provided by local authorities or other authorities created by statute for the purpose of supplying services. The legal position is that the authorities derive their power to act from the statutes creating them. Any action outside the power granted to them by the statutes will be *ultra vires*. The relationship between the servicing authority and the user of the service may be contractual. Any contract is, however, subject to the terms imposed by the servicing authority. To enable the servicing authorities to function properly they are usually given power to enter and lay services in private land and to carry out maintenance at any future date. Where this power is used land must, so far as is possible, be returned to its original state and in certain cases compensation may be paid. Since each service has individual features it will probably be best if we consider each separately.

Gas

The Gas Act, 1972, which is the chief statute dealing with the supply of gas, created area boards whose responsibility is to see that there is a supply of gas in their areas. The supply of gas to any premises in the board's area can be demanded by the owner or occupier of the premises, provided the premises are within twenty-five yards of a main belonging to the board. A service pipe connecting the premises to the main is laid and maintained at the expense of the owner or occupier of the premises for that part of the service pipe that is on his property or is more than thirty feet from the main. The supply of gas is obtained by giving notice to the area board stating the date by which the supply is to begin, which must be a reasonable time, and agreeing to pay the charges for the supply of gas – a deposit may also be required for the board's expense of the cost of laying the service pipe. If an area board fails to provide a gas supply where there is entitlement to such a supply a fine may be imposed. A defence is that the failure was by reason of circumstances beyond the board's control.

Electricity

The Electricity Act, 1947, which governs the supply of electricity to premises, set up an organization whereby a central body is responsible for the generation of electricity sold to area boards who are empowered to supply electricity within their areas. An owner or occupier of premises in a board's area may give notice to the area board that a supply is needed to these premises, and the board is required to lay an electric line from the distributing main of the board to the premises which are the subject of the notice. The cost of the electric line on the property of the owner or in the possession of the occupier, or of the electric line which is more than sixty feet from the distributing main, may be charged to the owner or occupier. The notice served on the area board must specify the premises to be supplied, and the date the supply is to begin, which must be a reasonable period – if required by the board a deposit must be made for the payment of the cost incurred in laying the electric line. The board may also require that there shall be a contract to take and pay for a minimum supply for two years at the normal charge such that the board will get 20 per cent each year of its own outlay on the electric line. A fine may be imposed subject however to a number of defences if the board fails to supply electricity.

Water

There are a number of statutes dealing with water supply, some of which are private statutes applicable only in certain areas. The chief statute is, however, the Water Act, 1945. In general it may be said that there is a duty to supply wholesome water sufficient for domestic purposes of owners or occupiers of premises within the area of the supply authority. A sufficient supply of water for domestic purposes can be demanded by the owner or occupier of premises and a fine may be imposed by a court for failure to provide the supply. The supply may be made subject to conditions regarding the taking of the supply for at least three years and to payment in order to recover the supplier's expense in laying a water main. The charge for the supply of water to a house is different from the charge made for the supply of gas or electricity: the amount of water consumed is not measured, instead a charge is made based on the rateable value of the house.

Drainage

The duty of water authorities to provide public sewers is set out in Section 14 of the Water Act 1973. This requires every authority to provide sufficient public sewers for the proper drainage of its area. There is no duty on the authority to see that every house is provided with an accessible public sewer: it would, for example, be unreasonable to provide a public sewer to an isolated cottage. Section 23 of the Public Health Act 1936 requires every water authority to maintain, cleanse and empty all public sewers vested in it. Section 34 of the Public Health Act 1936 gives an owner or occupier of premises the right to have his drains or sewer connected to a public sewer on giving the proper notice to the authority. This right does not mean that where there are separate public sewers for foul water and for surface water connection can be made in any way other than that authorized by the water authority. The authority may reserve the right to itself to make the actual connection to the public sewer and recover the cost from the person seeking the connection.

14

Building Contracts

A building contract is a contract made between a person known as the employer, who wishes to have building work carried out, and a person known as the contractor, who agrees to carry out the building work. This definition covers such works as the construction of porches and minor alterations to the erection of large buildings. Most building contracts for minor matters are formed verbally; others are made in writing – usually by a letter to the builder asking for an estimate for some stated work. The builder's estimate constitutes the offer and the contract is formed when a letter of acceptance is sent. Finally, some contracts are made by the use of a special form of contract designed for use in building work. The use of this special form of contract is usually reserved for the more expensive work where it is felt that either of the other two methods would be inappropriate. It is with this last method of contracting we are more concerned; but the fact should not be forgotten that building contracts may arise from the two other methods.

The formation of a building contract is governed by the normal principles of contract law: offer, acceptance, consideration, mistake and misrepresentation. Offer, which it will be recalled must be distinguished from an invitation to treat, arises when the builder offers to carry out work – the word 'estimate' is more frequently used but this does not affect the legal consequences. A common practice is to invite tenders to carry out work. The tenders submitted in reply to this request constitute offers, but the employer is not bound to accept the lowest or any tender. The position is that the employer is trying to find out at what cost he can have the work carried out; the advertisement inviting tenders usually states that the employer does not bind himself to accept the lowest or any tender but there is no legal necessity for this. Acceptance, to be valid, must be acceptance of the offer made. Acceptance subject to conditions is a rejection of the original offer and constitutes a counter-offer. Consideration, it will be remembered, is essential to any simple contract – without consideration such a contract is not enforceable in the courts. Mistake and misrepresentation if found in a building contract will operate in the normal way to make the contract void or voidable.

The contract when formed will usually contain express terms which are inserted with the intention of defining each party's rights and duties. There are, however, a number of matters which the courts will imply as being terms of the contract. Terms are only implied as being part of a contract where the court is satisfied that this is necessary to enable the contract to operate and a term will not be implied by the courts if its effect would be to conflict with an express term of the contract. So far as these matters concern building contracts the courts will imply that the workmanship shall be of a proper standard and that any materials used shall be of a reasonable standard. There is also an implied term that where a house is built without plans and specification, that the house when finished will be fit for human habitation. The application of implied terms was demonstrated in the case of *Hancock & Others v B. W. Brazier (Anerley) Ltd.*, 1966, where a builder constructed a house, the hardcore filling of which contained certain salts which had a damaging effect at a later date. The court decided that the house had not been constructed with suitable materials and that this was a breach of an implied term of the contract.

It should not be forgotten that a builder may well be held liable in tort for damage resulting from his negligent work. This liability in tort is additional to the builder's liability under the contract, and in fact may apply where there is no contractual relationship.

Architects and Surveyors

In the more costly building work it is the usual practice to engage an architect and a quantity surveyor. The position of these persons in the building contract must be clearly understood.

The architect has a contract with the employer for the performance of his professional services which is separate from the building contract itself. The contract of employment of the architect usually contains terms which define the duties of the architect; it may well be that the contract provides for the provision of plans and no further service. The general practice however is to engage an architect to prepare plans and to supervise the work, so protecting the employer's interests. When the building work has begun the architect is an agent for the person for whom the building work is being carried out. His authority may be clearly expressed in the contract document but the appointment of an architect without express terms of authority will create a position where the architect has implied or ostensible authority to bind his employer. Where an architect acts outside his implied or ostensible authority his action does not bind his employer and he is placed in a position where he can be sued for breach of warranty of authority. An example of implied or ostensible authority is seen in the case of *Carlton Contractors* v *Bexley Corporation*, 1962, where, before a contract was signed, the borough surveyor of a local authority drew the contractor's attention to the absence of certain matters from the contract documents. There was verbal agreement to vary the contract, and this the contractor confirmed by letter, but the contract when it was signed did not contain the agreed alterations. The court decided that the borough surveyor had implied or ostensible authority to negotiate the terms of the contract and so the contract had to be rectified to take account of the alterations.

The quantity surveyor may be appointed by the architect as part of the architect's services where the building work is to be tendered for on a bill of quantities. The rule in law appears to be that such appointment is within the architect's authority and so binding on the employer. The employment of a quantity surveyor, when the building work has begun, for the purpose of measurement of variations is usually a term of the contract; in this case the employment of a quantity surveyor without that express authority appears to be outside any implied or ostensible authority the architect possesses; any such engagement would therefore not be binding on the employer.

Standard Form of Contract

From what we have considered we can see that a building contract may be formed by verbal agreement or by a series of letters, and that the terms of a contract formed in this manner may be so indefinite as to cause difficulty. Building contracts are frequently concerned with work which extends over a long period of time and may also be of a complex nature. In these circumstances it is essential to set out all the details of the work in a proper form of contract and to state each party's rights and obligations; failure to do this may cause difficulties and possibly lead to litigation. For these reasons the practice has arisen of building contracts being made on a standard form of document. The advantages to the use of a standard form of contract are many: the building contractor is familiar with the use of the document; he is aware of his rights and obligations under the contract; and the document has been drafted for the specific use of builders with the aim of keeping disputes to a minimum and providing a means of settling disputes without the use of the courts. Many building contractors are now unwilling to accept work which is of any value unless the standard form of contract is used. From the employer's point of view the use of a standard form of contract may be advantageous, certainly the employer may benefit by any saving in expense in settling a dispute by arbitration.

The standard form of contract used in the construction industry was first produced by the Joint Contracts Tribunal which was set up in 1931. The edition used in recent years has been that produced in 1963 with later revisions, eventually being revised on a yearly basis. A number of criticisms were made of various clauses in this edition of the contract and the need for a substantial review became apparent. This review took place over a number of years and eventually resulted in the production of the 1980 edition.

In earlier years the standard form of building contract was known as the Royal Institute of British Architects form. In recent years however it has more accurately been known as the Joint Contracts Tribunal (JCT) form.

There has always been a need for a standard form of contract to suit a particular purpose. For example, not all building work is done on a bill of quantities, so there is need for a form of contract which does not make reference to a bill of quantities. The Local

Authorities Edition was drafted to take account of local government law and practice.

This practice of having slightly different types of the standard form of contract has continued with the issue of the JCT 1980 Edition. There are now 1980 Editions of Local Authorities Without Quantities, With Quantities, and With Approximate Quantities; the Private With Quantities, the Private With Approximate Quantities and the Private Without Quantities. There is also a Sectional Completion Supplement 1980 Edition for use where a building is to be completed in phased sections.

It must also be noted that on occasions a party to a contract using the standard form of contract may amend the wording of a clause or clauses of the contract.

The JCT 1980 Edition is a complex form and detailed consideration of the document and the relevant law is beyond the scope of this book.

What can be done, however, is to comment on the provisions in the 1980 Edition Private With Quantities. The possession of a copy of this document will therefore be of some assistance to the reader.

The 1980 Edition JCT Private With Quantities

The first point to note with this edition is the use of a decimal system of numbering to the various parts of the document.

The document starts with the articles of agreement. This sets out the agreement made between the employer and the contractor. The works the employer wishes the contractor to carry out are described briefly and reference is made to drawings and bills of quantities, which are described as 'the Contract Bills' and 'the Contract Drawings'. The amount the employer will pay to the contractor for the completion of the works is stated and described as 'the contract sum'. The architect and the quantity surveyor are described and provision is made for the appointment of a replacement by the employer in certain circumstances.

Article 5 of the articles of agreement sets out the procedure to be followed in the event of a dispute arising under the contract. This is to be by arbitration. The arbitrator is to be appointed by agreement of the parties to the contract and if no such agreement can be made within 14 days of the written request either party has given to the other to appoint an arbitrator the President or Vice-President of the Royal Institute of British Architects shall make the appointment. If, however, the dispute raises issues which are similar to or are connected with a dispute under the standard sub-contract forms, and that dispute has already been referred to an arbitrator, then that arbitrator may, with the agreement of the employer and contractor, deal also with that dispute. Although this measure is designed to save time and expense it is not compulsory. Either the employer or contractor may require that a separate arbitrator be appointed to resolve the dispute under the main contract.

The reference of a dispute to arbitration whilst the work is still in progress could be a substantial impediment to the completion of the contract. Article 5 therefore states that, with certain exceptions, there shall not be a reference to arbitration which is enquired into until there has been practical completion of the works or practical completion has been claimed. Matters which can be the subject of arbitration without having to wait for practical completion include such matters as: whether an architect's instruction is a valid instruction under the conditions, and whether a certificate has been improperly withheld. Subject to these exceptions, where there is justifiable reason for immediate arbitration, there cannot be arbitration until there has been practical completion of the works or that is claimed.

Article 5 also sets out certain power the arbitrator is to possess in order to allow him to carry out his arbitration properly. The award of the arbitrator is to be final and binding on the parties.

Article 5 concludes by stating that the law to be used in dealing with any dispute under the contract shall be English law. Without this provision there could be great difficulty in deciding what was the appropriate law to use. For example, the contract may relate to a building project in France for a Dutch employer. If the parties so agree the law of some other country may be substituted for English law.

The articles of agreement conclude by the signatures and seals, where appropriate, of the parties being attached to the document. If the contract is to be a simple contract only it is signed by the parties and their signatures witnessed. If, however, the contract is to be by deed – a specialty contract which it will be recalled is a contract made in a special way by being signed, sealed and delivered by the parties to the contract and thus has a higher status than a simple contract –. then the parties will sign, seal and deliver the document. Where a company is executing a contract under seal then the company's seal is used.

Although there is no requirement in law that a building contract shall be a specialty contract, in practice this is usually the case. The advantage to the employer is that under the Limitation Act 1980 he has the right to bring an action for breach of contract up to twelve years after the breach occurred. This is an important matter to an employer since building works are often complex and take some time to complete: defects therefore may not become apparent for some time. A further feature with a specialty contract is that statements in the contract are conclusive evidence against the parties, where a contract is a simple contract only the period within which an action may be brought is six years only and the statements in the contract are presumptive evidence only.

The Conditions

1. *Interpretations, definitions etc.*
This clause requires that the article of agreement, the conditions and the appendix are to be read as a whole document. This provision prevents any dispute arising as to whether for example, the articles override the conditions. It also means that certain modifications or qualifications are to apply.

The clause also defines what certain words or terms are to mean in the document. This it does by either defining the word or term or by stating the condition, article or appendix where the definition may be found. By this provision the exact meaning of a word or term is fixed; both parties know this and therefore no dispute should arise on the meaning of a particular word or term.

2. *Contractor's obligations*
This clause requires the contractor to complete the works in accordance with the contract documents, using materials and workmanship of the quality and standard specified in those documents. Where the quality of materials or standard of workmanship is something on which the opinion of the architect is relevant then those matters must be to the architect's reasonable satisfaction.

The contract bills of quantities are to be prepared in accordance with the 7th edition of the Standard Method of Measurement of Building Works. If in preparing the bills of quantities there is a failure to follow the Standard Method or there is some other error then that fact is not to end the contract but is to be remedied by the architect issuing a variation order.

The clause also states that if the contractor discovers any discrepancy or divergence between the contract drawings, the bills of quantities, architects instructions and drawings or documents supplied by the architect, then the contractor is to notify the architect in writing informing him of the divergence or discrepancy. The architect is then to give the contractor instructions on the matter.

3. *Contract sum – additions or deductions – adjustment – Interim Certificates*

This clause requires that where any adjustment has been made under the conditions to the contract sum that adjustment is to be taken into account when the next interim certificate is issued.

4. *Architects' instructions*

The contractor is required to comply with the instructions issued by the architect provided the architect is acting within his powers under the conditions. A contractor however need not comply with an architect's instruction requiring a variation under 13.1.2, that is varying the access to to site or the use of a particular part of the site, limitation as the the hours of work or working space or the carrying out of the work in a particular order. In any one of these cases the contractor must make reasonable objection in writing to the architect.

The purpose of this last provision is to allow a contractor who has tendered to the contract on this basis, say, of being allowed certain access to the site, finding that the architect's variation is going to change that access substantially to the contractor's disadvantage, to make reasonable objection to the variation and to decline to comply with it.

Where the contractor does not comply within seven days with the written notice from the architect requiring compliance with his instruction, the employer may employ some other person to carry out the work. Payment for this person's work may be recovered from the contractor or be deducted from money due to him under the contract. The contractor has the right to request the architect to state in writing which condition in the contract gives the architect power to issue that instruction and the architect must comply with this request. The matter may be referred to arbitration and is one of the matters which may be dealt with even though work is still in progress.

Instructions from the architect are to be in writing. Where an architect gives a verbal instruction the contractor can confirm the instruction in writing within seven days of the verbal instruction, and if the architect does not, within seven days, dissent in writing the confirmation takes effect seven days after the contractor's notice. Where the architect gives his instruction verbally and then within seven days confirms that instruction in writing, the contractor need take no action. Where a contractor acts on an architect's verbal instruction without confirmation, the architect may give his confirmation in writing at a later date.

5. *Contract Documents – other documents – issue to certificates*
The contract bills of quantities and drawings are to be kept by the architect or quantity surveyor but are to be available at all reasonable times for inspection by both the contractor and the employer.

The clause requires the architect to provide the contractor with copies of the contract documents, drawings and bills of quantities, and during the course of the work the architect is to provide such further drawings and details as may be necessary to complete the works.

On the part of the contractor, he is to provide the architect with copies of his master programme for carrying out the contract works and such revisions as become necessary from time to time as a result, for example, of the architect granting an extension of time.

The contract drawings, documents and bills of quantities are to be returned to the architect if he so requests when the final payment has been made. The contractor is required not to make use of the contract documents, drawings or bills of quantities or to divulge their contents except in connection with the contract.

At this point it is probably convenient to make mention of the law of copyright which concerns, among other things, the use of plans of a building. The law concerning copyright is found in the Copyright Act, 1956 which restricts the reproduction of certain works. The works we are concerned with are original artistic works such as works of architecture and original literary works, which include plans of a building. The Act grants to the holder of the copyright, who is usually the author of the original work, a right to restrict publication, subject to certain exceptions, without his consent. This restriction is effective for the life-time of the author and fifty years thereafter.

A copyright is a legal right which may be assigned in whole or in part to another. Licences may also be granted for the use of the copyright by persons other than the owner of the copyright.

Infringements of copyright give the owner of the copyright the right to protect his copyright by legal action. An action is often brought for an injunction to restrain further infringement and for damages for the infringements.

The question of ownership of copyright sometimes creates a problem. Who owns the copyright of plans for a building when there is a contract of employment? Who owns the copyright of the plans of a building when an architect has been commissioned by a client? Where there is a contract of employment the copyright is held by the employer. So the copyright of plans prepared by an architect who is employed by a company belongs to the company. In the case of an architect engaged by a client to prepare plans the position is that the copyright of the plans is retained by the architect unless the contract between himself and the 'client' stipulates otherwise.

6. *Statutory obligations, notices, fees and charges*
The provisions in this clause make the contractor responsible for giving all notices required by law in connection with the works, for example, the giving of notice to the local authority that certain works which require inspection have been completed. Where a contractor must make a variation in the work in order to comply with some legal requirement he must, before making the variation, give written notice of the fact to the architect. The architect is then to give instructions, within seven days of the contractor's notice, with regard to the matter. In an emergency the contractor may undertake work at once but he must immediately inform the architect of the emergency and what he has done. The fees and charges are to be extra to the contract sum unless they were included in the contract sum.

7. *Levels and setting out of the works*
This clause requires the architect to determine levels required in the work and to supply drawings to the contractor so that he may set out the work at ground level. The contractor is liable for any errors arising from his own inaccurate setting out, unless the architect otherwise instructs.

8. *Materials, goods and workmanship to conform to description, testing and inspection*
The purpose of this clause is to require materials, goods and workmanship to be so far as procurable in accordance with the specification. The architect is given power to require the contractor to furnish vouchers showing that the materials and goods are of the proper standard. The architect may also require the contractor to open up work to test materials or goods in order to determine that they are to the specification. The cost of testing or of opening up work is an extra to the contract sum unless the test or inspection reveals materials or goods not to be of the standard specified. Any goods, materials or work may be required by the architect to be removed from the site if they are not in accordance with the contract. The architect may also require the removal of any person employed on the works, but this power is not to be used unreasonably or vexatiously.

9. *Royalties and patent rights*
The use of patented articles, processes or inventions requires the payment of royalties. This clause requires the contractor to indemnify the employer from claims made for any infringement of patent rights; the contractor must also pay the royalties as part of the contract sum. If, however, the architect gives instructions requiring the use of patent articles, processes or inventions, then the contractor is not liable for any infringement and any royalties are added to the contract sum.

The payment of royalties and the use of patents require mention of the law concerning patents. A patent is a grant made to a person who invents an article or process. The grant which is by means of a document known as 'letters-patent' is made under the Patents Act, 1949–77, but the power was formerly a prerogative of the Crown. The effect of the grant is to give the holder of the patent a monopoly of manufacture of the article for a limited period of time. The Act limits the monopoly to twenty years with a provision for extending this time where it appears the holder of the patent will be inadequately rewarded for his invention. A practical example of a patent in the building industry would be where a builder invented a new method of scaffolding. He could obtain a grant of a patent by following the necessary administrative procedure and thereby acquire a monopoly of that invention for the next twenty years.

The holder of a patent may take action against any person who infringes the patent. The action would be for an injunction to restrain further breaches of patent and may seek damages; innocent infringement of a patent does not lead to an award of damages.

An invention may be of such a nature that the inventor does not wish to produce the article himself. He can obtain the benefit of the patent in this circumstance by authorising someone, by his licence, to make use of the invention. The person to whom the licence is granted pays a sum known as royalty to the holder of the patent.

The holder of the patent is the person in whose name the grant has been made. As we have already seen problems can arise when an employee perfects a new invention. The general rule is that where the employee has made use of his employment to perfect an invention the patent belongs to the employer.

10. *Person-in-charge*

This clause requires the contractor constantly to keep on the works a person-in-charge. The architect may give instructions to him or the clerk of works may give him directions. In either of these circumstances it is deemed to have been issued to the contractor.

By this provision the person appointed by the contractor to be in charge of the works is in the position to receive instructions and directions as if he were the contractor.

11. *Access for Architect to the Works*

The purpose of this clause is to provide the architect and his representatives with access at all reasonable times to the works and to any place of the contractor where work is being prepared for the contract. Furthermore, the contractor is required in any sub-contract he has to secure as far as possible similar rights in the workshops and other places of the sub-contractor.

12. *Clerk of Works*

Any building work on a large scale has a clerk of works who may be resident or visit the work at frequent intervals. This clause empowers the employer to appoint a clerk of works who acts on behalf of the employer under the directions of the architect. The clerk of works is to be given by the contractor all reasonable facilities for the performance of his duties. The clerk of works is usually in day-to-day supervisory control on behalf of the employer and therefore is in a position to deal with any difficulty which may arise in the course of the work. As however he is not the architect he cannot give instructions as the contract permits the architect to do. The clerk of works may however give directions to the contractor but these are of no effect unless they are within the powers of the architect to issue instructions and are confirmed by the architect in writing within two days of being given. If this procedure is followed the directions are deemed to be architect's instructions.

A recent development regarding the position of a clerk of works is to be seen in the case of *Kensington and Chelsea and Westminster Area Health Authority* v *Adams, Holden and Partners and Others*, 1984. In this case an extension was being built to a hospital. The clerk of works on the site was an employee of the Health Authority. Part of the work involved the erection of pre-cast concrete mullions. After the work was completed and the building put in use cracks were noticed in the mullions. Investigation showed that the mullions had had to be cut whilst on the site in order for them to fit to the structure. This was unknown to the architects and the clerk of works. The cost of the remedial work came to some £250,000. The Health Authority sued the architects and others for negligence. The architects were held liable and ordered to pay £200,000. The judge decided that the clerk of works had been negligent in failing to detect that the mullions were being cut and trimmed to make them fit and to report this to the architects for them to take action. He was held to be 20 per cent negligent. As he was an employee of the Health Authority this meant that they were liable for his negligence. So they were liable themselves for the remaining £50,000.

13. *Variations and provisional sums*

In the course of a building project, which need not be necessarily complex, there is likely to be the need to make an alteration to the contracted work. There may be a need for more work of a particular kind, such as more extensive foundations, or there may be a reduction in the need for some work. There is therefore a need to make provision for any such circumstance and this is what this clause does.

Variation has an extensive meaning under the section but it includes alteration to the work, materials or goods shown in the contract drawings and mentioned in the bills of quantities. Variations may occur as a result of the architect issuing instructions or by the architect sanctioning something done by the contractor. The clause states that no variation shall invalidate the contract.

The clause authorises the architect to give instructions for the expenditure of provisional sums under the contract and any subcontract. The term provisional sum is not defined but it may be taken to mean a sum of money allocated for some work which cannot be properly detailed at the time the contract was made.

The payment of the cost of the work done in a variation is governed by rules in the clause. In general, it may be said that if the work is similar to that that is already rated and priced in the bills of quantities, then those rates and prices apply. If those rates or prices are not applicable then day work rates are to be used. The contractor has the right to be present when the variation is being measured.

14. *Contract Sum*

The quality and quantity of work that is covered by the contract sum is to be taken as that which is set out in the contract bills of quantities. The contract sum is not to be adjusted except in the manner authorised by the conditions. The clause requires any error or omission in compiling the contract sum to be accepted by the parties unless it is something which can be corrected as a variation required by the architect.

15. *Value added tax – supplemental provisions*

This clause deals with VAT matters and states that the contract sum is not to include VAT, and that VAT may be recovered by the contractor from the employer. It also makes provision for payment by the employer to the contractor of any loss he suffers as a result of goods or services becoming exempt of VAT after the date of the tender.

16. *Materials and goods unfixed or off-site*
The system under the contract whereby a builder is paid in instalments for work done or goods delivered on the site or on adjoining land may cause some difficulty as to the ownership of goods and materials on or near to the site awaiting fixing. This clause removes any doubt by stating that goods or materials which have been paid for in an interim certificate are the property of the employer. Materials and goods on or adjacent to the site, not included in an interim certificate, which are to be used in the works are not to be removed except with the written consent of the architect which must not be unreasonably withheld.

17. *Practical Completion and Defects Liability*
This clause imposes a duty on the contractor to remedy defects which appear within a stated time. The architect is required, when he is satisfied that the works are practically completed, to issue a certificate to this effect naming the date of completion. The purpose of this is to name a day from which the contractor's duty to remedy defects shall run.

The period during which the contractor is under this duty is known as the Defects Liability Period; it is fixed according to the nature and size of the works – if no time is stated the period is to be six months and is set out in the Appendix at the end of the document. The architect can require the contractor to remedy defects and other faults at any time in the defects liability period. Frost damage occurring after the practical completion of the works is excluded, unless the architect certifies that the damage is due to injury occurring before the practical completion of the works. The clause gives the architect the right to deliver a schedule of defects to the contractor not later than fourteen days after the end of the defects liability period. These defects are to be remedied within a reasonable time by the contractor at his own expense, unless the architect directs otherwise. When the defects have, in the opinion of the architect, been made good he is required to issue a certificate naming the date of the completion of making good defects.

18. *Partial possession by Employer*

An employer sometimes wishes to take possession of parts of a building as soon as those parts become available for occupation; this enables him to have some use from the building at the earliest possible time. An example of this practice is often seen in office and shop developments in the centre of towns; the ground floors are occupied at the earliest possible moment even though work is still proceeding on the floors above so that rents are collected from the shops even before the building is completed. This clause sets out to deal with partial completion.

Briefly it may be said that where an employer takes possession of a part of a building before practical completion of works the employer must pay the contractor the amount, which is estimated by the architect, due to him for that part of the building. So far as the part of the building occupied by the employer is concerned the date for practical completion and for the defects liability period to begin shall be the date on which the employer occupied that part. The architect may require defects to be remedied to that part of the building and shall issue a certificate when this has been done. The duty of the contractor to insure the building is amended by a reduction in the amount of insurance to the value of the part of the building occupied by the employer. There is a similar adjustment to be made to the liquidated damages provision for partial possession by the employer.

19. *Assignment and Sub-Contract*

This clause prohibits both the employer and contractor, except with the written consent of the other, from assigning the contract. This is a matter of some importance to the employer since it is likely that he has selected the contractor to carry out the work, possibly on the ground of the contractor's experience in similar work or of his reputation for prompt completion or good workmanship. He would therefore be reluctant to see the contract transferred to another contractor whose experience or standing is not as good.

The clause also restricts sub-letting by the contractor but in this case the architect may give written consent and this must not be unreasonably withheld. This sub-letting is different from the use of a nominated sub-contractor, and a sub-contractor under this clause is referred to as a domestic sub-contractor. To enable the employer to have some control over the sub-contractors who carry out work under this clause there is provision for the employer to put in the bills of quantities a list of not less than three persons from whom the contractor is to make his selection for sub-letting part of the contract works. There are provisions in the clause for dealing with the situation when the list of names falls below three.

20. *Injury to persons and property and Employer's liability*
The contractor is required under this clause to indemnify the employer against any claim for death or injury to any person, and, with a certain exception, indemnify the employer against claims for any injury to any property which arise from the carrying out of the works.

21. *Insurance against injury to persons and property*
Although the provisions in the previous clause required the contractor to indemnify the employer against those stated risks that indemnity would be of little value if the contractor got into financial trouble. The indemnity would probably be worthless. There is therefore a need to have the necessary financial cover backing up the contractor's indemnity. The provisions in this clause requiring insurance provide that financial backing.

Without affecting his liability to indemnify the employer under the last clause, the contractor is required to take out insurances against injury to persons or property arising out of the work. The contractor must also cause any sub-contractor to maintain similar insurances covering his liabilities. The contractor and sub-contractor are required to produce the policies of insurance and receipts for the premiums when so requested by the architect. If the contractor or sub-contractor fails to effect the insurance required by the clause, the employer may himself take out the insurance and deduct the premiums from any money due to the contractor.

The liability of the contractor so far as persons is concerned is limited to death or injury arising out of, or in the course of, or caused by the carrying out of the works. Liability for damage to property is limited to that arising out of or in the course of or by reason of the carrying out of the works and caused by the negligence, omission or default of the contractor, his servants or agents.

The clause also deals with the possible liability of the employer for claims which may arise for damage to property, other than the works, caused by such things as vibration, collapse or removal of support where the contractor is not to blame. A provisional sum may be included in the contract bills of quantities for insurance against these risks in the joint names of the employer and the contractor. If any such insurance is taken out it is to be placed with insurers approved by the architect and the policies and receipts are to be deposited with him.

22. *Insurance of the Works against Clause 22 Perils*
It is standard practice for the owner of a building to insure it against certain risks, the main one being loss or damage by fire; without insurance of this nature the owner of a building has to stand the loss himself. The same need for insurance cover exists with regard to a building which is being erected or to an existing building where alterations are being carried out. Clause 22 deals with this matter of insurance cover. Two matters need particular attention in the clause. The first is that the risks to be insured are referred to as clause 22 perils and these are defined in clause 1. Not all these perils may be insured against in certain circumstances; in which case amendment to the clause is necessary. The second matter to note is the arrangement in the clause whereby there is a choice of either the contractor or employer insuring when a new building is being erected.

Clause 22A applies when a new building is to be erected and the contractor is to take out the insurance. The insurance is in the joint names of the contractor and employer. The architect is to have possession of the policy and the receipts of the premiums paid, and he is to approve the insurers. If the contractor defaults the employer may take out insurance at the contractor's expense. Where an event occurs which necessitates repair or replacement, the insurance money is to be paid to the contractor in the form of instalments on interim certificates of the architect.

Clause 22B differs from A in that the insurance for the erection of a new building is to be taken out by the employer. If the employer defaults the contractor may take out the insurance and add the premium to the contract sum.

Clause 22C is used where the work involved is alteration or extension to an existing building. The employer is to effect the necessary insurance. There is a right under this provision, where loss or damage occurs, for either party to end the employment of the contractor. This right may only be exercised if it is just and equitable to act in this manner. The matter may go to arbitration to determine whether it is just and equitable to end the employment of the contractor. Where his employment is not ended the contractor is to make good the damage.

23. *Date of Possession, completion and postponement*
This clause requires the contractor to work regularly and diligently from the date of possession of the site to the completion date. Both the date of possession and the completion date are set out in the appendix to the document. The architect is empowered by the clause to issue instructions postponing any of the contract work.

24. *Damages for non-completion*
This clause causes contractors concern when a delay occurs in the work for which extension of time cannot be granted. The delay may mean that the work will not be completed by the agreed completion date and the contractor will have to pay liquidated damages. Liquidated damages is a sum of money agreed by the parties to the contract at its formation as being the loss likely to be suffered by one of the parties in the event of a breach of contract by the other party. The agreement of liquidated damages avoids the need to sue for damages at common law in the courts in the event of a breach of contract. Building contracts of other than a minor nature invariably have a liquidated damages provision.

The clause requires that where the work has not been completed by the contractor by the completion date the architect is to issue a certificate stating that fact. That certificate empowers the employer before the date of the Final Certificate to deduct liquidated damages, at the rate set out in the appendix, for the period from the date when the building should have been completed to when the architect issues the certificate of practical completion. If the architect should later grant an extension, then any liquidated damages deducted by the employer from money due to the contractor shall be returned to him as is appropriate.

Difficulty has arisen in the past because of the amounts claimed as damages under contracts. The court will not enforce a condition for the payment of damages under a contract when the court is satisfied that the amount claimed is by its nature a penalty and not damages which properly result from the failure to complete by the agreed date. The reason for this is that a penalty is a form of punishment and the courts are not willing to help a person enforce a private punishment. Courts look to the intent of the matter and ignore the words used; so it is no use trying to conceal a penalty by referring to it as liquidated damages.

Certain rules have been evolved for determining whether a stated sum is a penalty or liquidated damages. These were given by Lord Dunedin in *Dunlop Pneumatic Tyre Co. Ltd.* v *New Garage and Motor Co. Ltd.*, 1915, as follows:

1. The sum is a penalty if it is extravagant and unconscionable in amount compared with the loss arising from the breach of contract.
2. Where the obligation of the contract is to pay a certain sum of money, the payment of a larger sum of money in the event of breach of contract is a penalty.
3. Subject to the two previous rules, if there is only one event upon which the sum is to be paid that sum is liquidated damage.
4. If a single lump sum is payable on the occurrence of one or more events, some of which may be trifling and other serious, there is a presumption that that sum is a penalty.

The fixing of liquidated damages in a building contract is in some cases a simple matter. For example, failure to complete the erection of a house by the agreed date will mean the employer will lose the rent of the house from the agreed date of completion until the house is actually completed; so the loss of the expected rent may be the agreed sum of liquidated damages. The circumstances where the loss of non-completion are not as easily calculated present some difficulty. The rule is that if the sum is a genuine pre-estimate of the expected damage the court will uphold the sum as liquidated damages. *Dunlop Pneumatic Tyre Co. Ltd.* illustrates this point. The facts of the case were that the Dunlop Co. sold tyres to the defendants under an agreement that the defendants would not sell the tyres below the list price, and that if they did sell tyres below the list price they would pay Dunlops £5 for every tyre sold below list price. Tyres were sold contrary to the agreement and in the subsequent action the defendants claimed that the sum of £5 was a penalty. The court said that the sum of £5 was a genuine pre-estimate of the loss likely to be suffered by Dunlops and so was liquidated damages.

The difficulty of knowing at the beginning of a contract the loss likely to be suffered because of delay leads some employers to consider not have a liquidated damages clause in the contract. In such a circumstance, the employer would sue in court for damages at large. In the case of *Temloc Ltd.* v *Errill Properties Ltd.*, 1987, the court had to deal with a dispute which arose from the employer writing the word 'nil' in the liquidated damages clause. The court decided that this was an agreement not to claim any damages for delay in completion. There was no right to claim unliquidated damages. By this action the employer had effectively denied himself any right to damages for delayed completion. From this case it would appear that to retain the right to sue for unliquidated damages the liquidated damages clause in a contract would have to be excluded in its entirety.

25. *Extension of time*
A delay in the building work may arise from a number of causes which may prevent completion by the agreed date. Some events are beyond the control of the builder and it is considered that not to take those events into account would be unfair. Without an extension of time, a delay on the part of the contractor puts him at risk to pay liquidated damages under the contract. The clause requires the contractor when it becomes apparent to him that the progress of the works will be delayed to inform the architect in writing of that fact. On receiving the written notice from the contractor the architect, if he is satisfied that the cause of the delay comes within one of a number of grounds listed, is to grant an extension of time. The architect fixes a new completion date which is fair and reasonable in the circumstances. The architect also has power to fix a new completion date after the date of practical completion of the building. The list of grounds for extension is wide but one common ground is that the delay has been caused by exceptionally adverse weather conditions.

26. *Loss and expense caused by matters materially affecting regular progress of the Works*
In the course of building work there may be circumstances arise which cause the contractor delay and which in turn cause him loss or expense. If the reason for this delay is the contractor's own fault then he cannot look to anyone to make up his loss. If, however,

the event affecting his regular progress with the work is not his fault it may be that there are provisions in the contract permitting him to make a direct claim for that event. There are however some circumstances where the contractor cannot under the contract receive a direct payment because his regular progress of work has been affected. The provisions in this clause deal with this situation.

The procedure is that the contractor makes a written application to the architect as soon as he has incurred or is likely to incur direct loss or expense for which he cannot receive a direct payment by some other provision in the contract. The architect then deals with the application, and in order to do this he may require the contractor to submit details. Once satisfied that the application is justified and there has been an event which has materially affected the regular progress of the work the architect assesses the amount of the direct loss or expense and this amount is added to the contract sum. The matters on which the contractor may base a claim are listed in the clause.

A nominated sub-contractor may also make use of these provisions by submitting his written application to the contractor who in turn submits it to the architect. The grounds for application are set out in the sub-contract but are the same as in this clause.

27. *Determination by Employer*

This clause gives the employer the right to determine the contract on the happening of any of a number of specified events. These events are: the contractor without reasonable cause suspending the work; failing to proceed regularly and diligently with the work; refuses or neglects to comply with the architect's written notice to remedy defective work; or assigns or sub-lets the work without permission. The procedure is that the architect on becoming aware of the existence of one of these events sends a notice to the contractor telling him of his default. If the contractor's default continues after fourteen days from the architect's notice or it is repeated the employer may within ten days by notice determine the employment of the contractor. In the event of the contractor becoming bankrupt or going into liquidation or certain other specified events occurring, the employment of the contractor is ended forthwith. The clause sets out certain rights of the employer when the employment of the contractor has been ended under this clause. Briefly these are that the employer may do those things necessary to enable the work to proceed. The contractor is to pay or allow to the employer the amount of loss or damage the employer has suffered as a result of the determination of the contract.

28. *Determination by Contractor*
This clause gives the contractor the right to determine the contract in the event of any of a number of specified events occurring. One important event is the failure of the employer to pay the contractor on a certificate within a specified time. The procedure is that the contractor may give notice to the employer or the architect determining the contract. On giving that notice the contractor must remove his plant, tools, goods and materials and he must be paid for the work completed at the date of determination. The contractor may also claim payment on certain other grounds.

29. *Works by Employer or persons employed or engaged by Employer*
In some circumstances an employer may want to carry out some works himself or use some person to do that for him. The provisions in this clause allow this. Provided there is sufficient information in the bills of quantities as to the work the employer wishes to do himself, so that the contractor can carry out his own work, the contractor is to allow the employer to carry out the work. Where there is no such information in the bills of quantities then the employer must obtain the contractor's consent, which consent is not to be unreasonably withheld. A person employed or engaged by the employer under this clause is a person for whom the employer is responsible.

30. *Certificates and Payments*
The system under the contract for payment to the contractor is that he is paid by instalments. This is subject to the right of the employer to retain for certain works a stated percentage in a retention fund which is held by the employer until all the work has been satisfactorily completed. The employer is entitled in certain circumstances to make deductions from this retention fund which otherwise would have been paid to the contractor.

The clause requires the architect to issue interim certificates of the amount due to the contractor and these certificates entitle the contractor to payment within fourteen days of their issue. The employer is entitled to make deductions from the money due to a contractor under an interim certificate if some provision in the contract allows the employer to deduct money from that due to a contractor. The quantity surveyor makes the valuations for the interim certificates. The certificates are issued at intervals stated in the appendix which is usually one month. These interim certificates are issued at the stated intervals throughout the course of the work up to the certificate of practical completion being issued. After that, interim certificates are issued as and when further amounts are found to be due to the contractor, and after the end of the defects liability period or the issuing of the certificate of completion of making good defects.

The way in which the amount due under an interim certificate is to be calculated is laid down in the clause. Certain items are listed as being ones which are subject to the retention rules and others which are not so subject, and on which therefore there is to be full payment by the employer to the contractor of the value of the certificate. In general the amounts to be included in an interim certificate cover work done by the contractor or a nominated sub-contractor, and goods or materials delivered to the site or to adjoining land and, subject to the discretion of the architect, goods or materials which are neither on the site or an adjoining land. This last matter is designed to allow the architects to sanction payment for goods which are still on the manufacturers' premises. Before these goods can be included in an interim certificate a number of conditions have to be satisfied, included in which are that the materials are intended for use in the contract works and that they are ready for incorporation into the contract works.

The rules in the clause with regard to retention empower the employer to deduct and reatain a percentage of the value of the interim certificate for certain works. The amount of the retention percentage is fixed in the appendix. This is 5% unless a smaller amount is agreed. Where the contract sum is at the tender stage £500,000 or more the retention percentage recommended should be not more than 3%. The rules empower the employer to deduct the full percentage, 5%, on the amounts on which such deductions can be made, up to the work reaching practical completion, then when the work has reached practical completion the employer may deduct at half that rate, that is 2½%, and when the certificate of completion of making good defects has been issued no retention may be deducted. What this means is that when an interim certificate is issued after the practical completion of the works one half of the money retained by the employer will be released to the contractor, subject to any right the employer has to make a deduction from money due to the contractor. On the payment of the interim certificate after the end of the defects liability period or after the issue of the certificate of completion of making good defects, which ever is the later, the rest of the retention fund is paid to the contractor.

As can be readily appreciated the retention fund on a large building project can amount to several thousand pounds. This is money the employer is holding but which in fact is the contractor's subject to certain rights. The clause therefore puts the employer in the position of a trustee for the retention fund but the employer does not have to invest the money in the way a trustee usually has to do. A contractor or sub-contractor can require the employer to put the retention money he holds into a separate bank account. The interest earned by that money belongs to the employer.

In order to allow the correct contract sum to be calculated the contractor is required either before or within a reasonable time after practical completion of the works to send to the architect or quantity surveyor all the documents needed to make the final adjustment to the contract sum. The contract sum is then adjusted in accordance with the rules in the clause. A copy of the computation of the contract sum is to be given to the contractor. At least twenty-eight days before the final certificate is issued the architect is to issue an interim certificate which deals with the sub-contract sums for nominated sub-contractors.

The clause requires the architect to issue the final certificate before three months have expired from the end of the defects liability period, or from the completion of making good defects or from the receipt by the architect or quantity surveyor of the documents necessary for a final adjustment to the contract sum. The final certificate states the amount already paid under interim certificates, what the adjusted contract sum is, and then it strikes a balance which may mean money being paid by the contractor to the employer or by the employer to the contractor.

The effect of the final certificate, subject to certain exceptions, is that it is conclusive evidence in any proceedings that the work has been carried out and completed in accordance with the contract and that all the necessary adjustments under the contract have been made to the contract sum. The exceptions to the conclusiveness of the final certificate include, where there has been fraud, or with regard to the contract sum where there has been an accidental inclusion or omission. An important exception is where either of the parties to the contract have started proceedings before the final certificate has been issued. In this case once the proceedings have been concluded the final certificate is conclusive subject to any judgment or award or any settlement of the proceedings. If proceedings have been started but neither party takes any further step in the proceedings for a period of twelve months then the final certificate is conclusive subject to any terms which may be agreed between the parties. Where proceedings have been started within fourteen days of the final certificate being issued, the final certificate is conclusive evidence to those matters which are not the subject of the proceedings. The clause ends by stating that other than what has been considered with regard to the final certificate no architect's certificate shall be conclusive evidence that the work materials or goods are in the accordance with the contract. This means that interim certificates are not conclusive evidence that some work has been done in accordance with the contract. If, for example, payment is made on an interim certificate for some work which is later found to be defective, the fact that an interim certificate had been issued authorising payment for that work is not conclusive evidence that the work had been done properly.

31. *Finance (No.2) Act 1973 – Statutory tax deduction scheme*
In order to prevent the avoidance of the obligation to pay income tax, which a number of sub-contractors in the construction industry were doing, the above Act was introduced. The Act requires an employer to deduct income tax at the appropriate rate from a sub-contractor unless the sub-contractor has a tax certificate issued by the Inland Revenue which exempts him from this tax deduction. This clause contains a number of rules which are designed to ensure that the legal provisions on this matter are observed.

32. *Outbreak of hostilities*
This clause deals with the situation where there is an outbreak of hostilities during the currency of the contract. Provided certain matters, which are defined in the contract, are satisfied both parties have the right, by giving written notice, to end the employment

of the contractor. The contractor is to be paid the value of the completed work.

33. *War damage*

The possibility of the works or unfixed goods or materials receiving war damage is something for which there must be some provision. This clause makes provision for the architect to issue instructions to the contractor requiring the removal of damaged work and the carrying out of protective work. This contractor is to make good war damage and proceed with the work; he is to be given an extension of time and the making good of war damage is to be treated as a variation required by the architect.

34. *Antiquities*

During the carrying out of work or excavation on sites, antiquities and other objects of value have on occasion been found. The ownership of such objects has in the past caused the courts some problems. Was the finder the owner or did the owner of the land have a stronger claim to the ownership of the objects?

This clause gives ownership of all objects found to the employer. The contractor is required to deliver the objects to the architect or clerk of works. Where the finding of an object has caused loss or expense to the contractor that amount is to be added to the contract sum. The architect may also grant an extension of time.

Nominated Sub-Contractors and Nominated Suppliers

There has been a practice in the construction industry for many years whereby an employer selects a person to do some work or to supply some goods for a building project he is to have carried out. Often the person who is to carry out the main work, the main contractor, is unable to undertake work of that particular description because of its specialized nature. In that case the appointment of another person with that specialized skill and experience is essential. In some cases however the main contractor may have the necessary skill and resources to carry out the work. An employer, or more likely his architect, selects a person to undertake special work because of that person's skill, experience and reputation. In most cases this person is selected and negotiations entered into before the main contractor is appointed. Where special goods are needed it may be necessary to instruct such a person to start work early so that the goods will be ready for installation in the building when the appropriate stage of construction is reached. Much the same applies to a supplier of materials, particularly at a time of shortage. For example, when steel has been in short supply it has been necessary to place the order for the steel in the early stages of the design of the building well before a main contractor was appointed.

This practice has led to a procedure for an appointment of sub-contractors and suppliers being incorporated in standard forms of contract. The JCT 1980 Edition contains such a procedure.

35. *Nominated Sub-Contractors*

The clause defines who is to be treated as a nominated sub-contractor. The most important one of the list is the person selected by the employer under the contract bills of quantities. A main contractor who in the ordinary course of his business carries out work of the nature which is included in the bills of quantities as likely to be done by a nominated sub-contractor is allowed to submit a tender for that work. If the tender is accepted he is not allowed to sub-let the work.

The Joint Contracts Tribunal has produced a number of standard forms relating to nominated sub-contractors. The reader is recommended to have these forms. These are: nominated sub-contract tender and agreement – tender NSC/1; employer/nominated sub-contractor agreement – agreement NSC/2; nomination of a sub-contractor where NSC/1 has been used – nomination NSC/3; form of sub-contract where contractor has tendered on NSC/1 and executed agreement NSC/2 and been nominated under NSC/3 – NSC/4. Where the tender has not been submitted on NSC/1 then the agreement between the employer and nominated sub-contractor is to be on form NSC/2a, with the sub-contract being on form NSC/4a.

A main contractor is given the right to prevent the nomination of a sub-contractor if he has reasonable objection to that person's nomination. Where NSC/1 and NSC/2 are used the contractor's reasonable objection is to be made at the earliest practicable moment but any case before he sends the NSC/1 to the architect.

In general only those persons who have tendered on NSC/1 and entered into an agreement under NSC/2 are to be nominated under the contract. Before the architect nominates the sub-contractor he has to send the various forms to the main contractor for him to settle any remaining detail with the sub-contractor. If these details cannot be settled then the architect is to be informed and he must issue instructions on the matter. On the settlement of the details the architect is to nominate the sub-contractor on NSC/3.

Where the above procedure has not been used in that no tender was submitted on NSC/1, then the employer makes an agreement with the sub-contractor on NSC/2a. Following which the architect instructs the main contractor to enter into a sub-contract with the person nominated on NSC/4a.

The procedure secures payment to a nominated sub-contractor by the architect including in each interim certificate any amount due and directing the main contractor to pay that amount to the sub-contractor of what he has done. Further interim certificates are to be subject to the architect being satisfied that the main contractor has paid the sub-contractor on the previous interim certificate. The contractor is to provide the architect with reasonable proof that payment has been made. Failure to do so, other than because of some fault of the nominated sub-contractor, means that the architect issues a certificate stating the amount which the main contractor is unable to prove he has paid to the nominated sub-contractor. The employer then pays that amount to the nominated sub-contractor direct and future payments to the main contractor are reduced by this amount.

The matter of delay under a nominated sub-contract is dealt with in NSC/4 and NSC/4a. The main contractor is not to grant any extension of time unless the architect gives his written consent to that action. The main contractor and the nominated sub-contractor are to send a written request to the architect for this consent.

If there has been a failure by the nominated sub-contractor to complete the sub-contract work within the agreed time, or such extended time as the architect has granted, then the architect is to certify that fact in writing to the main contractor and the sub-contractor. The issue of this certificate enables the main contractor to deduct liquidated damages under the sub-contract from the sub-contractor. When the architect is satisfied that there has been practical completion of the work by the nominated sub-contractor he is to issue a certificate to this effect.

When the certificate of practical completion has been issued by the architect the nominated sub-contractor is entitled to his final payment. This is done by means of an interim certificate to the main contractor; this is subject to the architect and main contractor being satisfied that any defects the nominated sub-contractor is liable to remedy under the sub-contract have in fact been remedied. Where a nominated sub-contractor who has received final payment from the main contractor fails to remedy defective work under the sub-contract which appears before the architect issues the final certificate under clause 30 the architect is to issue an instruction nominating a substitute sub-contractor who shall carry out the remedial work. The employer then recovers this expense from the defaulting nominated sub-contractor and if he is unable to recover the whole of this amount then the balance is to be paid by the main contractor. A final payment by the main contractor to the nominated sub-contractor does not remove liability from the main contractor for those works for which he remains responsible until the date of practical completion of the works or until the employer takes possession and the insurance under the contract must be maintained.

In dealing with a nominated sub-contractor an employer may get him to design the sub-contract works or select the materials or goods, and in turn the nominated sub-contractor may seek to limit his liability under the sub-contract. In these circumstances the main contractor is not liable for matters concerning design or the selection of materials and goods and where liability has been so limited the main contractor's liability is not to exceed that limited liability.

Where a proposed nomination does not proceed, the architect is either to select another person to be nominated as a sub-contractor or to issue a variation instruction omitting that work from the contract. Where a nominated sub-contractor has made default in one of a number of matters, and the architect is of that opinion, or the nominated sub-contractor becomes bankrupt or anyone of a number of other events occurs the architect is to take the following action. In the case of a defaulting sub-contractor, require the contractor to give the sub-contractor notice of his default and require him to remedy it. Failure to remedy the default entitles the main contractor to determine the sub-contract and the architect will make a further nomination of a sub-contractor. In the case of a sub-contractor's bankruptcy or one of the other stated events occurring, then the architect is to make a further nomination of a sub-contractor. The rights possessed by a main contractor under the sub-contract to determine the employment of the sub-contractor are not to be used without an instruction from the architect.

36. *Nominated Suppliers*

As we have seen it is common practice for an employer to select those persons he wishes to carry out work of a specialised nature to the building he intends to have erected. These are nominated sub-contractors. It is also the practice of an employer to select the person he wishes to supply him with materials or goods. These are nominated suppliers.

In the clause the term nominated supplier is defined. In general, it means the person named in the bills of quantities as the supplier of materials or goods where a prime cost sum or provisional sum is to be expended or where the architect names that person in an instruction issued by him.

Since the main contractor is required by the employer to enter into a contract with a person selected by the employer alone there is a need to give some protection to the main contractor. The clause therefore requires that the architect will only nominate a supplier who will enter into a contract with the main contractor on terms which do not reduce his liability unduly. If the contract between the nominated supplier and the main contractor does contain restriction, limits or excludes the liability of the nominated supplier and the architect has specifically approved in writing such restrictions, limits or exclusions then the liability of the main contractor to the employer is similarly restricted, limited or excluded.

37. *Fluctuations*

This clause states that one of clauses 38, 39 or 40 is to apply to the contract. Whatever clause is selected is to be mentioned in the appendix to the contract. Each of these clauses contains detailed provisions designed to deal with changes in the price of materials or goods or in the rates paid for labour. The purpose is to ensure that the main contractor is properly reimbursed for any change in these prices or rates which have occurred since the contract was made.

15

Building Sub-Contracts

As we have seen, it is the usual practice in building projects, particularly those of a substantial size, to make use of sub-contractors and suppliers. By this means those special skills and experience possessed by such as a heating and ventilating engineering contractor may be used. The main contractor almost invariably not possessing those skills and experience and so being unable to undertake that kind of work.

The system of using sub-contractors, particularly with large scale work where the JCT form of contract is used, gives the employer the opportunity of selecting the sub-contractor he wishes to undertake that work. That person selected by the employer is known as a nominated sub-contractor. There is, however, the system where a contractor who has undertaken the performance of the whole of a building project may sub-contract parts of the work out to other contractors. In this case the employer is not concerned with the selection of the sub-contractors.

With the nominated system of sub-contracting there is a standard form of sub-contract in use which comes within the JCT 1980 edition system. Where the system does not make use of nominations by the employer or his architect the relationship between the main contractor and a sub-contractor is based either on the ordinary rules of contract law or on a special sub-contract form. The law with regard to the rules of contract law will be considered first.

Although a contract may be made by a main contractor with a sub-contractor using the ordinary rules of contract law, this would only be done for work of an ordinary nature having a short period for completion. The reasons for this are that ordinary contract law does not make provision for payments at intervals during the work, this is something the parties have to agree to specifically; it does not make provision for liquidation damages, which again must be expressly agreed between the parties; nor does it make provision for any dispute to be settled by arbitration, the courts are the normal bodies to settle contract disputes.

Where, however, a sub-contract is made using ordinary contract law then all the contract provisions considered previously must apply. That is there must be offer and acceptance, an absence of illegality to the contract, the necessary capacity of the contracting parties, genuine consent of the parties, consideration or be made by deed.

A not uncommon practice however is for a sub-contract to be made on a form drawn up specifically for that purpose either by the main contractor or by the sub-contractor. Whichever party draws up the contract document it is inevitable that he has done so in such a way as to protect his own interests. If the main contractor draws up the contract document he will seek to put the sub-contractor under, at least, the same obligations as he the main contractor is under to the employer. If the sub-contractor draws up the contract document he will seek to minimise his obligations by means of exclusion and limitation clauses. It is up to each of the contracting parties to ensure that he understands fully all the terms of the sub-contract before he enters into the contract. The importance of this may be seen from the case of *A Davies & Co. (Shopfitters) Ltd.* v *William Old Ltd.* 1969. Here Davies had been sub-contractors for the shop fittings of a new store. The value of the sub-contract was £18,296 and all the work had been completed properly. The employer who had been having the new store built became insolvent and the main contractors, Olds, were still owed some £5,000. Olds had paid Davies all of the £18,296 except £457 which they kept back when they realised that they were not going to be paid all that was owed to them. Olds had done the work under the standard form of contract then in use, the RIBA form 1963 edition, with Davies being nominated by the architect as sub-contractors. Olds had sent to Davies a sub-contract form which had the main clauses on the front of the form. One of the clauses on the front stated that the whole was subject to the terms and conditions 'overleaf'. On the back in small type was a condition that Olds would not be liable to the sub-contractors until they themselves had been paid by the employer. On the basis of this Olds withheld the £457. In the court action by Davies to recover the £457 the judge held that Olds were entitled to withhold the money and that they were not at fault in not having done more to bring the clause to the attention of Davies. Davies had ignored, or failed to read, the clause at their own risk.

This matter of a main contractor being able to withhold money due to a sub-contractor has given rise to considerable litigation in recent years. The principal reason for the main contractor with-holding payment has been a dispute as to the satisfactory com-pletion of the sub-contract work. Sub-contractors have objected strongly to being denied payment when some independent person, usually the architect, has indicated by means of a certificate that he was satisfied that the work had been done properly and by the certificate payment has been made to the main contractor for payment by him to the sub-contractor. A further reason has been that the main contractor was owed money by the sub-contractor and he had set-off this debt against the payment due.

The litigation started with the case in the Court of Appeal of *Dawnays Ltd.* v *F G Minter Ltd.* 1971. Here Dawnays were nomi-nated sub-contractors under the standard sub-contract form then in use for the steelwork to an office block to be built by Minters as main contractors. There was a delay in the start of the steelwork and some of the work was said by the main contractor not to be right. Some alterations were made as a result of which further delay occurred to other work. Minters said that this delay had caused them loss and that they had a claim against Dawnays.

The main contractors put in a claim to the employer for work done in the normal way and this included the sum of £27,870 which was due to the sub-contractors Dawnays for the steelwork. The architect issued an interim certificate for the £27,870 which was payable to the sub-contractors. The sub-contractors were noti-fied of the payment but this notification said that the payment had not taken into account any claims the employers might have for damages for delay in the erection of the steelwork, and the main contractors were similarly notified. The £28,870 was paid to Min-ters but they did not pay it to Dawnays and furthermore they claimed £61,000 from Dawnays as damages for delay.

Dawnays sued Minters for the £28,870 to which Minters cross-claimed for delay. Minters applied to stay the action on the ground that it was a matter which ought to be settled by arbitration under the sub-contract. This was granted to Minters but Dawnays appealed to the Court of Appeal.

The Court of Appeal decided that Minters were not entitled to withhold payment of the £28,870 since the sub-contract required the main contractors to make payment within fourteen days of the issue of the certificate, less only certain specified sums. The court held that under the sub-contract the only sums which could be deducted were those which were liquidated and ascertained sums established or admitted to be payable. As Minters were not able to satisfy the court that their claim was for a certain sum which was not disputed they were ordered to pay the sub-contractors the £28,870.

The decision in this case which became known as 'the rule in *Dawnay's* case', was followed in a number of similar cases which quickly came before the courts. What it did was to say that a sub-contractor's claim for payment under the standard sub-contract form was not to be denied by any main contractor's counter claim or set-off unless the amount deducted was a certain sum which was not disputed.

This matter came before the House of Lords for consideration in the case of *Gilbert-Ash (Northern) Ltd.* v *Modern Engineering (Bristol) Ltd.* 1973. Here Gilbert-Ash were main contractors and Modern Engineering the sub-contractor for the steelwork. The sub-contractor was not on the standard form but on a form drafted by Gilbert-Ash. The sub-contract contained a number of provisions which differed from the standard form with regard to payment to the sub-contractors. In particular these provisions stated that the sub-contractor was not to be paid until a certificate had been issued under the main contract and the main contractors had received the money; that if the sub-contractor failed to comply with any of the conditions of the sub-contract the main contractors had the right to suspend or withhold payment of money due or becoming due to the sub-contractor; and the main contractors reserved the right to deduct from any payment certified as due to the sub-contractor any bona fide claim the main contractors may have against the sub-contractor in connection with the sub-contract or any other contract. The sub-contractor carried out the steelwork but there was a delay in its completion and the main contractors said that some of the work was not satisfactory.

The architect issued an interim certificate for £14,532 to the main contractor for payment to the sub-contractor. The main contractors paid the sub-contractor £10,000 only and claimed that they were owed £3,137 for the delay and £1,862 for defective work. The sub-contractor claimed that full payment had to be made under the rule in *Dawnay's* case. The Court of Appeal agreed with the sub-contractor. Appeal was then made by the main contractors to the House of Lords.

The House of Lords decided that the terms of the sub-contract were such that the main contractors were entitled to withhold payment received from the employer provided the claim to withhold the money was made bona fide. Since the amounts for delay and defective work had been properly calculated the main contractors were entitled to deduct the sums claimed. In doing this the common law rights of set-off and counterclaim were being exercised. The House of Lords in reaching this decision commented on the rule in *Dawnay's* case and the subsequent cases, all of which had been where standard forms of contract had been used. They said that those cases had been wrongly decided and that those standard forms of contract did not take away the main contractor's right to make deduction for set-off or counterclaim.

This right of a main contractor to make deduction from payment due to a sub-contractor must be based on a properly calculated sum; the right cannot be used to make deduction of an amount which cannot be shown to be properly due. This may be seen in the case of *Ellis Mechanical Services Limited* v *Wates Construction Limited* 1976. Here Ellis Mechanical Services were sub-contractors for heating pipes and other services for Wates the main contractors of a large development. The main contract was determined and this meant that the sub-contractors were entitled to be paid for the work they had done. The sub-contractors believed that they were entitled to some £187,000 but they recognized that they could only show an undisputed claim to £52,437. The balance of the £187,000 was a matter they recognized was open to dispute. They therefore made a claim, using the Order 14 procedure to obtain summary judgment without the matter going to trial, for the £52,437. Wates disputed this claim and wanted the whole of the sum of £187,000 to be the subject of arbitration. The matter eventually came before the Court of Appeal, where the decision was that the sub-contractors were entitled to the £52,437 they had claimed under the Order 14 procedure. The basis for this decision was that engineers for the employer had certified that that work had been done and as the employer was the ultimate paymaster that sum ought to be paid. The balance of the £187,000 was to be dealt with by way of arbitration.

Standard Forms of Sub-Contracts

There have been a number of standard forms for sub-contracts used in the construction industry, some of which were used solely by sub-contractors of specialized services. The most important standard form has been the one designed to be used in conjunction with the then RIBA standard form of contract. Because of the colour of the paper on which the document was printed it was usually referred to as the 'green' form. Two points arose in the use of this document which require attention since they have played a part in the new form of sub-contract now in use.

The first point is that as the parties to the sub-contract were the main contractor and the sub-contractor the employer, who ultimately was to pay for all the work, was not a party to the contract and could therefore take no direct action against the sub-contractor. This is based on the principle of law that, in general, only the parties to a contract may either benefit from or take action under the contract. The absence of a contractual link between the employer and a nominated sub-contractor or supplier was considered to be a deficiency which had to be remedied. This was done in 1969 by the Royal Institute of British Architects issuing forms of warranty which could be used to create a direct contractual relationship on certain matters between the employer and a nominated sub-contractor or supplier. These matters are now covered by the provisions in NSC/2, the agreement between an employer and nominated sub-contractor.

The second point was the need to clarify, so far as it could be clarified, the right of the sub-contractor not to be kept out of his money while at the same time protecting the main contractor with regard to his rights. This was done by the introduction in 1975 of an amendment to the green form. The amendment required that where a sum was disputed that matter should be resolved by an adjudicator. The adjudicator's powers included deciding that the contractor was entitled to retain the amount, in whole or in part; or that the sub-contractor was to be paid, in whole or in part; or that the matter should go to arbitration with the amount in the meantime being deposited with a trustee-stakeholder. These matters are now covered by the provisions in NSC/4, the sub-contract.

NSC/1

This document constitutes the tender submitted by a sub-contractor for the work he is to do. The document gives the sub-contractor the right to withdraw his tender in certain circumstances, included in which is the right to withdraw on the name of the main contractor being made known. The document contains two schedules which contain information on which the sub-contractor is to make his tender and other information regarding the carrying out of the sub-contract work.

NSC/2

This document creates a contractual link between the employer and the nominated sub-contractor as the RIBA warranty forms formerly did. The document requires the sub-contractor to settle with the main contractor certain matters in the second schedule of NSC/1, and having done so to notify the architect of that fact. The important part of the document for the employer is in clause 2 where the sub-contractor warrants that he has exercised and will exercise all reasonable skill and care in the design of the sub-contract works; in the selection of materials and goods for the sub-contract works; and satisfaction of any performance, satisfaction or requirement of the sub-contract works. By this provision an employer may under the contract obtain damages when, for example, a heating engineer sub-contractor has failed to use reasonable skill and care in the design of a heating system with the result it is inadequate for its known purpose.

The document also gives the employer a legal right against the sub-contractor if the sub-contractor delays in his work so that the main contractor becomes entitled under the main contract to an extension of time. The sub-contract also places other obligations on the sub-contractor, including the remedying of any faulty sub-contract work after proper notification from the architect.

The architect is under a duty to notify the sub-contractor of any interim certificate he has issued to the main contractor which certifies that a payment be made to the sub-contractor.

In the event of any dispute arising under the document the matter is to be referred to arbitration. If the dispute is substantially the same as a dispute under the main contract or the sub-contract then, with the agreement of the parties, the arbitrator who is already dealing with that dispute may deal with the dispute under the document. A reference to arbitration shall not be opened until practical completion or practical completion of the main contract works is claimed, or until the contract is otherwise ended, unless the employer or the architect on his behalf and the sub-contract otherwise agree.

NSC/3

This document informs the main contractor which sub-contractor has been nominated by the architect for specified sub-contract works.

NSC/4

This document is the sub-contract between the main contractor and the sub-contractor. It follows the pattern of the main contract in defining the obligations and rights of each party.

The articles of agreement define the parties to the contract and the work which is the subject of the sub-contract. The various procedural steps, such as nomination by the architect, are stated to have been complied with. The contract sum is stated to be that set out in the tender or as finally ascertained in accordance with the contract. The procedure for settling disputes it to be by arbitration with the provision that if the dispute is substantially the same as one under the main contract which is already being dealt with by an arbitrator then he may deal with the sub-contract dispute. This arrangement is subject to the agreement of the parties. Arbitration is not, except in certain circumstances, to be until there has been practical completion of the works or such is claimed. The award of the arbitrator is to be final and binding on the parties.

The articles conclude with the signatures or seals of the contracting parties as is appropriate to the contract being made.

1. *Interpretation, definitions, etc.*
This clause defines certain words and terms which are used in the sub-contract.

2. *Sub-Contract Documents*
This clause states that the tender and any documents annexed thereto and the sub-contract shall be the sub-contract documents. In any dispute the sub-contract is to prevail. Any restriction, limitation or exclusion negotiated by the contractor and approved by the architect in respect of work, materials or goods in turn limits the liability of the sub-contractor to the same extent.

3. *Sub-Contract Sum – additions or deductions – computation of Ascertained Final Sub-Contract Sum*
The final payment to the sub-contractor is to be the adjusted sum after deduction or addition in accordance with the sub-contract.

4. *Execution of the Sub-Contract Works – instructions of Architect – directions of Contractor*
The sub-contractor is to carry out the sub-contract work and to comply with written instructions of the architect and any reasonable direction in writing of the contractor. The sub-contractor may make reasonable objection to a variation. Where the sub-contractor receives instruction from the architect or direction from the main contractor which is not in writing then that is of no effect unless the sub-contractor confirms it in writing to the main contractor within seven days and the main contractor does not dissent in writing within seven days. A sub-contractor can ask for the architect to specify the provision in the main contract which gives him authority to issue an instruction. Failure of a sub-contractor to comply with a written direction of the main contractor means that some other person may be employed to comply with that instruction and the contract sum is adjusted.

5. *Sub-Contractor's liability under incorporated provisions of the Main Contract*
The sub-contractor is to comply with the provisions in the main contract which relate to the sub-contract works. He is also to

indemnify the main contractor from breaches or non-performance of the relevant provisions of the main contract.

6. *Injury to persons and property – indemnity to Contractor*

This clause follows the pattern of the corresponding clause in the main contract with in this case the sub-contractor indemnifying the main contractor for certain events.

7. *Insurance – Sub-Contractor*

Again a similar provision to that in the main contract. In this case the sub-contractor is to secure the necessary insurance cover.

8. *Loss or damage by the 'Clause 22 Perils' to Sub-Contract Works and materials and goods properly on site*

This clause deals with the sub-contractor's liability for loss or damage by those risks referred to as 'clause 22 perils'. Where the main contractor or the employer has taken out the appropriate insurance under clause 22 of the main contract the sub-contractor is protected by that insurance and is to receive payment for any loss or damage for 'clause 22 perils'. Other than these risks the sub-contractor is to be responsible for loss or damage to materials or goods on the site ready for incorporation into the sub-contract works. When materials or goods have been incorporated into the sub-contract works the main contractor is responsible.

9. *Policies of insurance*

The sub-contractor is to take out the necessary insurance under the sub-contract and to produce the policies and receipts when so required. Where the sub-contractor defaults the main contractor may take out the necessary insurance and deduct the premium from money due to the sub-contractor.

10. *Sub-Contractor's responsibility for his own plant, etc.*

With certain exceptions, the sub-contractor is to be entirely responsible for his plant, equipment and other property which is not properly on the site for incorporation in the sub-contract works.

11. *Sub-Contractor's obligation – carrying out and completion of Sub-Contract Works – extension of Sub-Contract time*
This clause enables a sub-contractor in certain circumstances to obtain an extension of time for the completion of the sub-contract. In order to get an extension of time the sub-contractor is to notify the main contractor in writing of the likelihood of a delay. The main contractor notifies the architect who is to grant an extension if the delay arises because of one of the relevant events described in the clause occurring. In the event of the architect refusing an application for any extension of time the sub-contractor can go to arbitration.

12. *Failure of Sub-Contractor to complete on time*
In the event of the sub-contractor failing to complete the sub-contract on time the main contractor is entitled to recover the loss or damage he has thereby incurred but this is subject to the architect certifying in writing that there has been a failure to complete on time.

13. *Matters affecting regular progress – direct loss and/or expense – Contractor's and Sub-Contractor's rights.*
The provisions in this clause are similar to those in the main contract. In this case the sub-contractor is entitled to payment for direct loss or expense for which he cannot claim payment under any other provision of the contract provided the claim comes within one of a number of stated grounds. A fault on the part of the sub-contractor which causes direct loss or damage to the main contractor permits the main contractor to make deduction from money due to be paid to the sub-contractor.

14. *Practical completion of Sub-Contract Works – liability for defects*
On notification of practical completion in writing by the sub-contractor to the contractor, and from the contractor to the architect, the architect may then certify practical completion. The sub-contractor then becomes liable for defects in his sub-contract work.

15. *Price for Sub-Contract Works*
The sum payable for the sub-contract work shall be in accordance with the tender and any alterations in accordance with the sub-contract.

16. *Valuation of Variations and provisional sum work*
Where the sub-contract sum is stated in the tender, all variations and all work done by the sub-contractor on the instructions of the architect as to provisional sum work is to be valued by the quantity surveyor in accordance with the rules laid down in the clause. Where appropriate the prices in the bills of quantities are to be used. The sub-contractor is entitled to be present when the valuation is made by the quantity surveyor.

17. *Valuation of all work comprising the Sub-Contract Works*
Where the sub-contractor has in his tender quoted a contract sum which is subject to complete re-measurement the provisions in this clause apply. The quantity surveyor is to value the work in accordance with the rules in the clause. The sub-contractor is entitled to be present during the valuation.

18. *Bills of quantities – Standard Method of Measurement*
As in the main contract, the bills in the sub-contract are to be prepared in accordance with the Standard Method of Measurement of Building Works, 7th Edition. Any error in the bills of quantities shall not invalidate the contract but shall be corrected by the architect issuing a variation instruction.

19A to 20B. *Value added tax etc*
The provisions in these clauses are designed to ensure that the legal requirements concerning VAT and income tax are observed. In particular they deal with the deduction of tax when a sub-contractor does not possess a tax certificate issued by the Inland Revenue.

21. *Payment of Sub-Contractor*
The main contractor is required to pass on to the architect a request from the sub-contractor for payment for work done or materials or goods on the site or on adjoining land for incorporation in the sub-contract works and materials and goods elsewhere. The architect will include, as is appropriate such amount for payment in an interim certificate to the main contractor. Within seventeen days of the date of issue of an interim certificate the main contractor is to pay the sub-contractor. The sub-contractor is to give the main contractor written proof of payment so that that may be produced for the architect. The rules with regard to retention set

out in clause 30 of the main contract apply in the sub-contract payment. The clause includes rules which are to be observed in calculating the final contract sum.

22. *Benefits under Main Contract*
The clause requires the main contractor if requested by the sub-contractor to obtain for him any rights and benefits of the main contract so far as such apply to the sub-contract.

23. *Contractor's right to set-off*
As we have seen, the main contractor's right to make deduction from money due to a sub-contractor gave rise to litigation and caused an amendment to be made to the then standard sub-contract, the 'green' form.

The clause entitles a main contractor to deduct from money due to a sub-contractor the amount awarded to him by an arbitrator or court from a matter concerning the sub-contract. Where no such award has been made, the main contractor may still set-off any claim he had for loss or expense against the sub-contractor provided that where he wishes to make deduction for delay in completion he must have the certificate of the architect issued under clause 12, and the amount to be deducted must be calculated in detail and with reasonable accuracy by the main contractor. The main contractor must also give notice of his intention to make deduction at least twenty days before the money from which the deduction is to be made becomes due. Even if the main contractor uses this right to deduct from money due to the sub-contractor both contractors may seek to change the amount claimed and deducted by negotiation, arbitration or court proceedings. The clause states that the rights of the parties to the sub-contract to set-off claims are those set out in the sub-contract only.

24. *Contractor's claims not agreed by the Sub-Contractor – appointment of adjudicator*
Where a sub-contractor disputes the main contractor's claim to make deduction from money due to the sub-contractor he must, within fourteen days of receiving the main contractor's notice of intended deduction, send the main contractor a written statement giving the grounds for his disagreement and details, calculated with reasonable accuracy, of any counterclaim he has against the

main contractor under the sub-contract. At the same time he is to give notice to the main contractor of arbitration and request action by the adjudicator.

The adjudicator, who is named in the tender, then deals with the matter. The main contractor has fourteen days from receipt of the notice of arbitration from the sub-contractor to send a written statement to the adjudicator setting out his defence to any counter-claim of the sub-contractor. The adjudicator is to make his decision within seven days of receiving the written statement from the main contractor. He may decide that the whole or part of the amount shall be retained by the contractor; or until arbitration be paid by the main contractor to a trustee-stakeholder; or be paid by the main contractor to the sub-contractor; or his decision may be a combination of any of the above. The adjudicator shall do what is fair, reasonable and necessary in the circumstances and his decision binds the main contractor and sub-contractor. Both have to be notified in writing of the decision. When the decision of the adjudicator is known the main contractor is to obey it by paying the sub-contractor or depositing money with the trustee-stake-holder as is appropriate.

The trustee-stakeholder holds the money until the arbitrator otherwise directs or until in a joint letter the main contractor and sub-contractor otherwise direct. The trustee-stakeholder puts the amount into a bank deposit account so that it earns interest. He is entitled to a fee for his services, to be paid by the sub-contractor unless the arbitrator otherwise directs.

25. *Right of Access of Contractors and Architect*
The sub-contractor shall, unless the architect otherwise certifies in writing, provide access to the sub-contract works to the main contractor, the architect and other persons they authorize.

26. *Assignment – sub-letting*
The sub-contractor must have the written consent of the architect and main contractor to assign the sub-contract. He must also not sub-let any part of the sub-contract without the written consent of the architect and main contractor and such consent must not be unreasonably withheld.

27. *General attendance – other attendances, etc*
This clause sets out the obligations of both the main contractor and the sub-contractor with regard to these matters. In general the main contractor is to permit the sub-contractor to use such things as scaffolding, hoists, lighting and water supplies.

28. *Contractor and Sub-Contractor not to make wrongful use or interfere with the property of the other*
This clause places obligations on each of the parties to the sub-contract to obey the relevant law and to act properly with regard to such things as plant.

29. *Determination of the employment of the Sub-Contractor by the Contractor*
If a sub-contractor without reasonable cause suspends the sub-contract works; or fails to proceed with the sub-contract works in accordance with the programme or main contract works; or refuses or persistently neglects after written notice from the main contractor to remove defective work or improper materials or goods or wrongfully fails to put right defective work; or wrongfully assigns or sub-lets the work or fails to pay fair wages, then the main contractor is to inform the architect in writing. The architect may instruct the main contractor in writing to give notice to the sub-contractor requiring within fourteen days the sub-contractor's default to be remedied. Within ten days of that period expiring without the default being remedied the employment of the sub-contractor may be determined in writing. In the event of the sub-contractor's bankruptcy or other stated financial event occurring the sub-contractor's employment is determined automatically. The uncompleted sub-contract work may then be completed by another sub-contractor. Payment to the sub-contractor whose employment has been determined is not to be made until the sub-contract work has been completed and then account is to be taken of any direct loss or expense caused to the employer by the determination.

30. *Determination of employment under the sub-contract by the Sub-Contractor.*
This clause has provisions which follow the pattern just considered. The occurrence of one of a number of stated grounds allows the

sub-contractor to end the sub-contract. He is then to be paid in accordance with rules in the clause.

31. *Determination of the Main Contractor's employment under the Main Contract*

Where a main contractor's employment is ended under certain provisions in the main contract the employment of the sub-contractor is also determined. The sub-contractor is then to be paid in accordance with rules in the clause.

32. *Fair Wages*

This clause requires that where the main contract contains the requirements in clause 19A that fair wages be paid then similar provisions are to apply in the sub-contract.

33. *Strikes – loss or expense*

Where either the main contract works or the sub-contract works are affected by a strike or lockout which affects the trades on the works or those trades engaged in the supply of goods to the works then neither the main contractor nor the sub-contractor is entitled to payment for any loss or expense suffered by that action. The main contractor is to take all reasonably practicable steps to keep the site open for the sub-contractor, and the sub-contractor is to take all reasonably practicable steps to continue with the sub-contract works.

24, 35, 36 and 37. *Fluctuations, etc.*

It is now standard practice in contracts of any lengthy duration, whatever the work is, to have a clause which allows the contract price to be adjusted for any change in the price of materials or goods or in the wage rates of workers. Without such provision at a time of inflation a contractor would quickly be in financial difficulty. The sub-contract therefore follows this standard practice. Clause 34 states that the provisions in clauses 35, 36 or 37 shall be used as selected. Where no selection is made clause 35 is to be used. Whichever clause is used there is a detailed procedure for the calculation of changes in prices, wage rates and other financial charges. The sub-contractor is to give notice of the changes and of his request for the contract sum to be altered to take account of these changes.

Use of Alternative Method of Sub-Contract

This method makes use of the NSC/2a form and the sub-contract form NSC/4a. The use of this alternative method cuts out the submission of the sub-contractor's tender on NSC/1 and the subsequent negotiation and settlement between the main contractor and the sub-contractor to ensure that the work will be completed within the main contractor's programme. Since the tender in the form of NSC/1 is not used the sub-contract form NSC/4a, which is basically similar to the sub-contract NSC/4 just considered, does not make reference to the tender or to any of the procedures and matters which arise from its use.

In general it may be said that the alternative method is a simpler procedure used where the employer does not need to negotiate in great detail with the sub-contractor he intends to nominate.

Appendix

It is inevitable in a book such as this that some topics have been dealt with in less depth than the reader might wish. It may be, therefore, that the reader wishes to study some topic in greater depth for his own particular purpose. In order to do this there will probably be need to consult the sources used by practising lawyers. Such sources are usually available in the libraries of the larger towns and cities and they are available to all. The advice of the library staff is always available but the following may be of assistance.

The law reports are a standard source to the practising lawyer and are usually on open shelves in the larger libraries available for the general reader. The law reports are divided into official and semi-official reports. The official are published by the Incorporated Council of Law Reporting. The volumes refer first to the cases in the House of Lords and the Court of Appeal of whatever nature the law was in the case. Then the volumes divide into the individual divisions of the High Court, so that for example, all the reported cases of the Queen's Bench Division of the High Court for that year are found in the volumes, usually three, published that year. The volumes themselves are marked Q.B.D. 1980 1, indicating that that is the first volume of the reports of the Queen's Bench Division of 1980. The required case may be found by consulting the index of the front under the name of the case. If the name of a case is known but not the year in which it was reported then the particular volume may be found by consulting the large index of cases which is published every few years. This large index may also be consulted under the particular legal topic if the name of the case is not known, or if a search is being made to discover if there has been any recent case on that matter.

The law reports are first published in a weekly series known as the *Weekly Law Reports*. This series enables new cases to be brought to the attention of lawyers as soon as possible. Later the more important cases in the *Weekly Law Reports* are put into the *Law Reports*. Again these are usually available in the larger libraries.

There are three semi-official law reports the reader needs to know of, and which he may find in his library. The first is the *All England Law Reports*, published by Butterworths of London. These reports unlike the official reports do not deal with the cases of the different divisions of the High Court, the Court of Appeal and the House of Lords by separate volumes. The cases in the *All England Law Reports* deal with all the different legal topics and all the courts. Finding a case in the reports if its full title is not known is by consulting the index in the individual volume or the general index published yearly and at intervals of several years.

The second semi-official law report is the *Lloyd's Law Reports* published by Lloyd's of London. These reports contain details of commercial cases in the main but they are often a useful source of decisions on arbitration which may not have been reported in any other law reports. Finding a case in the reports is similar to that previously described.

The third semi-official law reports which were introduced a few years ago are the *Building Law Reports* published by the Builder Group of London. These are particularly useful since they are written for the building industry and contain many cases which have not been reported in any other series of law reports.

A source of information widely used by practising lawyers, but which is likely to be found only in law libraries, is the publication *Current Law*, published monthly by Sweet and Maxwell of London. This monthly publication contains notes on all the different topics of law: new legislation, new cases, reports of cases by individual lawyers and articles in other journals which are of interest to lawyers. As this publication is produced every month it is used by practising lawyers to see if there has been any recent change in the law they are dealing with; the system of a cumulative index enables this to be done easily and speedily.

Another source of information widely used is the *Local Government Library* published by Sweet and Maxwell of London. These

are looseleaf encyclopedias on legal topics such as planning, highways, housing and environmental health. They not only deal with
the law of the matter but also the practice. The encyclopedias,
which are usually in several volumes, are kept up to date by
replacement sheets issued by the publishers several times a year.
An extension of this series of encyclopedias in another field, but
which is of interest to the building industry, is the *Encyclopedia of
Health and Safety at Work.*

An example of the way in which one of the encyclopedias may
be used will probably be helpful to the reader. Suppose some
problem arises with regard to a condition imposed by a local
planning authority in granting planning consent for a development.
By consulting the index it can be seen that section 29 of the Town
and Country Planning Act 1971 gives the local planning authority
power to grant planning permission subject to such conditions as
they think fit. The additional information provided by the publishers directs the reader to the relevant case law so that the law
reports may be consulted to see what the courts have decided on
the matter of conditional planning consents. As planning conditions may be part of the national planning policy there may be
a policy statement issued by the government. The index directs
the reader to Circular No. 1/88 issued in 1980 by the Secretary of
State for the Environment, on the use of conditions in planning
permission. The circular is set out in full in the encyclopedia and
may be read for an indication of the Secretary of State's view on
this matter. The granting of a planning permission subject to a
condition gives the applicant a right of appeal to the Secretary of
State for the Department of the Environment. Since the decisions
of the Secretary of State in planning appeals on this matter will
indicate his policy, knowledge of his previous decisions will therefore be helpful. On this matter the index directs the reader to the
part of the encyclopedia entitled Selected Planning Appeals.

It can be seen therefore that the ordinary reader by proper use
of the index, and the information in the encyclopedia, can learn
for himself the legal position of the matter. This is, what legal
powers are the local planning authority using, are they using them
properly in accordance with past judicial decisions, what is the
Secretary of State's policy on this matter and how have appeals on
conditional planning permissions been dealt with previously?

A final point to note for the reader who seeks further information is the existence of textbooks on legal topics of special interest to the building industry. Probably the best example of this is *Hudson's Building & Engineering Contracts*, 10th Edition published by Sweet and Maxwell. There is also a supplement to this edition. Whatever textbook is consulted it is important to check that it is the most recent edition and whether a supplement has been issued. Since law changes so rapidly it would always be prudent to check in *Current Law* that the law in the textbook on a particular matter is still unchanged.

Index